New International

A MAGAZINE OF MARXIST POLITICS AND THEORY

NUMBER 12   2005

EDITORIAL BOARD

EDITOR
Mary-Alice Waters

MANAGING EDITOR
Steve Clark

CONTRIBUTING
EDITOR
Jack Barnes

———

INTERNATIONAL
CONSULTANTS
Anita Östling
Ron Poulsen
Michel Prairie
Ólöf Andra Proppé
Samad Sharif
Jonathan Silberman
Mike Tucker

Contents

Copyright © 2005 by New International

All rights reserved
First printing, 2005

ISSN 0737-3724
ISBN 0-87348-967-5
Manufactured in Canada

New International is distributed internationally by Pathfinder Press:
www.pathfinderpress.com

Cover design: Eva Braiman

Cover photograph: Saudi commandos landing on roof of compound housing foreign oil company employees, Khobar, May 2004. Four Islamic jihadists had taken hundreds of hostages, killing twenty-two. Photo taken from Al Arabiya television.

by Jack Barnes

T HIS ISSUE OF *New International* opens with "Their Transformation and Ours," a resolution prepared in the last several months by a commission of the Socialist Workers Party National Committee. It is based on political reports and summaries I gave in November 2004 that were discussed and adopted by an expanded meeting of the SWP National Committee in which leaders of Communist Leagues in a number of countries, including Australia, Canada, Iceland, New Zealand, Sweden and the United Kingdom, participated.

The resolution has been submitted to the party's membership for discussion, leading to a vote at a convention scheduled for June 2005. Centered on several decisive points of world politics, it has been drafted to be read and discussed together with—as an integral component of—"Capitalism's Long Hot Winter Has Begun," the political report adopted by the party's 2002 convention and the central article in this issue of *New International*.

"Their Transformation and Ours" analyzes the sharpening interimperialist conflicts fueled both by the opening stages of a world depression and by the most far-reaching shift in Washington's military policy and organization since its preparations in the late 1930s to transform the nearly decade-long war in Asia and the European war of 1939–41 into a world war. Class-struggle-minded workers and farmers must face—fully—this historic turning point for imperialism (and cataclysmic crisis for "the West" and "Christendom"). And draw satisfaction and enjoyment from being "in their face" as we chart a revolutionary course to confront it.

The resolution weighs the importance of the beginning political transformation of militant workers who, impelled by these momentous changes, are taking the lead to reach for, organize, and use *union power*. As the social consequences of capitalist crises grow, as inevitable political conflicts sharpen between and within classes, and as probes to restrict political and democratic rights used by working people increase, these vanguard militants will join with other workers to resist accelerated employing-class assaults in the plants and the political arena, at home and abroad.

❖

As an appendix to "Capitalism's Long Hot Winter Has Begun" we are running two reports debated and approved by the Third Congress of the Communist International, held in Moscow in 1921, which I referred to several times in the 2002 convention report. Included here are "A Very Unstable Equilibrium: Report on the Tactics of the Russian Communist Party" by V.I. Lenin, and "The World Economic Crisis and the Tasks of Communists" by Leon Trotsky. These merit a few introductory comments.

In preparing the party's 2002 convention, the SWP National Committee recognized that we were addressing a special challenge: Not only how to orient the party to act in face of the "long, hot winter" world capitalism has now entered, but how to lead it to act confidently and responsibly. When enough indications accumulate that the direction of capitalist development, and thus the class struggle, has shifted, communist workers must act on that knowledge, and act now. We do so even when concrete manifestations of the unfolding political logic—accelerating financial and economic crises, increased militarization, spreading wars, intensifying interimperialist conflicts, and increasing social and economic pressures on a growing majority of the working class—are still visible only in partial, scattered, and partly disguised ways.

Once we understand the algebra, we need to act before it's possible to do all the arithmetic. If, before acting, we wait until we can substitute constants for most political variables, it will be too late. In the midst of these changing conditions, we will have squandered opportunities to act as part of a small but recognizable emerging working-class resistance, to join with others in affecting its outcome and politicizing its militants, to learn from the experiences, and to transform the revolutionary workers movement in the process.

What tools do worker-bolsheviks have at hand to better understand and act on today's shifting long-run trends and the consequences for communist strategy and party building? It was with that question in mind at the 2002 convention that we called to delegates' attention the reports by Lenin and Trotsky to the 1921 Comintern congress. Those reports ended up sparking considerable interest both during and after the SWP convention, and the editors decided it would be useful to include them here.

The Bolshevik leaders' analysis was developed in the heat of revolutionary activity, applying what they had internalized from studying similar, earlier efforts by Karl

Marx and Frederick Engels, the founding leaders of the modern communist movement, to apply the materialist dialectic to turning points in history. Mastering this historical materialist method is necessary if we are to orient ourselves politically to such shifts.

A revolutionary proletarian party not only organizes its own members and supporters to act on the evidence of such changes and their logic; it takes responsibility for encouraging other class-struggle-minded, fighting workers and farmers to do the same. Militants won to this perspective may occasionally overreach what the relationship of class forces allows. Such mistakes will be made. But we remain convinced by 150 years of revolutionary working-class history that the costs of political indecision and delay are far more dangerous and difficult to correct.

EXTRACTING LESSONS FROM Lenin and Trotsky's analysis in the reports printed here is made more complex by the fact that the turning point vanguard workers act on today bears little resemblance to the concrete historical period more than eighty years ago during which the Bolsheviks were inspiring, educating, and leading millions in class combat. The Communist International, organized in 1919, was a product of the most exhilarating event of the twentieth century: the victorious conquest of power by the Bolshevik-led workers and peasants of Russia in October 1917, and the extension of this power to large parts of the tsarist empire in Europe and Asia to become the first union of soviet socialist republics.

Working people worldwide were drawn to the possibility of learning from and emulating a living proletarian revolution and its leadership, which had shown for the first time ever how to educate and organize workers, peasants, soldiers, and sailors to conquer—and defend—workers power.

In March 1918, just four months after the conquest of power, the Bolsheviks proudly took the name *Communist*. In doing so, they were signaling their unequivocal break with all elements of the world socialist movement that, with the guns of August, either had politically gone over to imperialism, or had vacillated in face of the Second International's capitulatory course. They were redoubling their intransigent opposition to these "socialists" who had ceased subordinating their lives and work to advancing the proletarian struggle. They were underscoring the fact that the toilers of the expanding union of soviet socialist republics were reknitting continuity with the revolutionary proletarian world movement that Marx, Engels, and their comrades—not only from Germany but from France, Belgium, Switzerland, and the United Kingdom—had begun building at the London convention that in 1847 voted to issue the Manifesto of the Communist Party.

The Bolsheviks were taking a name synonymous with being in the front ranks of the proletariat—among "the most advanced and resolute section," in the words of the Manifesto—in its march toward power, toward the dictatorship of the proletariat. They were proclaiming a new kind of movement, one "in no way based on ideas or principles that have been invented, or discovered by this or that would-be universal reformer," but on "clearly understanding the line of march, the conditions, and the ultimate general results of the proletarian movement." Communism merely expresses, "in general terms, actual relations springing from an existing class struggle, from a historical movement going on under our very eyes."

"Insofar as it is a theory," Engels had explained a year earlier, communism "is the theoretical expression of the position of the proletariat in [the class] struggle and the theoretical summation of the conditions for the liberation of the proletariat."

Between 1918 and 1920 revolutionary or prerevolutionary situations erupted in Germany, Hungary, and Italy, and mighty battles were fought by workers and farmers in Britain, France, Japan, the United States, and elsewhere. As the Comintern's Third Congress opened in June 1921, workers and peasants in Soviet Russia and worldwide were still celebrating the Red Army's recent crushing of the counterrevolutionary, landlord-capitalist armies that had waged a brutal three-year civil war to turn back the revolution. Invading forces from fourteen countries, including France, the United Kingdom, the United States, and other imperialist powers, had also been repelled.

In the wake of World War I, capitalism had entered a period "of prolonged and profound depression," Trotsky told the 1921 Communist International congress. The roots of that convulsion, he added, could have been seen "as far back as 1913," the eve of the interimperialist slaughter in which 8.5 million soldiers died, another 21.2 million were wounded, and factories, livestock, and railroads across Europe were decimated.

As it turned out, despite ebbs and flows, neither that social and economic crisis, nor the wave of revolutionary opportunities impelled by the Bolshevik victory, were to run their course for another twenty years: a period marked by the triumph of fascism in Italy; the Great Depression of the 1930s; a murderous political counterrevolution in the Soviet Union; the victory and bloody consolidation of National Socialism in Germany; and, most importantly, renewed opportunities for the socialist revolution—that is, prerevolutionary and revolutionary situations in Europe and Asia—that were exhausted only with the defeat of the Spanish revolution in 1939, making the simmering imperialist world war inevitable.

The concrete character of the historic turning point today, analyzed in "Capitalism's Long Hot Winter Has Begun," is very different from that of 1921. As is the world relationship of class forces. One difference is the international political standing of communism among workers, farmers, youth, and others. In the years following the October Revolution, the political respect the Bolshevik leadership had earned, and the confidence millions of workers worldwide had in it, became a powerful objective factor in the international class struggle.

TODAY, MORE THAN three-quarters of a century later, broad mass political attraction to communism among militant working people and youth has—for the moment—been exhausted. At best, communism is seen as a perhaps heroic and historically interesting, although bypassed, movement. At times it is put forward by academic "Marxists" in eviscerated form, its revolutionary working-class heart—the inevitable march toward state power—cut out. At worst, it is identified with the Stalinist counterfeit of Marxism and all the counterrevolutionary, political crimes against and betrayals of the working class and peasantry—and communists—committed in its name around the world.

The political course and communist continuity hammered out by the Comintern in Lenin's time, however, are revolutionary and working-class to the core. The reports by Lenin and Trotsky printed here are among the finest examples of the materialist dialectic used as a guide to revolutionary action by working-class leaders. Our job is to learn from and apply Lenin and Trotsky's living, practical example of how Marxists approach the interrelationship between deep-going economic and financial trends in international capitalism, shifts in long-term patterns of imperialist politics and the worldwide class struggle, and sea changes in working-class resistance. Our responsibility—and opportunity—is to act accordingly, in response to today's trends, and build revolutionary proletarian parties as part of a world communist movement.

Using these tools enables us to shape "Their Transformation and Ours" as a complement to "Capitalism's Long Hot Winter Has Begun," to affirm the central political conclusion they share, and to act on its implications for the organization and activity of proletarian revolutionists today:

> We find ourselves in the very opening stages of what will be decades of economic, financial, and social convulsions and class battles. . . . Like most other workers, communists participating in this convention must internalize the fact that this world—the likes of which none of us have known before in our political lives—is not only the world that must be faced today, but the one we will be living and fighting in for some time. By *acting* on this reality today, we will not be caught short politically as wars erupt, deeper social crises explode, pogroms are organized and attempted, and union conflicts become life-and-death battles. The proletarian party that exists tomorrow can only grow out of the proletarian party we put together *today*.

❖

During the final preparations of this issue, *New International* editor Mary-Alice Waters has been in Cuba—in Havana, Matanzas, and Cienfuegos—covering the annual international book fair there, preparing future publications, and participating in book presentations in each of these cities.

In Havana Waters spoke at an event celebrating the recent release of *Somos herederos de las revoluciones del mundo*, Pathfinder Press's Spanish translation of *We Are Heirs of the World's Revolutions* by Thomas Sankara, the central leader of the revolution in the West African country of Burkina Faso between 1983 and 1987. Also presented at that meeting was *Nueva Internacional* no. 7, the Spanish-language translation of *New International* no. 13, featuring the report "Our Politics Start with the World."

The Matanzas and Cienfuegos gatherings were sponsored by the Association of Combatants of the Cuban Revolution—the "Combatientes"—an organization spanning multiple generations of Cubans who have fought, wherever and however needed, to make and defend the first socialist revolution in the Americas. The meetings presented nearly a dozen Pathfinder titles, all of which were completed with collaboration from leaders of the Combatientes. These titles range from *Episodes of the Cuban Revolutionary War* by Ernesto Che Guevara to *Pombo: a Man of Che's 'guerrilla'* by Harry Villegas, from *Playa Girón/Bay of Pigs: Washington's First Military Defeat in the Americas* by Fidel Castro and José Ramón Fernández to *From the Escambray to the Congo* by Víctor Dreke, *Aldabonazo* by Armando Hart, and numerous others.

Steve Clark, the managing editor, in addition to overseeing much of the final work on the magazine, has traveled to Tampa, Atlanta, Newark, and San Francisco. There he worked with the leadership of the almost 200-person worldwide volunteer team of revolutionists who organize the formatting, proofreading, and numerous other steps necessary to produce and print not only *New*

International, Nueva Internacional, and *Nouvelle Internationale,* but books and pamphlets published by Pathfinder,
as well as the shipping and handling of orders and efforts
to get these titles onto bookstore and library shelves
around the globe. In Newark and Tampa Clark spoke at
regional socialist conferences to prepare an international
meeting in New York at the end of March to politically
launch the campaign to get these two new issues, in English and Spanish, into the hands of working people and
youth worldwide.

As a result, I took responsibility for drafting "In This
Issue," which is the final, nail-in-the-coffin piece for each
issue of the magazine. In reviewing and editing several
formatted articles over the last two months, I had become
increasingly convinced that the pages were irritatingly
hard to read. The type was too small. There was too little
space between the lines. They attracted you too little and
made you strain too much. I was assured the pages would
look better, that the type would be more readable in the
printed magazine. That was not the case. So, taking advantage of the accidental and temporary editorial powers I held, I instituted an increase in the type size—in the
readability—of each of the two new issues of the magazine in both languages. The editor had already insisted
that the ads be reworked to better complement, not compete with, the text, photos, and political content.

THESE SEEM TO ME POLITICAL QUESTIONS, class questions, not solely a matter of style or appearance, let alone
taste. Every issue of *New International* contains political
and theoretical articles that are challenging to read and
absorb, regardless of age or eyesight. Most of us are not
used to doing this kind of reading. It's not easy. It takes

hard, concentrated work. We're not trained to do it. For most of our waking hours, we're not asked or expected to do it. The truth is, under capitalism, we're not supposed to do it.

We're supposed to go to work, do our job, produce a profit for a boss, and not disturb the placidity of the homeland. That's the long and short of it. Education is a class institution aimed at instilling obedience, on the job and off, not "educating" for a lifetime, not teaching us how to read and write—or to think as the makers of history we can be. Even if at one point in our lives we did learn to read in this way, over time we lose that capacity if we don't keep using it. Simple exhaustion, or temporary illness, increases the difficulty. But the need for each of us to do so does not recede under these circumstances.

Ease of reading is connected to the effective political selection and presentation of photographs. Over the past ten to fifteen years, the communist movement has made substantial progress in preparing photo sections that visually walk readers through the books we produce: "We've improved our use of the 'universal language,'" as it's put in "Capitalism's Long Hot Winter Has Begun." Readability is of a piece with the care we take in preparing ads. It's the reason we never excuse bad printing (the first limited, digital printing of *New International* no. 13 was terrible). Were we to accept this, the rigor of our copyediting, proofreading, and other crafts we are proud of would slide too. Everything each of us strives to do *well,* individually and collectively, in every book we produce is to the same end: to get rid of obstacles to having fighting workers and farmers, and young people attracted to their struggles, read and consider *the politics,* and together use those books to help change ourselves as we change the world.

James P. Cannon, a longtime central leader of the communist movement in the United States going back to its founding in 1919, taught me something about the class question of readability almost forty years ago when I was a recently graduated young socialist and a newly elected member of the leadership of the SWP. I was in Los Angeles on a speaking and organizational tour, and Jim invited me to stop by to talk politics. Shortly beforehand, the editor of one of our publications had decreased the type size in order to squeeze in a little more copy, and, among other things, Jim expressed his opinion that the type was now too small—way too small. And the periodical was thus also unattractive.

Like all the self-taught, pioneer worker-bolsheviks who founded the communist movement in North America, Jim was a voracious reader all his life. He asked me if I had any idea how many people in the United States alone had vision problems that made reading an extra effort. This was above and beyond the big majority who need glasses by middle age. I didn't and was surprised when Jim reeled off the figures his secretarial staff had gathered and checked. Even four decades ago, the number was in the many, many millions.

That fact alone would settle the question for any class-conscious worker. Even more, however, English is not the first language of many in our class—not only in recent decades, but at the time Jim Cannon joined the socialist movement at the opening of the twentieth century. Reading and studying theoretical material in your second or third language is always even more challenging.

For all these reasons, beginning with *New International* 12 and 13 and *Nueva Internacional* 6 and 7, all being launched in early 2005, the type is substantially larger. As earlier issues come up for reprint, each will be reformatted in this larger type size. I'm confident Pathfinder's editors will initiate a review of the books and pamphlets it publishes, as well, and henceforth organize to meet the same standards in every book and pamphlet, new and reprint, that comes off the press. And there's a good chance that if readers think these considerations have merit and bring them to the attention of the worker-bolsheviks who edit other revolutionary publications, comparable progress can and will be made on those fronts too.

February 25, 2005

THEIR TRANSFORMATION
AND OURS

THEIR TRANSFORMATION AND OURS

Socialist Workers Party Draft Resolution

February 2005

"The underlying contradictions of world capitalism pushing toward depression and war did not begin on September 11, 2001. Some were accelerated by those events, but all have their roots in the downward turn in the curve of capitalist development a quarter century ago, followed by the interrelated weakening and then collapse of the Stalinist apparatuses in the Soviet Union and across Eastern and Central Europe at the opening of the 1990s. . . . One of capitalism's infrequent long winters has begun. With the accompanying acceleration of imperialism's drive toward war, it's going to be a long, hot winter."

—Capitalism's Long Hot Winter Has Begun
Jack Barnes, July 2002

SUMMARY PREFACE

As WE ENTER 2005 the employers' offensive, begun in the early 1980s, continues and intensifies. Pressing factory by factory, industry by industry, they have driven down workers' wages, increased differentiation among wage earners, and diluted seniority. The bosses have intensified speedup, extended hours of work, and made pensions and medical care more expensive, less secure, and narrower in coverage. In doing so, they keep weakening the union movement.

At the same time, these "conquests" have not been

enough to enable the employing class

• to push labor off center stage of politics in the United States;

• to break the spirit of vanguard workers in packinghouses, sewing shops, mines, and other workplaces where the capitalists have pressed their offensive the farthest for the longest time; or

• to reverse the sea change in working-class politics, marked by renewed rank-and-file resistance to antilabor assaults.

Progress limited to companies and workplaces, however, has not been, and will not be, sufficient for the employers to establish a new economic, social, and political relationship of forces between the capitalist class and working class. The owners of capital must achieve a much greater shift in class relations if they are to successfully dominate rival imperialist powers, organize to meet and withstand financial crises and depression conditions, pay for increasing war spending, and stabilize state finances. The U.S. rulers have been unable to push back far enough either the living standards workers and farmers have come to expect or the Social Security benefits they consider a *right.* These class expectations remain an untested social and political terrain of battle. They are an obstacle that cannot be bypassed by the employers, an obstacle that, unless surmounted, guarantees continued failure in their efforts to open a new period of sustained world capitalist expansion.

To try to accomplish such goals, the capitalists must slash the social wage wrested from them by working people in the course of class battles beginning in the mid-1930s. These gains culminated in the great advances of the late 1960s and early 1970s: the extension of Social Security benefits, establishment of Medicare and Medicaid, and the addition of escalator clauses protecting retirement, medical, and disability benefits against inflation. But starting a fight over programs that tens of millions of workers, farmers, and broad layers of the middle classes not only consider their right, but also feel less able to sacrifice than at any time in their memory, is a necessity in face of which the rulers still flinch. They recognize that such a fight, by its very nature, will have to be waged not just in the factories, mines, and mills but simultaneously on the terrain of a nationwide political struggle.

Coming after a brutal, decades-long offensive by hundreds of thousands of individual employers, the sea change in working-class politics has been punctuated by scattered pockets of workers trying to organize unions effective enough to defend themselves. These rank-and-file militants are seeking to use *union power.* The transformation of this atomized but ongoing resistance into a broader fighting vanguard of the labor movement will not begin solely by worker militants learning from each other's struggles, emulating them, and reaching out to one another in solidarity; it will gain ground as militants start to recognize that what they achieve through any strike or organizing drive can be defended and consolidated only by actively *extending* union power to other workplaces in their industry and in their region. Through the spread of class-struggle experience of such a scope, moreover, a growing number of workers—as well as youth drawn to the possibilities of what strengthened unions can do—will also be attracted to the disciplined activity and program of communists with whom they are fighting shoulder to shoulder in the front lines of such battles.

In face of the rulers' mounting financial and economic vulnerability, the political and military challenges they confront worldwide, and the inevitable sharpening of class conflict these conditions entail, America's proper-tied families and their political representatives in both the Democratic and Republican parties have become increasingly conscious of the need to *use* both the eco-nomic *and* the military power of U.S. imperialism. Gone is the illusion that the outcome of the Cold War in itself was a victory that would bring global stability under the domination of a Pax Americana, together with a cushion in state finances provided by a permanent "peace divi-dend." The rulers sense—even if they do not see clearly or understand—the uncontrollable forces carrying them toward a future of sharpening crises, with its intertwined faces of depression, war, and increasingly violent class battles with higher and higher stakes.

The frustration born of a vague but growing awareness of this vulnerability, combined with the inability to find a self-confident course to decisively surmount it (there *is* none), is the single greatest source of the deepening factionalism, demagogy, and degradation of political dis-course—what can accurately be called its "pornographi-cation"—that characterize all bourgeois politics in the United States, not only between but increasingly within the dominant ruling parties and their peripheries.

To prepare to defend their more and more crises-rid-den global order, the U.S. rulers, led by Bush, Cheney, and Rumsfeld with broad bipartisan backing, are carry-ing out the most profound transformation in Washing-ton's military policy, organization, and initiatives in more than half a century. No longer facing down massed War-saw Pact troops and tank divisions across northern Europe, U.S. imperialism has begun implementing a fundamen-tal shift in the strategy, global deployment, structure, and leadership of its armed forces.

This military "transformation," as they call it, barely

begun by the Clinton administration and Congress in the closing years of the last century, can be accelerated and secured by the U.S. rulers only through war. The history of the twentieth century demonstrates, moreover, that only in the midst of deep-going economic crisis and spreading war, with patriotic appeals for "national unity," "mobilization," and "equality of sacrifice," can the capitalists convince substantial layers of working people and the insecure middle classes, at least for a time, of the need for "temporary" but sweeping "mutual" economic concessions. This includes radical reductions in the social wage, as much of the care of the young, the ill, and the elderly is pushed back on the family, aided by the church and charitable institutions.

Struggles bred by attempts to impose these conditions, however, are the very ones through which a growing vanguard of the working class will test itself and become steeled and politically experienced in class combat. This long, hot winter of economic and social crises and wars, whose opening stages we have already entered, inseparably intertwines their transformation and ours.

THEIR TRANSFORMATION

1. A historic shift in the global deployment of U.S. imperialism's armed forces, its military strategy, and its order of battle is being sharply accelerated. Championed by the White House and pushed forward by the Defense Department, this transformation aims at preparing for the character of the wars the imperialist rulers know they need to fight—at home as well as abroad. No substantial wing of either the Democratic or Republican parties has a strategic alternative to this course. And it is already too far advanced to be reversed.

"This is the most significant change of your Army since 1939," Gen. Richard Cody, deputy to Army Chief of Staff Gen. Peter Schoomaker, told the House Armed Services Committee in February 2005.

Between the beginning of 1939 and December 1941, when the Roosevelt administration declared war on Tokyo simultaneous with Germany's declaration of war against the United States, the U.S. Army was increased from 125,000 troops to 1,640,000 (and finally to 8,300,000 during the war itself); a major expansion of ship construction, as well as establishment of the first Atlantic patrol, was begun by the U.S. Navy (which increased from 300,000 to more than 3 million sailors and officers by the end of the war); and the Army Air Corps (later the Air Force) began its massive enlargement.

Underscoring the changing character, geographic scope, and accelerating frequency of U.S. imperialism's military operations, Cody pointed out: "From 1950 to 1989 the size of the total Army ranged from 64 Divisions during the Korean War, to 40 Divisions during the Vietnam War, to 28 (18 Active Component and 10 National Guard) Divisions when the Cold War ended. During this 39-year period, the Army participated in 10 distinct operations including those in the Dominican Republic, Vietnam, and Grenada. In the 14 years since the end of the Cold War (1989 to 2003), the size of the total Army further decreased from 28 Divisions to 18 Divisions; however, the operating tempo increased dramatically as the Army answered this nation's call in 57 distinct operations . . . including Panama, Desert Storm, Somalia, Haiti, Macedonia, Bosnia, and Kosovo, as well as commitments in Iraq, Afghanistan, the Philippines, the Horn of Africa, and many other locations."

Percentage of world military spending

TOTAL: $950 BILLION (2004)

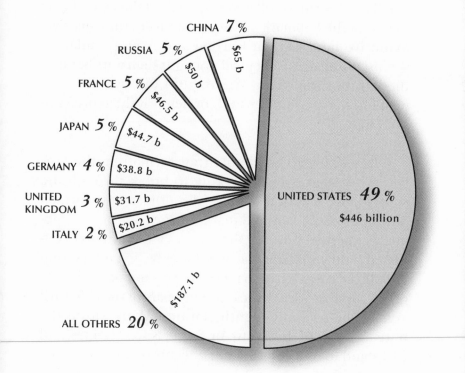

CHINA **7** %

RUSSIA **5** %

FRANCE **5** %

JAPAN **5** %

GERMANY **4** %

UNITED
KINGDOM **3** %

ITALY **2** %

$65 b

$50 b

$46.5 b

$44.7 b

$38.8 b

$31.7 b

$20.2 b

$187.1 b

ALL OTHERS **20** %

UNITED STATES **49** %

$446 billion

SOURCE: GLOBALSECURITY.ORG

"Peace will be the exception and war will be the norm for this Army," Cody pointedly told representatives of military production industries a few weeks later.

2. The U.S. rulers will never again fight the kind of wars that were the hallmark of the twentieth century: massive, extensive land wars in Europe and Asia, population against population. They will not fight such wars because they cannot win them. Washington will use whatever weapons necessary, offensively or defensively, to preempt such wars.

3. In seeking to accelerate transformation, the U.S. rulers are aggressively working to break through the conservative bias of the imperialist officer caste formed during the Cold War and marked especially by their political experience during the war in Vietnam. This determined push is sparking the most bitter factionalism within the officer corps of the armed forces—and of the intelligence services—since the opening years of the U.S. Civil War in the mid-nineteenth century. Many within the bureaucracies of the Army, Air Force, Navy, Marines, and CIA stand to lose (or win) not only promotions but control over big resources. Never before have so many generals and intelligence officials gotten away with publishing so many politically partisan "tell it like it is" books in so short a period, often within a few months of resigning or retiring from active duty. They line up on one side or another in these turf wars and openly join the factional and electoral struggle for control of the executive and legislative branches of the government.

4. There can and will be no repeat of a war conducted in the manner of the 1990-91 assault on Iraq, waged by a large U.S.-organized coalition under the flag of the "peacekeeping" United Nations. Nor will there be a re-run of the strategy used by Washington to half-heartedly wage the first European wars since the end of World War II—in Bosnia in 1994–95 and Kosova in 1999, brutally employing cruise missiles and aerial bombardment from afar against the toiling classes of the Balkans. The consequences of these Balkan wars are made even more explosive by the fact that the political questions at their root remain unresolved and are building toward further conflict.

These wars, fought in the 1990s, registered the decisive need for a transition from the command structure and order of battle established some fifty years earlier by U.S. imperialism to promote its "free world" interests.

5. The second Bush administration has accelerated transformation by mobilizing patriotic support for its course through the Afghanistan and Iraq wars. The concrete challenges the rulers confronted during these wars, and the initial experience gained in the course of fighting them, reinforced their commitment to structuring and carrying through this fundamental transition.

The place of U.S. special operations forces has been qualitatively upgraded. Army Rangers and Delta Force troops, Navy SEALs, Marine Expeditionary Units, and Air Force special operations wings collected on-the-ground intelligence, conducted combined combat maneuvers with allied indigenous forces (the Northern Alliance in Afghanistan and Kurdish peshmerga militia in Iraq), selected real-time bombing targets, and directly called in U.S. air strikes and naval firepower.

The Pentagon field-tested new weapons systems under battle conditions, including unmanned aerial reconnaissance planes and attack drones and Stryker light-armored vehicles. The U.S. rulers, to a degree undreamt-of in previous wars, pressed forward joint command and operations by the Army, Marines, Navy, Air Force, and their special forces, down to the company level.

6. The thirty-three existing U.S. Army brigades are being restructured into between 43 and 48 faster, more mobile, more lethal, light-armored brigades called Brigade Combat Teams (Units of Action). The announced goal is to be able by 2010 to put a combat-ready brigade into action anywhere in the world within 96 hours, a full division within 120 hours, and 5 divisions (some 75,000 troops) within 30 days. Substantial powers of command are being devolved from the division to the brigade level, including joint command, as needed, across all four services (including, in all probability, any CIA covert operatives in the field).

In a major shift from the post–World War II configuration of the U.S. armed forces, top Pentagon officials are projecting the need for a new "strategic triad," prioritizing the Army, Marines, and special operations forces relative to the Army, Air Force, Navy triad. Air Force fighters and bombers, as well as Navy carriers and other battleships, will remain decisive, but as part of, and subordinate to, joint operations across all the services under centralized command. The new triad builds on and consolidates two changes in the command structure instituted by the U.S. government in 1986 (the Goldwater-Nichols Act), during the closing years of the Cold War: (1) that combatant commanders report directly to the secretary of defense, not to the top officer of their respective service on the Joint Chiefs of Staff; and (2) that no officer is promoted to general or flag rank without prior experience in commanding joint forces.

The Pentagon's press release on its 2006 budget projections and "the restructuring of U.S. forces" points to the centrality of "the increase in combat units in the Army and Marine Corps," as well as initiatives to strengthen special operations forces, which "have been critical to the fight against terrorism." At the same time, the budget proposes measures so "the Navy can deploy more aircraft carriers and supporting ships more rapidly," including further reductions in Navy personnel, as well as a restructuring of Air Force expeditionary forces so they "can rapidly provide the right mix of capabilities . . . to U.S. Combatant Commanders across the globe."

7. To advance these goals, the Pentagon is reshaping the "global footprint" of the U.S. armed forces.

With the end of the Cold War, U.S. imperialism no longer confronts Warsaw Pact tanks and troops across the Fulda Gap in central Germany. Another 70,000 troops and 100,000 family members stationed at massive, sprawling "little Americas" in Europe and Asia, especially in Germany and South Korea, will be relocated to the United States. This includes the recall of all four heavy combat brigades in Germany (the better part of two divisions) to be replaced with one lighter brigade. Washington has already announced the withdrawal of 12,500 of its 37,000 troops in south Korea, recognizing that defense of U.S. imperialist interests on the peninsula can no longer rely on massing infantry and artillery as a "trip wire" along the border with north Korea. The sizeable cut in U.S. overseas-based troop deployments, especially in Western Europe, carried out during the first Bush and Clinton administrations will be further extended in the course of Washington's "global force posture review."

Among the 35 percent of U.S. bases and installations abroad scheduled for closure over the coming decade, Washington intends to pull back from those in countries, and those at locations within countries, where U.S. troops are the object of particularly strong popular hatred and resentment—beginning with the Prince Sultan Airbase near Riyadh, Saudi Arabia (from which they have already withdrawn), downtown Seoul, and Vieques in the U.S. colony of Puerto Rico.

Instead of stationing large numbers of U.S. troops and their families at bases abroad, the Pentagon is negotiating with governments to establish smaller "Forward Operating Sites," sometimes referred to as "lily pads," and others called "Cooperative Security Locations." Along with "sea-based" launching pads and matériel reserves, these installations will be situated closer to parts of the world where Washington anticipates a greater need to use its military might—primarily in the Middle East, Africa, Central Asia, former Soviet republics, and Eastern and Central Europe, with proximity to oil resources among the explicit criteria.

Most "lily pads" will support small numbers of frequently rotated troops, unencumbered by families, and maintain equipment depots to provision fighting units deployed from North America or elsewhere on short notice. Such installations are already operational in Oman, Honduras, Kyrgyzstan, and elsewhere, and Washington is holding talks with governments for sites in Bulgaria, Romania, and São Tomé and Príncipe (Gulf of Guinea), among a dozen or so others. "Cooperative Security Locations," like those under negotiation in Senegal and Uganda, will be maintained by "contractors" or "host nation personnel," according to the Pentagon, and involve no permanent, substantial U.S. military presence.

Through such negotiations, Washington is moving to establish its military presence in oil-rich West Africa at the expense of its imperialist competitors in Paris and London (and its aspiring rivals in Moscow and Beijing).

Under the banner of anti-drug-trafficking operations, the U.S. rulers are also strengthening themselves militarily in Latin America, expanding cooperation with Colombia especially (already the world's third-largest recipient of U.S. military aid, surpassed only by Israel and Egypt). In mid-2004 Congress doubled the authorized size of the U.S. military mission there to 800. Among other things, these moves are being accelerated in preparation for coming "border" conflicts and oil pipeline disputes with Venezuela.

8. The U.S. rulers are committed to maintaining an all-volunteer armed forces. Their opposition to reinstituting a draft today is not a public relations trick. It is based on their judgment of the kind of armed forces they need to prepare for the coming decades of wars they intend to fight; on lessons from the broad decline of military discipline and morale in the conscript army during the closing years of the Vietnam War; on attempts to raise the average intelligence and aptitude test scores of recruits, which have climbed with the volunteer army; and on their judgment about how best to mobilize patriotic support for a draft when they do inevitably need it in face of future, more large-scale wars.

The U.S. rulers recognize that filling recruitment quotas becomes more difficult during wartime, as deaths and injuries mount. As a result, the U.S. government is raising salaries of armed forces personnel; increasing bonuses for recruitment, reenlistment, combat theater deployment, and skills-upgrading; increasing benefits for

Some 70,000 U.S. troops at massive, sprawling "little Americas" in Germany will be relocated to the United States. Meanwhile, the Pentagon is negotiating with governments to establish small "Forward Operating Sites," sometimes called "lily pads." These will be closer to parts of the world where Washington anticipates greater need to use its military might—in the Middle East, Africa, Central Asia, former Soviet republics, and Eastern and Central Europe.

BOTTOM: U.S. base, Wiesbaden, Germany. **TOP LEFT**: U.S. Army Special Forces officer teaches counterinsurgency techniques to Colombian army unit; growing numbers of U.S. troops have been sent there since 2000. **TOP RIGHT**: U.S. troops in Uzbekistan (2004), where Washington first established a base in preparation for 2001 Afghanistan war.

GARRY LEECH

U.S. AIR FORCE / TIM VINING

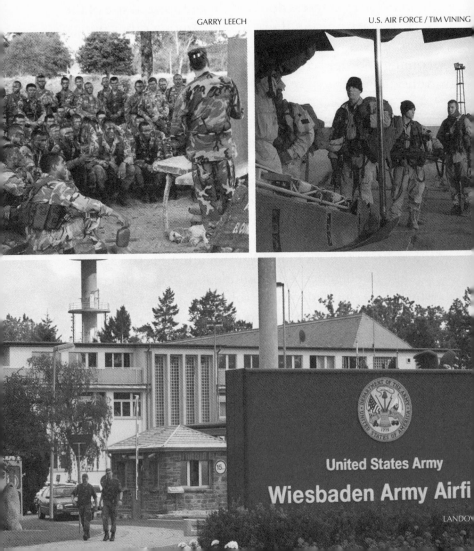

United States Army
Wiesbaden Army Airfi

LANDOV

Where U.S. imperialism has military bases or installations—2004

EUROPE	EAST ASIA & PACIFIC	NORTH AFRICA, MIDEAST, SOUTH ASIA*	SUB-SAHARAN AFRICA, SOUTH ATLANTIC
Belgium	Australia	Afghanistan	Djibouti
Bosnia	Guam	Bahrain	Kenya
Denmark	Hawaii	Diego Garcia	St. Helena
France	Hong Kong	Egypt	
Germany	Indonesia	Georgia	**WESTERN HEMISPHERE**
Greece	Japan	Iraq	
Greenland	Johnston Atoll	Jordan	Alaska
Iceland	Kwajalein Atoll	Kuwait	Antigua
Italy	New Zealand	Kyrgyzstan	Aruba and Curaçao
Kosova	Samoa	Oman	Bahamas
Luxembourg	Singapore	Pakistan	Canada
Netherlands	South Korea	Qatar	Colombia
Norway	Wake Island	Turkey	Cuba
Portugal		United Arab Emirates	(Guantánamo Bay)
Spain			Ecuador
United Kingdom		Uzbekistan	El Salvador
			Honduras
			Peru
			Puerto Rico
			United States (Continental)
			Virgin Islands

* Many U.S. military installations in these areas—set up since 2001 to wage the U.S. wars in Afghanistan and Iraq—are among the first "lily pad" bases of the kind Washington plans to spread. The same is true of bases in Djibouti in Africa, as well as Colombia, El Salvador, and elsewhere in Latin America.

SOURCES: AP, CENTER FOR DEFENSE INFORMATION, AIR FORCE ASSOCIATION, LOS ANGELES TIMES, UPI, PRAVDA.

U.S. "global posture review"

Additional countries under consideration by Washington for Forward Operating Sites ("lily pads") or Cooperative Security Locations

EUROPE	EAST ASIA & PACIFIC	NORTH AFRICA, MIDEAST, SOUTH ASIA	SUB-SAHARAN AFRICA
Bulgaria	Malaysia	Algeria	Ghana
Hungary	Philippines	Azerbaijan	Nigeria
Poland	Thailand	India	Mali
Romania		Morocco	São Tomé and Príncipe (Gulf of Guinea)
		Tunisia	Senegal
			Sierra Leone
			Uganda

SOURCES: FY2004 DEFENSE DEPARTMENT BASE STRUCTURE REPORT; U.S. STATE DEPARTMENT; PBS; AP; GLOBALSECURITY.ORG

SEE MAP NEXT PAGE ▶

U.S. military bases around the world

◄ SEE LIST ON PREVIOUS PAGE

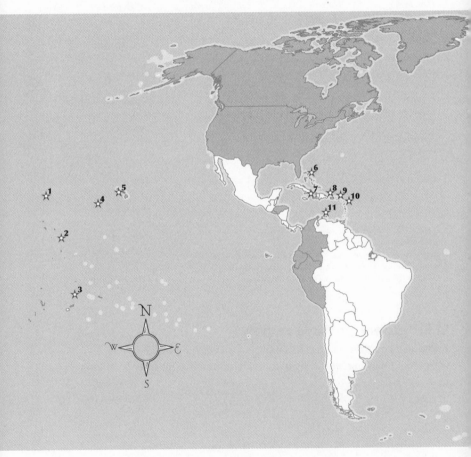

COUNTRIES WITH A U.S. BASE (2004)

☆ U.S. bases in **1.** *Wake Island* **2.** *Kwajalein Atoll* **3.** *Samoa*
4. *Johnston Atoll* **5.** *Hawaii* **6.** *Bahamas* **7.** *Cuba (Guantánamo Bay)*
8. *Puerto Rico* **9.** *Virgin Islands* **10.** *Antigua* **11.** *Aruba and Curaçao*
12. *St. Helena* **13.** *Diego Garcia* **14.** *Singapore* **15.** *Hong Kong* **16.** *Guam*

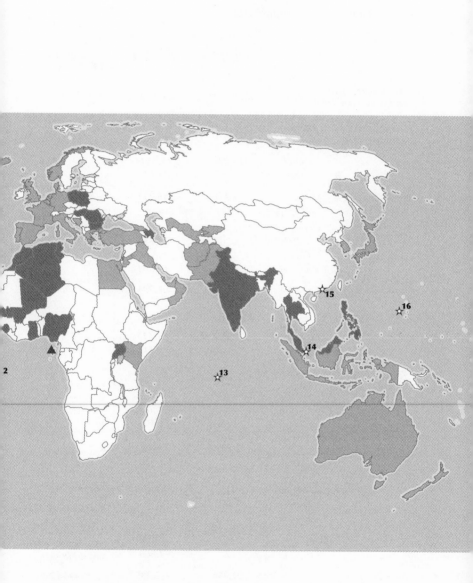

ADDITIONAL COUNTRIES UNDER CONSIDERATION FOR "LILY PADS"
OR "COOPERATIVE SECURITY LOCATIONS."

▲   *São Tomé & Príncipe*

U.S. imperialism's military "global posture review"

ACTIVE DUTY U.S. TROOPS
Regional and selected country totals

	1989	**2004**	**DoD POSTURE REVIEW PROJECTIONS**[1]
TOTAL ACTIVE DUTY (Including in/around Iraq)[2]	2,130,229	1,425,887	
TOTAL ACTIVE DUTY ABROAD (Excluding Iraq)	509,873	257,692	~190,000
Land	*452,916*	*233,544*	
Afloat	*56,957*	*24,148*	
EUROPE	**336,416**	**~114,200**	**~45,000**
Bosnia	*—*	*250*	
Germany	*248,621*	*75,603*	
Italy	*15,706*	*13,354*	
Kosova	*—*	*~2,000*	
United Kingdom	*27,639*	*11,801*	
EAST ASIA & PACIFIC	**134,912**	**97,724**	**~85,000**
Australia	*717*	*205*	
Japan[3]	*49,861*	*40,045*	
South Korea	*44,461*	*40,258*	*~28,000*
Philippines	*14,745*	*144*	
NORTH AFRICA, MIDEAST, CENTRAL AND SOUTH ASIA	**8,070**	**~31,100**	
Afghanistan	*—*	*~20,000*	
Bahrain	*168*	*1,496*	
Diego Garcia	*1,048*	*491*	
Egypt	*1,182*	*350*	
Kyrgyzstan	*—*	*1,000*	
Qatar	*—*	*3,432*	
Saudi Arabia	*416*	*291*	
Turkey	*4,862*	*1,863*	
Uzbekistan	*—*	*~1,300*	
SUB-SAHARAN AFRICA	**333**	**~1,800**	
Djibouti	*7*	*~1,600*	
AMERICAS	**21,448**	**~2,495**	
Colombia	*42*	*~800*[4]	
Cuba (Guantánamo Bay)	*2,467*	*700*	
Honduras	*1,158*	*413*	
Panama	*12,719*	*16*	

1. *Overall Department of Defense posture review projections are over roughly 10 years; south Korean reductions by end of 2008.*

2. *According to the DoD, as of early 2005 there are roughly 150,000 U.S. troops in Iraq. There are also 40,000 troops in Kuwait and elsewhere around Iraq.*

3. *Some 30,000 of the U.S. troops in Japan are on the island of Okinawa.*

4. *In October 2004, the U.S. Congress authorized doubling U.S. forces in Colombia from 400 to 800.*

SOURCES: DEPARTMENT OF DEFENSE, GLOBALSECURITY.ORG, CENTER FOR DEFENSE INFORMATION, AND VARIOUS WIRE SERVICES

Active duty U.S. troops
(1989, 2004, future)

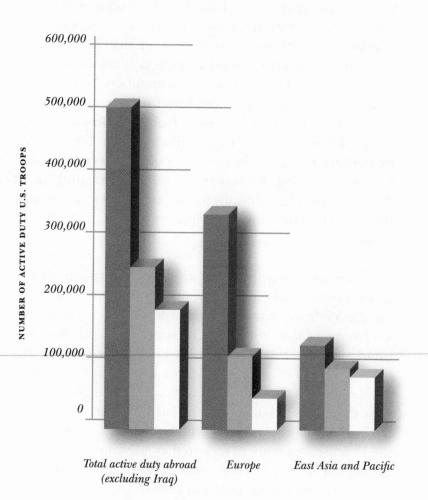

NUMBER OF ACTIVE DUTY U.S. TROOPS

600,000
500,000
400,000
300,000
200,000
100,000
0

Total active duty abroad
(excluding Iraq)   Europe   East Asia and Pacific

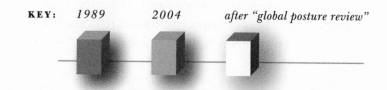

KEY: 1989   2004   after "global posture review"

families; continuing to expand ROTC programs on campuses; improving education and housing benefits; and increasing National Guard and Army Reserves inducements. Signing up for the Guard or Reserves is no longer a guarantee of one weekend a month and two weeks a year in return for college tuition. As of December 2004, when the Pentagon tripled retention bonuses for the Guard to $15,000, a quarter of its members had served in Iraq, nearly a third were deployed abroad, and 40 percent of U.S. troops in Iraq were from the Guard or Reserves. These and other rising military expenditures will exacerbate the battle in the U.S. ruling class over state finances, upping the stakes for them in winning the American people politically to support the "sacrifices" in their standard of living that must soon accompany these outlays.

9. Lessons from the class and racial divisions that eroded military discipline and undermined morale during the Vietnam War remain sharply etched in the consciousness of the military high command. With that in mind, since the 1991 Gulf War the Pentagon has reduced the assignment of GIs who are Black to combat units. The composition of those killed in action in Iraq registers the impact of these changes. As of early January 2005, 11 percent of those killed in action were African-American, the Defense Department reported, down from 17 percent during the 1991 Gulf War (Blacks make up roughly 13 percent of the U.S. population today).

The U.S. rulers have also made a concerted effort in recent decades to build an officer corps whose racial and national composition more closely resembles the ranks.

More than 8 percent of active-duty officers in the armed services today are Black, versus 2.4 percent in 1973. In the army, Blacks comprise 12 percent of the officer corps, up from 4 percent in 1973. Weighty support from within the upper echelons of the officer corps for the University of Michigan Law School affirmative action program was a determining factor in the decision of the Bush Justice Department attorneys to present only a limited challenge to that plan before the Supreme Court, which largely upheld the program in 2003.

10. In 2005 the Defense Department's Base Realignment and Closure Commission (BRAC) will release a list of bases in the United States to be shut down, an estimated 25 percent of current military installations on U.S. soil. Selected Army, Air Force, Navy, and Marine bases will be consolidated to facilitate joint training and operations.

The Bush administration plans to redirect much of the projected $3–5 billion in savings to increase spending on military salaries and bonuses, as well as to expand research, development, and deployment of what the Pentagon calls its "network-centric" Future Combat Systems: advanced communications devices and global positioning systems, designed for real-time battlefield command and control by small units; unmanned reconnaissance planes; laser-guided artillery and bombs; Light Armored Vehicles; and attack helicopters. In the process, Washington is scrapping or cutting back weapons programs carried over from Cold War combat priorities. The Comanche helicopter and Crusader artillery system have been canceled, and substantial reductions planned in the F/A-22 "Raptor" fighter jet program, as well as the Navy's aircraft carrier fleet. In an era of U.S. air dominance, fighter-bombers are the future; "dogfights" are the past.

Base closings and cutbacks in weapons systems produced by U.S. war manufacturers are particularly sensitive pork-barrel issues. They will generate more vocal opposition among both the Democratic and Republican party politicians than closing U.S. installations abroad.

11. Before attempting to increase the size of the U.S. armed forces, the Defense Department is expanding the number of combat-ready troops—what they call "war fighters"—by transferring soldiers out of noncombat tasks and replacing them with civilian employees under Pentagon supervision. The weakened union and civil service protections of Pentagon employees are already being imposed on workers in the Department of Homeland Security and presented by the Bush administration as a template to "reform" pay scales and hiring, firing, and promotion policies for increasing numbers of employees of the federal government.

The Defense Department is also "rebalancing" needed skills and responsibilities in the armed forces, among other things transferring many military police, drivers, and "civil affairs" troops from Guard and Reserves units to active-duty units.

12. Among the central aims of the transformation of the U.S. military is the creation—under the banner of antiterrorism measures—of the command structures and operational capabilities needed to respond to the resistance the capitalists know will inevitably deepen inside the United States as the consequences of their economic course bear down on workers, farmers, and other working people. The employing class's preparations register their awareness of the cumulative social and political consequences of more than three decades of stagnating capital accumulation, stiffening world trade competition, and mounting assaults on living standards and job conditions.

In contrast, during the mid-1960s and early 1970s, when U.S. imperialism was waging the Vietnam War, the rulers were still able, in response to a mass proletarian movement in the streets, to grant major social and economic concessions such as Medicare, Medicaid, and the indexation of Social Security benefits. Average hourly wages were still continuing to rise. The employers, their government, and their twin parties felt no pressing need to ready themselves for sharpening conflicts with workers, farmers, and the union movement.

Not so at the opening of the twenty-first century and the years that lie ahead. As U.S. finance capital wages war abroad, it is simultaneously advancing more and more openly on its front at home. Laying the groundwork for stepped-up militarization of civilian life, as needed, is central to their transformation.

Toward this end, in October 2002 the Northern Command was established, one of nine "war-fighting" commands of the military's global Unified Combat Command structure. For the first time in U.S. history, a military command has responsibility for the continental United States and the rest of North America. NORTHCOM, as it is called, shares facilities and a common commander with NORAD, the joint U.S.-Canadian North American Aerospace Defense Command that since the late 1950s has had the authority, by signed agreement, to place the Canadian air force under U.S. command as needed. NORAD is the center of the "missile defense" of North America.

The Northern Command also encompasses Mexico, the first time Washington's southern neighbor has been included under any of U.S. imperialism's global combat commands (including the Southern Command, long responsible for the Caribbean and Central and South America).

Under the rationalization that civil disorder is a national security matter since "terrorists" and their supporters and sympathizers exploit such situations, dealing with civil disorder within and along the borders of the U.S. has by law—for the first time since the aftermath of the Civil War—now been made a *military* matter for the federal government, not solely a *police* matter for city, state, and federal authorities.

13. The establishment of an armed forces command for the continental United States is combined with other, more publicized preparations to meet worker and farmer resistance at home. The capitalists deliberately drape these preparations in civilian, not military, trappings. Like NORTHCOM, elements of such measures—dubbed "Homeland Defense" since 9/11, and centralized through a new civilian cabinet department of that name—were initiated by the Clinton administration. Avoiding the xenophobic Americanism the rulers will inevitably nurture among layers of the population as conditions of social crisis and broader war require, they present the preparatory steps they need to take today as matters of "civic duty" and as minor intrusions of privacy required of "us all" in face of "terrorists" imperiling hearth and home.

These measures range from increased federal centralization of "surveillance" of "suspected terrorists" both at home and abroad, to a de facto national identity card system in the guise of Social Security numbers; from omnipresent "security" controls at airports, in office buildings, and elsewhere, to appeals to report "suspicious" packages in public places or behavior that's "out of the ordinary" in your apartment building, neighborhood, or on the streets; from curtailment of habeas corpus and even Fifth Amendment protections of the accused and spying on individuals' library use, book purchases, and bank accounts, to stepped-up targeting of foreign-born residents, whether "legals" or "illegals."

The decks are being cleared of restraints placed on military intelligence operations within the United States following the 1975–76 Senate Church Committee reports that detailed sweeping constitutional rights violations by military and other federal intelligence units carrying out often brutal operations against opponents of the Vietnam War, supporters of the Black and Chicano movements, the women's liberation movement, the labor movement, communists, and others. The FBI's domestic "counter-terrorism" work is once again being rapidly expanded.

These spying operations, which sooner or later include political disruption efforts, will be centralized by a cabinet-level "Director of National Intelligence" directly responsible to the president. Equally important, *exempted* from the purview of this centralization, in fact, are the massive armed forces intelligence operations organized by and responsible to the Pentagon. The intelligence "reform" bill, pushed through Congress in December 2004 by a campaign led by the Democrats, was crafted before final adoption to meet Bush and Rumsfeld's demands.

The big majority of workers and farmers in the United States do not yet directly feel, or politically understand, that what is happening today and in recent years at Guantánamo, what is happening with the "preventive detention" of U.S. citizens, what is happening with the curtailment of the right to appeal deportations is targeting *us* above all, not primarily pockets of suspect "foreigners." Even to all but a minority of foreign-born workers and other immigrants, any threat still seems several times removed. As throughout the history of the U.S. class struggle, from the Palmer Raids to the Smith Act labor frame-ups to Cointelpro, however, new and increasingly more militarized probes by the rulers will be recognized for what they are—and resisted—as working people and the labor movement are pressed into struggle to defend ourselves and our toiling allies against accelerated assaults by the employers and the state that represents and defends their class interests.

'The Mission Defines the Coalition'

14. Following the disintegration of not only the Stalinist regimes of Eastern Europe and the Soviet Union, but also of the Council for Mutual Economic Assistance (Comecon) and Warsaw Pact—through which trade and military ties among the Soviet Union and European workers states had been structured—triumphalist talk of a new era of "peace," "democracy," "stability," even "the end of history," was accompanied by massive reductions in the size of the U.S. armed forces and cuts in military spending. The "peace dividend," used by the Treasury on behalf of U.S. bond traders, laid the basis for the exaggerated rise of the dollar and stoked the fire beneath what became the financial balloon of the late 1990s and opening decade of the twenty-first century.

The end of the "peace dividend" and the beginning of transformation came with the rulers' growing recognition, beginning during the closing years of the Clinton administration, that they themselves would have to compensate for the fact that it was no longer possible for Stalin's heirs to police the toiling masses. Or for the fact that Moscow no longer has the political standing in the working-class movement needed to get a response to rationalizations for dampening the class struggle across vast areas of the globe.

15. "Liberation" not "stabilization," "freedom" not the "balance of power," register not just a change in watchwords but a historic shift in world political strategy under the second Bush administration, compared to Clinton and his predecessor.

What is decisive in this reshaping of U.S. imperialist foreign policy, often called the "Bush doctrine," is the administration's post–September 11 concretization and accelerated implementation in combat of the transformation of the U.S. armed forces. Those changes, in and of themselves, register the reversal of what a broad layer of the U.S. ruling class in both imperialist parties now agrees was a quarter century of politically and militarily inadequate responses to "terrorist" attacks on U.S. targets and belated action against states deemed capable of developing weapons and delivery systems endangering Washington's imperial interests.

The U.S. rulers' overturn of the Taliban and Saddam Hussein regimes in Afghanistan and Iraq, and the ongoing threats and pressures against Iran and north Korea— the two countries, along with Iraq, on Bush's "axis of evil"—are meant, among other things, as object lessons. These demonstrations of military might are aimed at "persuading" bourgeois forces in Syria, Libya, Palestine, and elsewhere from North Africa through Central Asia and Latin America that continuing to get crosswise with Washington is not only against their class interests but contrary over any extended period to their own survival. The Iraq war and its ongoing repercussions have displaced the Israel-Palestinian conflict as the center of politics in the Middle East, its effects radiating east, north, even all the way across to West Africa.

16. Neither NATO, an alliance born of the Cold War, nor the coalitions Washington patched together in the

1990s under UN or NATO fig leaves to fight wars in the Gulf and Yugoslavia, can serve the evolving purposes of U.S. imperialism. Nor can the coalition that was put together—or better, declared—to support the Anglo-American war against Saddam Hussein's Baathist apparatus.

As the U.S. government prepares to engage battles around the world that it won't be able to avoid (and in its majority no longer wants to avoid), in each and every case Washington's armed forces command will be the centerpiece. "The mission will define the coalition," not vice versa, in Rumsfeld's words.

17. The Proliferation Security Initiative (PSI), described by the State Department as "an activity, not an organization," is a prime example of Rumsfeld's dictum. Some sixty governments have so far signed on as part of this Pentagon-led and -organized worldwide piracy operation. Its purpose is to "interdict" shipments to "rogue states" and "hostile regimes" of materials the imperialist powers claim might possibly be used to produce or deliver weapons of mass (or "substantial") destruction.

Since the PSI was announced in May 2003, ships have been boarded on the high seas and cargoes confiscated in port. The governments of the United States, the United Kingdom, France, Australia, Canada, Japan, Mexico, Singapore, and numerous other countries have participated in one or more of the dozen joint exercises held as of the opening of 2005. The most recent have been Team Samurai 2004 in October in the Pacific not far from the territorial waters of north Korea, and Exercise Chokepoint '04, the first such exercise in the Americas, organized in November in the Caribbean between Key West and the island of Hispaniola, shared by Haiti and the Dominican Republic, just to the east of Cuba.

18. In Iraq the backbone of the imperialist-dominated coalition has been the governments of the United States and United Kingdom, plus those of Australia, Italy, Denmark, Poland, the Netherlands—more than thirty in all, from Europe, Asia and the Pacific, and Central America.

To these governments, the U.S. rulers are making the demand (with offers to assist those who cooperate) that they transform their own armed forces to fit the logistical, training, and special operations tasks, as well as international leadership example, they will increasingly be called on to provide in supporting U.S.-led operations.

Tokyo especially is using its dispatch of some 600 troops to Iraq on a "noncombat" mission to accelerate the breakdown of post–World War II barriers to Japanese imperialism's exercise of military power in the Pacific and beyond. At the center of this historic shift is a sharp increase in Nippon nationalism at home, greater overt support for Taiwan, and a tighter military alliance with Washington in face of China's military buildup, especially its naval expansion. The Pentagon "is concerned about and is attentive" to Beijing's growing naval power, said Rumsfeld, with classic understatement, in testimony before the Senate Armed Services Committee in February 2005. "[W]e hope and pray [China] enters the civilized world in an orderly way," he added. Not answered prayers, however, but self-fulfilled fears will be the order of the day.

19. Washington's course toward the shifting state alliances and conflicts called the European Union is to press for a more rapid expansion of that political relationship, from Turkey to Ukraine to the Black Sea.

In doing so, the U.S. rulers aim to have the biggest and most heterogeneous pool possible of potential allies; to further reduce the political weight of Russia; and to accelerate the displacement of the EU's long-standing Franco-German center. The goal of U.S. finance capital is to undermine the euro's ability to act as a competitor to the dollar as the dominant reserve currency as well as medium in world trade and finance, and to force Washington's rivals to bear the costs of integrating into the world capitalist market and imperialist military alliances the countries of Central and Eastern Europe where capitalist social relations were overturned in the wake of World War II, and increasingly the former Soviet republics as well.

20. For U.S. imperialism, the geopolitical center of the world is shifting to the east, both within continental Europe and beyond. Poland, Ukraine, or Slovakia is each more important to the U.S. rulers than Belgium; Pakistan or India more important than France; Indonesia more so than Germany.

21. Whatever diplomatic minuets the U.S. rulers engage in at the United Nations or other international forums, they will accept no alliances, even temporary, that hobble achievement of *their* strategic objectives. Nor do they believe any longer in either the possibility or effectiveness of UN-sponsored "Desert Storm"–type coalitions, as during the 1990-91 Gulf War, which ranged from London and Paris to Riyadh, Cairo, Damascus, and Moscow, with tacit backing from Beijing. The second Iraq War has sharply accelerated the conflicts among former components of the Desert Storm alliance, giving further evidence that what sounded during the earlier Gulf conflict were indeed the opening guns of World War III.

22. The efforts by a bloc of imperialist governments led by Paris and Berlin to stop Washington's invasion of Iraq in 2003 registered the attempt of these relatively weaker imperialist powers to protect their economic, political, and military interests in the Middle East.

These moves by certain imperialist powers, in turn, became a pole of attraction for some semicolonial governments trying to resist Yankee domination. Middle-class radicals the world over—whose nationalist "strategy" more and more is simply "No to America!"—find it easy to adapt to this "benign" face of imperialism.

23. Washington's initial deployment and ongoing development of an anti-ballistic missile weapons system occupies a central place in its political offensive to shift the balance of forces against its imperialist rivals as well as vis-à-vis Russia and China. ABM systems are no longer a bargaining chip, used over decades of "arms talks" to pressure the Soviet Union to limit expansion of its nuclear arsenal. The Reagan administration's accelerated development of the "Star Wars" program in the 1980s marked the beginning of a fundamental shift. The affirmation of this course as bipartisan policy was completed more than a decade later with the Clinton administration's course towards abrogating the 1972 ABM treaty with Moscow and its decision to proceed with building the system. Whatever technological shortcomings these anti-ballistic missile systems may have today, Washington will continue to improve their effectiveness, and all the more rapidly under conditions of war.

Washington's imperialist "allies" are being given an offer they can't refuse and—in the case of London, Tokyo, and some others—don't want to refuse: "Ante up land, facilities, and support for ABM deployment, and you will have a say in decisions and be protected by the shield. If not, as missiles approach your sovereign territory, we will decide without you."

Bush's offer to Russia's President Vladimir Putin is straightforward: "Don't take your eyes off China! Come in under the shield. Accept the loss of your former Soviet republics. And when you run into real trouble with your own workers, peasants, and oppressed nationalities, the U.S. armed forces will be there to help." The faint undertone saying *"until we can replace you,"* however, makes negotiations with Moscow rocky going.

24. U.S. imperialism's objective in the Cold War was to ensure that in bringing down the regime in the Soviet Union, they would defeat the working class and its toiling allies on the land. The imperialist powers assumed that in doing so they could move rapidly toward establishing the bourgeois class relations, legal structure, and other preconditions for a stable capitalist Russia.

The imperialist rulers lost, however. The heirs of Stalin were felled, but the war with the working class has yet to be joined. Washington's military transformation is aimed at preparing for that war. The "cooperative security locations" from one end of the Silk Road to the other, the bases that will eventually be negotiated in Belarus following those in Bulgaria and Romania, the lily pads in Ukraine, even refueling rights in Russia—all that is, or will be, on the table. As will the offer to Moscow that when civil strife threatens to spread "terrorism," "drug wars," or "nuclear proliferation," the U.S. military will be there to prop up Moscow's wretched declining armed forces against the workers and peasants—as well as, Putin hopes forlornly, against bourgeois-democratic oppositions both inside Russia and along its retrenched borders. However, neither experiences in the former Soviet republic of Georgia at the opening of 2004, nor in Ukraine a year later, bode well for these illusions.

What the U.S. Rulers Have Accomplished; What They Cannot Achieve

25. There is a difference between problems the imperialist rulers face due to mistakes they can and will correct (underestimate them at your peril!), and those resulting from the dynamics of the world class struggle that they can affect to one degree or another but cannot avoid. The rout of the Taliban regime in Afghanistan in 2001, as well as imperialism's devastating, decade-long squeeze on Iraq topped off by the 2003 invasion, put the writing on the wall for governments and other bourgeois forces from North Africa through Southeast Asia that were at odds with U.S. imperialism.

a) The Pervez Musharraf regime in Pakistan—former protector of the Taliban, and organizer of a worldwide black market in nuclear technology—is being transformed into an unstable but staunch U.S. strategic ally. The Pakistani army is carrying out joint operations against the Taliban with U.S. special operations forces on both sides of the Afghanistan-Pakistan border, and has curtailed the international nuclear arms network organized through sections of Islamabad's military intelligence apparatus and A.Q. Khan, "father of the Pakistani A-bomb."

b) Even more important, for the first time the U.S. rulers have pulled the government of India, including its two main competing bourgeois parties, into their orbit. The shifts by Washington in relations with Islamabad and New Delhi alike have precipitated steps to deescalate the decades-old conflict over Kashmir between these two nuclear-armed regimes.

c) In a joint operation by London and Washington, the Muammar el-Qaddafi leadership of Libya has been "persuaded" to see the error of its ways. It is abandoning its nuclear and other weapons development programs, settling billions of dollars of claims from victims of past terrorist attacks attributed to Libyan government agents, and opening its vast natural resources to imperialist exploitation in a manner more amenable to international finance capital.

d) In the interests of its own self-preservation, the royal house of Saud, sitting atop the world's largest known oil reserves, is joining forces with imperialism to help destroy networks like Al Qaeda, for whom the Wahabi rulers of Saudi Arabia are the infidels controlling and profaning the holy sites of Islam. Each such step deepens the contradictions and shakes the stability of this corrupt, rentier regime, while the results for the princes will be even worse if these steps are not taken.

e) Evidence is also mounting that the U.S. rulers' escalating squeeze on Syria is having an effect , with repercussions spreading to Lebanon. Together with the impact of the Iraqi elections, the pressure is even beginning to be felt in Cairo.

The U.S. government is demanding that Damascus take action against émigré Baathist forces in Syria who organize and finance the flow of weapons and combatants into Iraq, and that the Assad regime continue its de facto acceptance of U.S. military operations inside Syrian territory along the Iraqi border. The U.S. rulers are also demanding that Damascus halt its efforts to obtain "weapons of mass destruction."

26. Washington is taking advantage of its military gains in the Middle East to further strengthen its ties to the

Israeli government, armed forces, and intelligence agencies. The U.S. rulers are increasing their pressure on leaders of Palestinian organizations, with the aim of deepening divisions within and among them. This process has accelerated with the election of Mahmoud Abbas as the first post–Yassir Arafat president of the Palestinian Authority. For imperialism, however, the exhaustion and defeat of the second intifada has been the decisive factor in its efforts to impose a bourgeois coalition on the Palestinians in agreement with Israel.

Advancing under cover of the assault on Iraq and the "global war on terrorism," the Israeli regime had devastated towns and camps that have been organizing centers of mortar attacks, "martyrdom" bombings, and other armed actions; pressed ahead with construction of the 400-mile-long wall deep inside the West Bank; systematically assassinated layer after layer of the Hamas leadership; and initiated the political battle within Israel to withdraw settlements from Gaza in order to consolidate occupied territories in the West Bank and establish a more secure border.

27. The imperialist powers have effectively nullified the 1968 Nuclear Nonproliferation Treaty by declaring, contrary to treaty provisions, that "nonnuclear weapons states" will be barred from developing technology and facilities needed to produce uranium sufficiently enriched to power reactors for energy production. The U.S. government, with varying degrees of success, is pressing the International Atomic Energy Agency (IAEA) to turn itself into an international police force targeting semicolonial countries deemed insufficiently compliant with imperialist demands to abrogate their sovereignty and treaty rights. Washington's campaign to replace Mohamed

ElBaradei as head of the IAEA is part of its efforts to accelerate that organization's police work on behalf of the U.S. rulers.

a) The Iranian regime has come under increasing pressure, above all from Washington, to agree to unconditional inspection of all its nuclear facilities and to abandon extensive nuclear power development—a program initiated with Washington's aid and blessings under the pro-imperialist dictatorship of Mohammed Reza Shah Pahlavi, overthrown in the revolutionary upsurge of 1979. London, Paris, and Berlin have joined in this squeeze on Tehran, whatever the disputes between them and Washington over how fast and how far to tighten the vise.

Wiping out Iran's nuclear potential remains a premier Israeli strategic objective, prompting frequent references to Tel Aviv's 1981 air strike that destroyed Iraq's nuclear reactor at Osirak. Tehran's nuclear facilities are more geographically spread out than were Baghdad's (a lesson learned from the Osirak strike), and only when Washington believes the odds of success are high—or comes to believe it has no choice—will it initiate military action against Iran, or agree to Israel doing so. As shown by the virtually simultaneous destruction of Iraqi antiaircraft positions in the opening hours of the 2003 war, however, U.S. special operations forces can locate and take out widely dispersed installations with devastating speed and effectiveness. They have long ago begun the reconnaissance, mapping, electronic surveillance, and other steps inside Iran to prepare for such an eventuality.

b) The Democratic People's Republic of Korea, the third country on Washington's "axis of evil"—together with Iran and the former Iraqi regime—withdrew from the Nuclear Nonproliferation Treaty in 2003. It has defended its right, and proclaimed its intention, to continue developing nuclear weapons for its defense. Pyongyang is the target of a multifront effort, which includes Beijing, to force the DPRK to halt development of its nuclear program. At the same time, Washington has aided south Korea's effort to sweep under the rug the fact that as recently as 2000 it produced weapons-grade plutonium and uranium in experiments hidden from the IAEA.

c) After months of insisting that IAEA demands for on-site inspection violated Brazil's right to protect patented technology, the government of Luiz Inácio Lula da Silva conceded, agreeing in late 2004 to allow access to suffi-cient-enough areas of its Resende nuclear facility to sat-isfy the agency.

28. The government that emerges from the January 30, 2005, Iraqi elections will have to balance the increasingly autonomous Kurdistan Region in the north and rival political forces from within the Shiite majority and Sunni minority. The Baathist regime was based among sectors of the Sunni population with a vested class interest in preserving the minority privileges whose consolidation was bestowed on them by British imperialism. Among the bloodiest dictatorships in Middle East history, over its more than thirty-five years in power it systematically or-ganized the wholesale slaughter of dissenting Baathist forces, Communist Party members and those accused of being communists, along with Shiite and Kurdish leaders.

Following the 1991 Gulf War, under protection of U.S. and British imperialism's no-fly zone, the Kurdish region functioned more and more as a separate country. Lead-ers of the Kurdish area, which has its own government and the best-trained and most disciplined indigenous armed force in Iraq, are determined to claim a substan-tial share of control over, and revenues from, the oilfields on the perimeter of its region. And they are demanding reversal of the Baathists' "arabization" of Kirkuk and other cities and towns in Kurdish areas.

With the U.S. presidential race safely behind it, the Bush administration in November 2004 relaunched the war in Iraq to consolidate power over the Baathist stronghold in the center of the country, which it had originally stopped short of carrying through to the end following the taking of Baghdad in April 2003. Well-financed forces from Saddam Hussein's elite Republican Guard and secret police used the time to regroup as Baathist irregulars and to link up with groups such as that headed by Abu Musab al-Zarqawi.

U.S. forces conducted this stage in the war with little opposition among the Shia population, who have themselves been targets for decades of Baathist terror, bombings, and assassinations. U.S. operations also enjoyed overwhelming support in Kurdish regions. Despite deep wells of hatred among the Iraqi toilers for the imperialist occupiers, the detested Baathist forces and their allies who are waging the war they didn't fight in 2003 are antagonistic to and incapable of mobilizing and leading a revolutionary national liberation struggle in Iraq. None has a class interest in uniting the workers and peasants of Iraq to advance their national sovereignty. None has a program to do so.

A telling confirmation of this fact has been the stunning absence of any broad outpouring of opposition to the imperialist invasion and occupation of Iraq anywhere in the Middle East, or in any predominantly Muslim country. To the contrary, governments from Morocco to Indonesia have been under little pressure at home to pull back from their course of lining up behind Washington and Baghdad to legitimize, however "critically," the U.S.-

installed regime and the government emerging from the January 30, 2005, elections. The surprising scope of the participating electorate and the impact of the turnout in Shia and Kurdish areas have dealt the biggest blow yet to the prospects of the Baathist-organized forces.

The unintended consequence of the imperialists' course, however, is to open up space in Iraq and throughout the region for the working class and peasants to organize and fight to advance their interests; to open up space for oppressed nations such as the Kurds; to open up space for the fight to advance women's rights; to open up space to advance the separation of religious institutions from politics and the state; to open up space for the circulation of propaganda popularizing and explaining proletarian politics. The unintended consequences throughout the Middle East, South Asia, North Africa, and beyond will continue to unfold. That is the future the imperialists can do nothing to avoid.

Capital, Wages, and Class Struggle

29. The more than quarter-century-long stagnation in the U.S. rulers' rate of capital accumulation is sharply accelerating interimperialist competition and increasing pressure to shift further to their favor the relationship of forces between capital and labor. As explained in "Capitalism's Long Hot Winter Has Begun": "In seeking to boost their profit margins, more and more employers have been unable to count on anything other than pressing to drive down wages and benefits, lengthening hours, and intensifying labor. This stretch-out and speedup is the 'secret' to the productivity growth that Greenspan exaggerates and brags about in order to reassure the capitalist class that something more is happening than a further

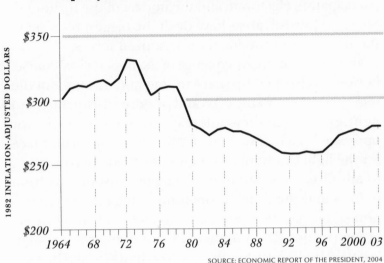

Average real weekly earnings of employed workers in U.S. (1964–2003)

1982 INFLATION-ADJUSTED DOLLARS

$350

$300

$250

$200

1964   68   72   76   80   84   88   92   96   2000 03

SOURCE: ECONOMIC REPORT OF THE PRESIDENT, 2004

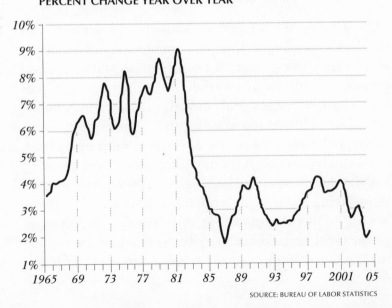

Average hourly earnings of employed workers in U.S. (1965–2004)

PERCENT CHANGE YEAR OVER YEAR

10%
9%
8%
7%
6%
5%
4%
3%
2%
1%

1965   69   73   77   81   85   89   93   97   2001   05

SOURCE: BUREAU OF LABOR STATISTICS

expansion of massive government debt and its private counterpart in corporate paper, mortgages, and credit cards."

30. Only in face of a social crisis triggered by depression and war has finance capital in the United States been able to mobilize the kind of patriotic appeals for "national unity" and "equality of sacrifice" that can convince broad sections of the population, at least for a time, to accept sweeping cuts in their living standards. It will take such circumstances once again for the rulers to mobilize, on a national political plane, a campaign that attempts to roll back wages and conditions further and to substantially reduce the social wage. Tens of millions in the working class and middle layers have come over decades to consider Social Security, Medicare, Medicaid, workers' compensation, and other benefits to be *rights*. Most depend on these benefits for survival after retirement, or after an injury or illness that has left them unable to work.

The progress thus far by individual employers in increasing the rate of exploitation through assaults on wages, hours, and conditions falls far short of what the capitalists must accomplish. The ruling class needs to slash payouts for Social Security pensions and other components of the social wage. It must shift more of the costs of education, public transportation, care of the young and old, and other government-funded services onto individuals and their families, making them more dependent on the church and charities.

Above all, the rulers must radically lower expectations bred over the last three decades by gains wrested from their hands during the 1960s and early 1970s that transformed Social Security into a modest but real inflation-protected pension to live on and medical coverage to fall back on.

When Social Security pensions were first won by workers in the course of labor battles in the mid-1930s, the monthly payments were at best a small supplement to individual family support and church and county charity. Average life expectancy in the United States at that time was six years *below* the retirement eligibility age set at 65. From the mid-1960s through the early 1970s, as a by-product of the mass proletarian struggle for Black rights, Social Security was significantly extended and strengthened. Benefits were indexed to inflation for the first time; Medicare was established for all those receiving Social Security; and Medicaid became available for those below a certain income level, and for many with physical disabilities, regardless of age.

Today life expectancy is twelve years—and rising—*above* the age at which most people become eligible for full Social Security benefits. The bosses are scrambling to devise ways to reappropriate more and more of even this small portion of the wealth workers create through our labor—a portion the capitalists, contrary to the assurances of the reformists, never intended to be settled for all time. Over several decades, however, as both jobs and increases in real cash money earnings have become more insecure, millions have come to believe they need a retirement income and emergency medical protection that are *less* vulnerable to risk, not more so. Thus, despite its need to slash these entitlements, the capitalist class recoils from the kind of social and political fight they know they'll be picking if they attempt anything more than takeback "reforms" around the edges.

In 1996 the Clinton administration took the initial slice out of the social wage, out of these "rights" of the working class, leading Congress to end federally funded Aid to Families with Dependent Children, which had been established as part of Social Security in 1935—the end of "welfare as we know it," in Clinton's cold and contemptuous phrase.

For more than a quarter century, both Republican and Democratic party politicians have escalated demagogic cries that Social Security is "going broke," implying that blame falls on growing numbers of "greedy geezers" who save too little, retire too early, and live too long. As far back as 1983, Democratic and Republican politicians joined together to raise the Social Security eligibility age, currently heading to 67, and hike the payroll tax—the most regressive and anti-working-class of all federal, state, or local taxes, aside from lotteries. What's more, despite the myth that these payroll tax funds are "put aside," are isolated from the flow of general tax revenues, they are in fact used by Washington year in and year out to fight its wars and prop up the dollar, one of the unspoken consequences of which is to subsidize massively inflated bourgeois consumption.

31. In order to prepare the ground to continue taking back what they can from the social wage, the U.S. rulers seek to undermine class solidarity. They aim to deepen divisions, pit younger working people against older, and win political support among layers of workers to place more of the burden for medical care, retirement, and other needs onto individuals and families. The capitalist parties play on insecurities fueled by the fact that, under cover of bankruptcy proceedings, growing numbers of companies—from coal operators, steel bosses, and garment and textile employers, to packinghouses, airlines, and others—are simply declaring null and void health insurance coverage and "defined benefit" pension plans supposedly guaranteed by contract to retirees.

The capitalists hope to convince not only broad sections of the middle class but "ambitious" workers and their families that they would be better off with individual "investment" accounts that won't "run out of funds" (as the rulers falsely claim Social Security is doing, even though there are no "dedicated" pension funds to run out of), that no employer or government "can take away," and that workers can "take with them" from job to job. The bosses rarely if ever mention that such "investment" accounts can be devastated by a sharp drop in the stock or bond markets, such as occurred starting in early 2001.

That such self-serving deceit and demagogy by the employing class gains a hearing among substantial layers of working people is the payoff for the post–World War II class-collaborationist course of the labor officialdom. For more than half a century, the union bureaucracy has blocked any social and political fight by the working class and our organizations for government-guaranteed universal health care, pensions, and other programs that return to all working people a greater portion of the wealth produced by our labor. Instead, they continue to pursue the class-collaborationist course of negotiating, or seeking to preserve, "fringe benefits" in union contracts that rely on the competitiveness and (hoped for) profitability of particular companies and some industries. Above all, "fringes" sharply differentiate "unionists" covered by such contracts from the big majority of our class and its toiling allies, lending credence to the employers' antilabor propaganda aimed at convincing workers that unions are job trusts, selfishly concerned only with maintaining the relatively better conditions of their own few members.

32. For nearly a decade following the end of the Cold War, the "peace dividend," combined with an overlapping federal tax revenue bonanza from the stock market bubble of the late 1990s, buffered the sharpness of the crisis in state finances confronting the U.S. ruling class. Over the ten years between 1989 and 1998, during the Bush senior and Clinton administrations, federal military spending was cut by nearly a third—by $135 billion, or close to 10 percent of the entire 1998 federal budget. Contrary to liberal mythology, the result was not to "free up" funds for education, food stamps, unemployment insurance, or other social needs, every single one of which was reduced during the eight years of the Clinton administration, but instead to help hold down real interest rates, prop up the "strong" dollar, and line the pockets of wealthy bondholders.

Between 1998 and 2004, however, Washington increased military spending by 50 percent, with the overwhelming bulk of the increase—$122 billion, or 41 percent—coming in the three years since September 11. These figures, moreover, do not include the annual $80–100 billion "supplemental" spending for Washington's ongoing wars in Iraq and Afghanistan, as well as untold amounts for what the Pentagon calls "black reconnaissance" by U.S. combined special operations forces in Syria, Iran, Saudi Arabia, Yemen, Colombia, the Philippines, and elsewhere. The rulers are already exploiting the return of federal budget and trade deficits to rationalize further "belt tightening"— our belts, not theirs—on social spending.

33. Since the 1970s Democratic and Republican administrations, on behalf of finance capital, have successfully used Federal Reserve Bank and U.S. Treasury maneuvers to postpone a financial crisis and depression spiral and to cushion the consequences of a social crisis. At the federal, state, county, and local levels, as well as through corporate, mortgage, and consumer lending, they have ted a debt balloon they depict as always expanding and never popping. This quarter-century-long accelerated debt creation has stretched out expansions and moderated slumps. It has done so, however, at the cost of inflating the dollar relative to many other currencies and to precious metals.

Since 1971, when the last vestige of the dollar's fixed convertibility to gold collapsed under the blows of Vietnam War–fueled inflation, all the world's currencies have become so-called fiat money—that is, none of them, including the greenback, has any labor value, and none has any price except relative to the others. They are nothing more than notations on a hard drive.

By creating more and more dollars to finance debt expansion, the U.S. rulers are inevitably and deliberately weakening their currency relative to that of their strongest rivals. Since what "stands behind" any currency, however, is the "full faith and credit" of the government issuing it, the dollar is and will remain first among fiat monies: it has the economic and military might of U.S. imperialism in its corner. No alternative national "brand name" can or will replace it as the dominant reserve currency in world finance and trade. The dollar's Pyrrhic victory, however, has destabilizing consequences for the capitalist system. It increases not only the odds of runaway inflation but also the likelihood of a world banking and monetary crisis, as rival finance capitals and state treasuries work to break the dollar's stronghold.

Exhaustion of Alternatives to Revolutionary Leadership

34. Underlying the absence of popular response to the U.S.-led invasion and occupation of Iraq in the Arab and Muslim world is the exhaustion of the bourgeois-nationalist leaderships that, over the span of some eighty years, came to power on the shoulders of anti-imperialist struggles involving hundreds of millions of workers, peasants, and youth across Asia, Africa, and the Americas.

Throughout much of the last century, these bourgeois currents filled a political vacuum left by political misleadership—if not outright betrayal—of worker and peasant battles and national liberation struggles by Moscow and its subordinate Stalinist parties in colonial countries themselves as well as the metropolitan centers of the respective imperialist overlords. If these bourgeois regimes in the oppressed nations toed the line sufficiently on matters of diplomatic importance to the Soviet bureaucracy, moreover, the caste in turn gave its tacit blessing to ruthless repression of workers, peasants, and national minorities, often including the local Communist parties themselves. In this way, governments such as that of Nasser in Egypt, Nkrumah in Ghana, or Sukarno in Indonesia gained some room for maneuver in conflicts with the imperialists and burnished their "radical" credentials for a time, both at home and through world forums such as the Movement of Nonaligned Nations.

With the end of the Cold War, even regimes that had still felt it in their interests in the closing decades of the century to retain some residual "anti-imperialist" verbiage found the cost-benefit equation abruptly altered to their disadvantage. Those in the state bureaucracy and officer corps hoping to "make it" as part of rising bourgeois layers were suddenly and involuntarily weaned from the largesse and privileges made possible by their former relations with Moscow. (The massive funds available through United Nations agencies and related "Non-Governmental Organizations" helped, but were nowhere near the scope of paradise lost.)

Too fearful of the revolutionary energy of the toiling masses, too desirous of siphoning to themselves crumbs from the table of the imperialist exploiters, too beholden to their former colonial masters, and now bereft of patrons in the former Soviet Union, these second-, third-, and fourth-generation bourgeois-nationalist layers are operating in different world conditions from those even a quarter of a century ago. For the bourgeois ruling classes in these countries, both the times and stakes have changed. They're different from the ones amid which—under pressure from the toilers' democratic and anti-imperialist aspirations and mobilizations—Nasser took back the Suez Canal from British and French finance capital in 1956, and other governments as recently as the late 1960s and early 1970s nationalized oil fields, refineries, and other natural resources owned by the propertied ruling families of U.S. and other imperialist powers.

35. A parallel and related exhaustion of revolutionary content marks the political evolution of petty-bourgeois and aspiring bourgeois leaderships of national liberation movements today: from the Palestine Liberation Organization (PLO) and other Palestinian organizations such as Hamas, to the Irish Republican Army (IRA) and the Basque Fatherland and Liberty (ETA).

These organizations arose (or re-arose) during the closing decades of the twentieth century on the basis of powerful opposition to national oppression among the Palestinian, Irish, and Basque peoples. Over the past four decades, however, the leaderships of these organizations have relied on spectacular armed actions, in combination (especially as such operations not only produced no gains but met intensified repression) with diplomatic and political maneuvers to reach a negotiated *accommodation* with the oppressors. Mobilizations organized by them were more and more used solely as pressure to better realize such an accommodation.

None of these leaderships ever proved capable of mobilizing and leading the workers and peasants as the backbone of a revolutionary democratic movement capable of fighting effectively for national liberation, freedom from imperialist domination, land to the tillers, the right to armed self-defense, and the organization of the working class to act in the interests of the producing classes. None developed a leadership of the revolutionary caliber and political capacity of the July 26 Movement and Rebel Army in Cuba, the National Liberation Front of Algeria, Sandinista National Liberation Front of Nicaragua, New Jewel Movement of Grenada, or the revolutionary movement in Burkina Faso.

Miseducated over decades by Stalinism, leaders of these organizations experienced repeated betrayals by Moscow and the world movement beholden to it. They were left high and dry when the regime of the Soviet caste and its European sisters collapsed at the opening of the 1990s. The military structure and internal methods of functioning they learned from Stalinist organizations, directly and indirectly, left them vulnerable to penetration by police agents and provocateurs. As the operations of the capitalist market have accelerated class differentiation within these oppressed nations (both bourgeoisification and proletarianization), the petty-bourgeois course of these leaderships has reached a political dead end. Frustration and demoralization are bearing fruit in intensified factionalism, including bloody internal score-settling.

These revolutionary national struggles themselves, the imperialist subjugation fueling them, and the self-sacrificing courage and determination of the toilers to fight are far from exhausted. The Palestinian people will continue to fight Israel because it occupies their land. Workers and farmers in northern Ireland and the Basque country will continue to resist oppression perpetuated by the ruling families of British and Spanish finance capital. But the political consequences of the crisis of leadership and its bourgeois corruption are posed more and more sharply.

36. What is often called "Islamism," "Wahabism," "jihad Islam," "Salafism," or "Islamic fundamentalism" (as distinct from the Islamic religion) has no revolutionary, let alone proletarian, content of any kind. Nor is it the wave of the future anywhere in the Muslim or Arab world. Its high point is behind us, not ahead.

September 11 marked a sensational blowoff, not a new beginning. These movements arose as a surrogate for revolutionary political leadership of the popular masses in face of the bankruptcy of Stalinist and bourgeois-nationalist forces.

The Iranian Revolution of 1979 was a profound political and social upheaval, not a religious jihad. It became a deep-going, modern, popular social revolution in city and countryside, a revolution against the pro-imperialist monarchy of the shah and the brutal despotism of his hated SAVAK police agents. It opened space for workers and landless peasants, for women, for oppressed nationalities, for youth—for communists. It made possible the flowering of political space, debate, and culture that to this day are far from being taken away.

The weight of religious figures and institutions grew stronger and more repressive as part of a political *counterrevolution,* stifling in the name of Islam the rebellion of the most intransigent workers in the oil fields and factories, peasants on the land, Kurds and other oppressed nationalities, women fighting for equality, revolutionary-minded soldiers, students, and other youth, and the boldest communists. The power and depth of that revolution is registered in the fact that the clerical-dominated bourgeois regime has never been able to come close to imposing suffocating political and cultural conditions of the kind the Taliban inflicted on Afghanistan or the Wahabi monarchists on Saudi Arabia.

The high point of "Islamist" action came with the seizure of the Grand Mosque in Mecca in late 1979, the year the Iranian Revolution brought down the shah. But the political content was the opposite. The armed units that laid claim to the mosque did so in the name of ousting royal Saudi infidels defiling Islam's holiest site. Over the subsequent two decades, this was followed up, among other actions, by the 1983 bombings of U.S. and French barracks in Beirut, Lebanon, killing 241 U.S. marines and 58 French paratroopers; the 1993 bomb planted in the basement of the World Trade Center, killing 6 and wounding thousands; the 1996 truck bombing of the Khobar military complex in Saudi Arabia, killing nineteen U.S. soldiers and injuring hundreds; the almost simultaneous 1998 bombings near U.S. embassies in Kenya and Tanzania, killing 224 people and wounding some 4,500 (few of them Americans); and the 2000 speedboat assault on the USS *Cole* in the Yemeni harbor of Aden, killing 17 U.S. sailors.

In terms of the scope of death and destruction inflicted, the September 11, 2001, terror attacks on the World Trade Center and Pentagon were the most sensational of these actions. And there will be others (such as the 2004 Madrid railroad bombings and attacks in Bali and elsewhere in Indonesia in 2002 and 2004), just as the kidnappings, assassinations, robberies, and bombings by anti-working-class groups such as the Red Brigades, Baader-Meinhof Gang, Black Liberation Army, and Weather Underground continued for years after the "armed struggle" ultraleftism of the 1960s had peaked and headed further into political eclipse.

The September 2001 attacks, however, were a registration of weakness, not growing social or political strength. Al Qaeda and other such organizations have become more politically isolated internationally, including among working people and the middle classes throughout Arab and Islamic countries. And the imperialist rulers learn from each of these attacks, making them more difficult to repeat.

37. The disintegration of the Stalinist apparatuses of Eastern Europe and above all the Soviet Union has had profound repercussions throughout the world for the petty-bourgeois forces within the workers movement that call themselves "the left": the popular front terrain within bourgeois politics defined since the 1930s by the Communist parties of the world Stalinist movement, social-democratic parties in their more "left" guises, and centrist organizations that have split from, adapted to, and/or vacillated between them.

It has now been some fifteen years since the collapse of the bureaucratic castes to whose diplomatic needs Stalinist parties around the world subordinated their program and activity, and on whom their recruitment, organizational structure, and resources were based. Over that period, some of these parties have literally dissolved, their former cadres drifting out of politics or deeper into imperialist liberal activism. Other former CPs, qualitatively reduced in size and resources, have changed their names to distance themselves from what they now view as a stigma, no longer providing any offsetting privileges and benefits.

Most, however, including the Communist Party USA, have kept the name for now. The day-by-day work of their members, however, has less connection with the ranks of the working class and union movement, as opposed to the labor officialdom and its staffs, than at any time since the end of the 1920s, when the political counterrevolution in the Soviet Union, including the bureaucratic strangling of the parties of the Communist International, was consolidated.

These counterfeit communist parties—which for more than sixty years sought to legitimize themselves among class-conscious workers by falsely posing as the continuators of Bolshevism—make fewer and fewer claims today to continuity with Marx, Engels, or Lenin. They are increasingly jettisoning even many of Stalinism's own legends and dogmas in order to integrate themselves more comfortably into the left wing of liberal bourgeois politics.

Less and less does the CPUSA acknowledge any political heritage separate and apart from the "progressive" wing of the Democratic Party and various labor, Black, and defense efforts from the New Deal on. They pride themselves on having been "the best canvassers for Kerry" in Ohio in 2004. Socialism has more and more explicitly become the extension of democracy.

38. Since capitulating to "their own" bourgeoisies at the opening of World War I in August 1914, the parties of the Socialist International have been imperialist labor or socialist parties. Unlike Stalinist parties that were politically subordinate to Moscow and to the needs of the Stalinist bureaucratic caste, the social-democratic parties are and have been loyal to their respective imperialist (or national) bourgeoisies and states.

The social democrats' relationship to Stalinist parties since the 1930s has been not only that of rivals within the labor movement but also periodic partners in popular frontism, especially amid financial, social, or international crises when CPs were under orders from Moscow to secure such blocs in order to gain greater diplomatic muscle. With the irreversible decline of international Stalinism, as social-democratic parties today pursue electoral opportunities to administer the "restructuring" and "reforming" of the bourgeois state and its finances, they will be able to rely much less than in the past on patching together governmental coalitions with parties shaped in the class-collaborationist politics of the world Stalinist apparatus.

Gone is another crutch, as well. Less and less can social democrats contrast themselves to a Stalinized Communist Party—the basis for the revival of "left socialism" in the 1930s—as a way to hold onto the allegiance of workers by presenting themselves as a lesser evil on the left.

The imperialist character of these "Social Democratic," "Socialist," and "Labor" parties has undergone no fundamental change for nine decades. They have, however, converged in their political character and functioning with imperialist bourgeois parties such as the Democratic Party in the United States. While maintaining an electoral base in the working class, they have sought, above all, to consolidate expanded support in the middle classes and have organized to weaken institutional controls—in fact or in form—by the trade union movement over their policies and course. The Blair government is today no more beholden to the program adopted at a Labour Party conference (much less that of the Trades Union Congress) than Democratic or Republican candidates to the platform of their respective party conventions. Like their U.S. counterparts, social-democratic party conferences today are increasingly scripted showcases for their apparatuses, higher state functionaries, and parliamentary leaderships.

39. For decades, Stalinism and its cadres were the popular front glue structuring the broader left of bourgeois politics. Communist and social-democratic parties intersected not only within the trade union officialdom, but also within an array of political, social, and cultural organizations—from those involved in struggles against racism, war, and sometimes women's oppression, to opposition to corporate abuse of the environment, support for "progressive" artists, and others. The political line and resources of the existing bureaucratic castes most often provided the motivation and inducements drawing centrist sects—the "far left"—into bourgeois politics as well.

Today, the glue has come unstuck. Within the international workers movement and broader radical milieus, even the pretense of any "culture of Marxism," involvement in the *ranks* of labor and their struggles, or colonization of the unions has melted away. Some currents subordinate themselves to figures in, or "progressive" caucuses of, the labor officialdom. *None*, however, organizes its cadres to become industrial workers or build industrial union fractions in order to join with other working-class militants to use, strengthen, and spread union power. The "industrial concentration" policy of the Communist Party USA had been more talked about than carried out for at least a quarter century. But it was finally dropped even

in word over the past half decade, with the death or in-
capacitation of the last of its central leaders going back
to labor struggles of the 1930s (who "kept the faith," but
made damned sure *their* children and grandchildren were
never part of the rank and file inside a factory, mill, or
mine).

Fewer and fewer individuals or organizations on "the
left" refer to themselves as communists. Some university
professors still say their writings are "informed by" what
they claim to be Marxism. But this is ideological and academic posturing shorn of any revolutionary working-class
content, always unconnected to the proletariat's fight for
power, let alone the inevitability of that struggle. Among
these petty-bourgeois radical layers, it is the ultimate scan-
dal (if it's of any interest at all) that the Socialist Workers
Party and others in our world movement continue to
judge everything we say and everything we *do* from how
best to advance as part of the fighting working class along
its line of march toward the dictatorship of the proletariat.

This turn away from the working class and even the
semblance of Marxism is the political trajectory of the
currents that make up the left in the United States: from
the Communist Party USA itself; to the Greens and "radical" supporters of Ralph Nader; to sects such as the Workers World Party, Freedom Socialist Party, International
Socialist Organization, and various "Trotskyist" groups;
to the assortment of other radical organizations. Many
enmesh themselves more and more in the attempt to
"politicize" the personal, intimate, sexual, psychological
life of the semiprofessional-acting-as-if-semibohemian
petty-bourgeois liberal left, with roots in the memories
of the radical movement of the late sixties and early seven-
ties—the "soixant-huitards," the generation of the '68ers,

as they are known in France.

Above all, what marks these organizations is not what they are *for* (few any longer even nod their heads to the proletariat's line of march) but what they are *against*. What marks them is their shared antagonism to American imperialism, or more precisely in most cases, their antagonism toward the wing of American imperialism associated with the Republican Party and, today, the Bush administration (or the "right wing" of the Democratic Party when it holds the White House or Congress). Orbiting around Paris, especially, and Berlin, they are the "left wing" of the bourgeois international "coalition to hate Washington" and to fear the "red state" masses who voted for the current incumbent. The rationalization, spoken or unspoken, is that the world has now "changed"; that socialism is a utopian fantasy; that there must be and is an alternative "third way" between socialism and imperialism, itself increasingly denied by euphemisms such as "globalization" or "neoliberalism"; and that the permanence of capitalism—hopefully a "reformed," increasingly democratic capitalism—is beyond challenge.

By rejecting the proletarian course insisted on by Lenin and Trotsky for the parties of the Communist International, by refusing to colonize basic industry, following the lines of resistance in the working class, all these political currents in the United States still identifying themselves to one degree or another as socialist have today moved beyond their long-standing rejection of the struggle for a proletarian party. Acting in accord with the class position and activity of their members and leaders, they are erasing from the historical memories of their organizations even the past forms of such a course. They are codifying what they carried out in practice many decades ago: turning away from the historic line of march of the working class toward state power, and from a proletarian orientation and discipline necessary to its victorious culmination.

OUR TRANSFORMATION

40. Since the closing years of the 1990s, renewed resistance in the workplace to the brutal effectiveness of the employers' antilabor offensive has led to the beginnings of important changes in the combativity and self-confidence of pockets of working-class militants. Members of the Socialist Workers Party and Young Socialists—working and building unions today in industries such as meatpacking, coal, and garment and textile, where the bosses' offensive has been among the fiercest for the longest—are among the workers taking the lead in learning to organize and use union power. Over the past half decade, we've been involved in such vanguard fights in packinghouses in the Midwest, the Point Blank Body Armor factory in Florida, and the Co-Op mine in Utah.

41. The seeds of labor's transformation that are being planted within this sea change in working-class politics are germinating at the same time that the trade unions in the United States continue to weaken, as they do throughout the imperialist countries. While still-atomized groups of workers are gaining greater experience, solidarity, and confidence through unionization efforts and strikes, the basic defensive institutions of the working class, as a result of the treachery of the class-collaborationist trade union officialdom, have been rendered less capable today than at any time since the early years of the

Great Depression of successfully organizing and fighting the bosses and their government institutions.

The labor movement remains hobbled by the decades-long class-collaborationist course of an officialdom focused on its own routines, its own daily creature comforts, and its own retirement benefits, as well as mergers solely designed to bolster the latter two, at least for the union tops. The unions continue to shrink as a percentage of the working class. They are bound hand and foot by the policies of these misleaders, who identify the interests of labor with those of capital—factory by factory, company by company, industry by industry—as well as through subordination of the unions to the election and reelection of capitalist, most often Democratic Party, politicians. Workers searching for effective tools with which to fight find themselves swaddled in bourgeois ideas advanced by union officials—reinforced by schools, churches, and the media—and often overlaid with the flotsam and jetsam of dead-end leftism picked up by "labor leaders" willy-nilly over the years from petty-bourgeois radicals.

42. At the same time, *labor remains at center stage of U.S. politics.* In face of ongoing employer attacks, and no matter how weak the labor movement has become, workers reach toward organizing unions and trying to use them to defend wages and job conditions against such assaults.

The employing class, even with its unrelenting offensive on the factory and industry level, still cannot radically alter relations between capital and labor, as they must do in order to reverse the downward pressures on rates of profit. Yet they continue to fear launching a social and political fight that takes a chance on spreading resistance and leading to a new intensity, unity, and solidarity of workers' struggles.

As these deep contradictions work their way to the surface, the postponed class battles will come.

43. Class-struggle-minded militants such as those who have been engaged in the UMWA organizing drive in Huntington, Utah, set an example of determination and solidarity for others. The decisive step in transforming such resistance into forging a broader vanguard of the working-class movement is the recognition by militants, as they gain class-struggle experience through such fights, that their initial victories, both small and large, will not be maintained or secured unless they *extend union power to other plants, mines, and mills in the industry and region.*

As a result of the Co-Op miners' struggle, the organization of Western coal has begun. It will advance, however, only as cadres of that fight and those influenced by them actively reach out to other mines and miners—union and nonunion—to strengthen the UMWA in Utah and also in Colorado, Wyoming, New Mexico, and elsewhere in the West. The same is true for workers who are leading fights in Midwest packing, in garment shops, textile mills, or wherever else the lines of resistance in the working class have and will spread.

44. Learning how earlier generations of workers gained experience in union combat—forging a class-struggle leadership in the process and, over time, winning increased numbers of workers to revolutionary conclusions—is necessary to strengthen the ability both of party cadres and other militants to take part effectively in struggles already unfolding, as well as those that lie ahead. Members of the Socialist Workers Party and Young Socialists who are an integral part of working-class resistance have advanced this understanding by introducing fellow militants to *Teamster Rebellion* by Farrell Dobbs, as well as organizing systematic classes on it in party units. The task ahead of vanguard workers today—captured well in the chapter title "The Struggle Widens" in *Teamster Power,* the second in the four-volume series—underlines the importance of systematically reading and discussing not only the first book but also *Teamster Power, Teamster Politics,* and *Teamster Bureaucracy.*

Read and absorbed together, the four-volume Teamster series describes how a growing workers vanguard put itself to the test in widening union combat, experienced inevitable differentiations, and advanced toward proletarian political consciousness: the capacity to think socially and act politically in the interests of the working class, independent of the employers, their political parties, and the capitalist state.

45. Learning the political realities of the class struggle—discovered and clarified through actions, intertwined with studying and absorbing the lessons of past fights to spread union power—is a precondition for a growing politicization of vanguard militants. Progress in extending and strengthening the union opens the door to start bringing labor's weight to bear in support of Black rights, women's equality, the rights of immigrants, defense of the social wage, and other social and political struggles. It opens the door to organizing education about, and opposition to, the imperialist rulers' militarization drive, expanding war budget, and increasing use of military might abroad and at home, including the fight to bring the troops home from Iraq and elsewhere in the Middle East—now!

46. Individual workers engaged in union struggles become interested in the ideas, program, and disciplined

political activity of fellow workers who are communists
and alongside of whom they are fighting, or whose paper they are reading. Some are attracted to a party whose
politics start not with elections, or with "reasonable" profit
needs of the U.S. imperialist rulers, but with the world.
They become interested in a party advancing a program
and strategy to close the gap in economic resources, social conditions, and political experience of workers and
farmers worldwide—from working-class communities,
factories, mines, and fields across the United States and
other imperialist countries, to those throughout Asia,
Africa, and Latin America.

This revolutionary political continuity—this integration of history, theory, and practice—can be maintained
and applied over time only by the cadres of a party that
is proletarian not just in program but also in composition, activity, and milieu. A party and world movement
of this kind is capable of ensuring that our class does not
"lose its memory"—that we do not lose the political *history* of the struggles of the revolutionary workers movement, the generalization of whose lessons is the foundation of communist *theory*, and of the continual renewal
of that theory in the course of ongoing revolutionary
class-struggle activity.

A century and a half of experience has confirmed, as
the Communist Manifesto explains, that trade unions are
bred by the very workings of capitalism itself. "The real
fruit of their battles," moreover, "lies, not in the immediate result, but in the ever-expanding union of the workers." So too the rebellion of the hanged—the irrepress-
ible struggles of oppressed nations and nationalities the
world over. But the class-conscious *political* organization
of the proletariat, the building of communist parties with
a program and strategy for the conquest of power, for the

dictatorship of the proletariat—that does not arise spontaneously from the operations of the law of value. As Lenin succinctly reminds us, "Without revolutionary theory there can be no revolutionary movement."

The struggle for a proletarian party is impossible without the generalization of lessons of working-class battles —not in any single factory or industry, not in any single country, nor at any given moment or even any single century. Only through the experiences of overlapping generations of workers and other toilers—youth new to the class struggle, together with those tested and trained over years—in many workplaces, spread geographically around the world, are those lessons accurately drawn.

47. Central to guiding the rounded political work of such parties today are the "six points" adopted by the 1990 Socialist Workers Party convention ("The Communist Strategy of Party Building Today: A Letter to Comrades in Sweden" by Mary-Alice Waters, in *New International* no. 11):

i) The turn to industry: Carrying out "consistent, professional communist work in the unions accompanied by the *deepening* proletarianization of the experience and composition of the party and its leadership." This is built on the foundation of active participation by the overwhelming majority of the members and leadership of the party in building industrial union fractions along the lines presented in *The Changing Face of U.S. Politics: Working-Class Politics and the Trade Unions* by Jack Barnes, including consolidating the gains of the third campaign for the turn begun in the late 1990s, described in "Capitalism's Long Hot Winter Has Begun."

ii) Political centralization: "The turn can only be real if it is the axis of work for an *organization* whose leadership is striving for political homogeneity and centralization, carrying out (in a particular country) an international political orientation…. [This] can't be done without having both strong, politically well-rounded, and confident branches *and* fractions. The two have some different tasks, but through the common political content of their work, they mutually reinforce each other."

iii) A weekly rhythm of working-class political life: This weekly rhythm, dictated by the capitalists' organization of wage labor, provides an "irreplaceable basis for the disciplined life of a centralized, combat party"—weekly Militant Labor Forums; participation in mass work, from labor battles and actions of social protest to solidarity with anti-imperialist vanguard struggles internationally; educational classes; sales of the *Militant, Perspectiva Mundial,* and books and pamphlets on street corners in working-class neighborhoods, at plant gates and mine portals, on campus, and at political events; and regular decision-making meetings of party branches, organizing committees, and union fractions to politically guide and centralize this ongoing activity.

iv) Expansion of broad propaganda work built around the distribution of books and pamphlets published or distributed by Pathfinder Press, including *New International*: Getting these hundreds of titles—which record lessons earned in blood by the international communist workers movement over more than a century and a half of struggle—into the hands of workers, farmers, and youth is a permanent axis of the work of a proletarian party. These works clarify "questions that are vital to the future of working people in every country."

v) Youth recruitment: "In everything we do our attention is directed above all towards those fighting young

workers who are the communist cadres of the future . . .
as well as students who are attracted towards working-class
battles and are open to joining a proletarian organization." Reaching out politically to young people, and attracting them to the Young Socialists and our movement, "is especially important given the increasing
average age of all our forces, and the increasing pressures this brings to adapt to the rhythms and norms of
the society in which we live, including the unions of
which we are members."

vi) Proletarian internationalism "under the banner of
the new international": Through every aspect of the work
of the Socialist Workers Party, Young Socialists, and our
sister Communist Leagues in other countries, organizing
to advance the rebuilding of an international communist
organization in continuity with the Communist International forged by Lenin and the Bolsheviks in the wake of
the victorious October 1917 Russian Revolution, subsequently corrupted and destroyed by the world Stalinist
movement.

Such is a summary of the strategic goal of the proletarian orientation. From 1959 to today, moreover, every
organization claiming to advance along that course has
had to meet—and continues to have to meet—"the 'acid
test' of the Cuban revolution . . . recognizing the place
of the communist *leadership* in Cuba and acting on that
understanding."

48. For the Socialist Workers Party and Young Socialists, joining with young people and other organizations
and currents to build the 16th World Festival of Youth
and Students in Caracas, Venezuela, August 7–15, 2005,
provides an opportunity to advance communist political
work along the axes of each of "the six points."

As with the last two youth festivals in Algiers (2001) and Havana (1997), the upcoming event enables our movement to reach out to, and engage in political work with, young workers and students who can be attracted to working-class resistance here and abroad and who can be won to seeing the need to make a revolution in the United States and to joining the communist movement to help achieve that objective. The fact that this festival is being held in Venezuela offers additional opportunities, and responsibilities, to organize events on campuses and elsewhere to present a political description and explanation of the class struggle that continues to unfold there today; to report on the internationalist work of volunteer Cuban teachers and medical workers; and to mobilize defense of Venezuela and Cuba in face of Washington's confrontational political course and military buildup in neighboring Colombia.

These are the revolutionary proletarian and anti-imperialist axes along which we organize to win young people to this effort. In doing so, we are primarily contending politically with the Communist Party and Young Communist League, in addition to a handful of other political opponents. During the heyday of world Stalinism's control of the festival movement from the late 1940s through the late 1980s, the CPs and their youth organizations dominated every aspect of the organization of delegations participating in these events. To this day, they fight to preserve the class-collaborationist political continuity of "peace and friendship," as well as the bureaucratic norms and methods designed to politically strangle, to narrow not broaden the involvement of young people.

The collapse of the Stalinist apparatuses in the Soviet Union and across Eastern Europe at the beginning of the

1990s opened up space for the first time for revolution-ary-minded young people previously barred from the festival movement to join with others in working to build these international gatherings as a way to meet radical-izing young people from around the world, learn from them, and help show how to use such get-togethers to advance the worldwide fight against imperialism. Since that time, the Socialist Workers Party and Young Social-ists have been doing so. Our collaboration in these efforts with, among others, leaders and cadres of the Union of Young Communists (UJC) in Cuba has been intercon-nected with U.S. speaking tours for Cuban youth lead-ers; cooperation in publishing books by Ernesto Che Gue-vara, Malcolm X, and other revolutionists for use in the United States, Cuba, and elsewhere; work with young people interested in learning firsthand for themselves the reality of the Cuban Revolution; and other political ac-tivity. We talk politics with, learn from, develop political relations with, and have a political influence on cadres of organizations from across the Americas and around the world.

Building U.S. participation in the 16th World Festi-val of Youth and Students as a central priority of a turn party means both working with student organizations, political opponents, and individual young people through the National Preparatory Committee (NPC) organizing the U.S. delegation. It means taking advan-tage of opportunities through our fractions and branches to involve young workers and unionists in political ac-tivity that broadens their horizons. It means designing Militant Labor Forums to join the many disputed po-litical questions that come out of discussions in this work.

As we contest with opponents, the political clarification

and differentiation will both educate and steel our own members as well as enhance opportunities for recruitment to the communist movement.

Historical Trends and Proletarian Strength

49. The prospects for forging a revolutionary proletarian political vanguard of the labor movement and building a communist international composed of disciplined combat parties are enhanced by six broad social and political trends that will increasingly mark the twenty-first century:

i) The size of the hereditary working class, both in absolute terms and relative to other social classes, continues to expand on a world scale. This increases the possibilities for proletarian participation in, and leadership of, revolutionary struggles for national liberation and socialism in the Middle East and worldwide. As new layers of toilers are proletarianized, the class struggle in Asia will intensify in a qualitatively new way from China to Pakistan, India, Indonesia, Russia, and beyond. In China especially, explosive contradictions are deepening as tens of millions of peasants, born and educated in a workers state however deformed it may be, pour into an urban factory workforce concentrated in rapidly expanding coastal industrial centers.

ii) Women continue to be integrated into the workforce, and barriers to women and men working alongside each other as equals, performing the same jobs, are progressively being breached in both imperialist and semicolonial countries. This proletarianization , the cornerstone for the realization of women's liberation, not only weakens the economic foundations of women's oppression and strengthens the working class. It also in-

"Supporters of the Socialist Workers Party 2004 presidential campaign began with our class and with the world. Our banner struck a theme that is decisive to strengthening the nucleus of a revolutionary proletarian movement in this country and worldwide: 'It's not *who* you're against, it's what you're *for*! Vote Socialist Workers in 2004!'"

SWP campaign stood out in contrast to other currents claiming to speak for workers' interests. **TOP LEFT**: "Stop Bush!" alliance, protesting at 2004 Republican convention in New York. Behind them, giant patriotic banner on UNITE HERE national union headquarters. **TOP RIGHT:** During convention, SWP campaigners carry "It's what you're *for*" and abortion rights banners in thousands-strong pro-choice march across Brooklyn Bridge into Manhattan. **BOTTOM**: Róger Calero (left), SWP candidate for president, campaigns at Point Blank Body Armor plant near Miami, where workers had recently won union representation fight.

AP   MILITANT

ballots "counted," which meant voting for Kerry where the election was "close"); to those who stood candidates but made no effort to win ballot status or carry out any aspect of a serious, nationwide campaign (such as the Workers World Party, on the ballot in three states with small petitioning requirements). Only campaigners for the SWP ticket—Calero, Hawkins, and more than forty other candidates in twenty-two states and the District of Columbia—were on the streets, day after day, reaching out to working people and youth with an independent working-class platform.

Calero, Hawkins, and their supporters began with their class and the world. They spoke on behalf of an international class that has no borders, one that has nothing to survive on for a lifetime but selling our capacity to labor to one or another employer. Our campaign banner struck a theme—unique, true, and timely—that is decisive to the broader strategic task of politically strengthening the nucleus of a revolutionary proletarian movement in this country and worldwide: "It's not *who* you're against, but what you're *for*! Vote Socialist Workers in 2004!"

Only from within the ranks of the industrial working class and unions, from within the ranks of labor militants in the front lines acting to organize and use union power to resist the bosses' offensive, can a proletarian political road be found to meet the consequences of the economic and military course the U.S. rulers are today pursuing. We gained confidence explaining this during the 2004 campaign. The first decisive steps toward independent working-class *political* action, toward a labor party based on the unions, will be taken as a by-product of organizing together with others to use and transform our most elementary class institutions—by organizing, strengthening, and extending union power. That point of departure is a precondition to *our transformation*—the forging of the broad political vanguard of which the communist movement is an irreplaceable component.

Decades of consistent work by the communist movement to build parties that are proletarian in composition, life, habits, and milieu is the only foundation that can make a difference as the working class enters the great furnace of historical battles ahead. Only parties tempered and trained on that basis will be prepared, through the course of tumultuous struggles, to draw millions into disciplined, class-struggle activity. That is the course our movement was founded on, the course being carried out by the Socialist Workers Party and the world movement of which we are part.

As stated in "Capitalism's Long Hot Winter Has Begun," communists, like other workers, find themselves "in the very opening stages of what will be decades of economic, financial, and social convulsions and class battles. . . . [We] must internalize the fact that this world—the likes of which none of us have known before in our political lives—is not only the world that must be faced today, but the one we will be living and fighting in for some time. . . . By *acting* on this reality today, we will not be caught short politically as wars erupt, deeper social crises explode, pogroms are organized and attempted, and union conflicts become life-and-death battles. The proletarian party that exists tomorrow can only grow out of the proletarian party we put together *today*."

THE TEAMSTER SERIES

FARRELL DOBBS, *a young worker who became part of the
class-struggle leadership of the Minneapolis Teamsters in the 1930s
tells the story of how the strikes and organizing drives by men and
women in the Twin Cities and throughout the Midwest paved the way
for the rise of the industrial union movement. They showed in life what
workers and their allied producers on the land can achieve when they
have the leadership they deserve.*

Teamster Rebellion

How members of Teamsters Local 574 in Minnesota during two 1934
strikes defeated not only the trucking bosses in Minneapolis but strike-
breaking efforts of the big-business Citizens Alliance and city, state,
and federal governments. $19

Teamster Power

How the class-struggle Teamsters leadership used the power workers had won during the 1934 strikes to make Minneapolis a union
town and launch an 11-state campaign that brought tens of thousands of over-the-road truckers into the union. $19

Teamster Politics

How the Minneapolis Teamsters combated FBI frame-ups, helped the
jobless organize, deployed a Union Defense Guard to turn back fascist
thugs, fought to advance independent labor political action, and mobilized opposition to U.S. imperialism's entry into World War II. $19

Teamster Bureaucracy

How the employing class, backed by union bureaucrats, stepped up
government efforts to gag class-conscious militants; how workers
mounted a world campaign to free eighteen union and socialist leaders framed up and imprisoned in the infamous 1941 federal sedition
trial. $19

www.pathfinderpress.com

INTRODUCTORY SUBSCRIPTION

THE **MILITANT**

$5 for 12 weeks

perspectiva
mundial

$5 for 4 months

The Militant and Perspectiva Mundial . . .

■ Present news and analysis on Washington's moves to transform its global military strategy and advance its world political interests.

■ Offer in-depth coverage of the capitalists' assaults on wages, job conditions, and social security.

■ Provide news from the front lines of union fights and organizing drives in coalfields, meatpacking plants, garment shops, and among other workers in North America and around the world.

■ Dissect, lie by lie, Washington's rationalizations for its war moves—from Iraq to Afghanistan, the Balkans, the Colombia/Venezuela border and beyond.

■ Follow Cuba's workers and farmers as they defend and advance their socialist revolution.

■ Report on anti-imperialist struggles in Africa, Asia, and Latin America.

■ Cover fights worldwide against police brutality and racist attacks, and for women's equality, including abortion rights.

■ Offer a socialist alternative to the big-business press.

"Published in the interests of working people"

FOR SUBSCRIPTIONS, WRITE TO:
The Militant
306 West 37th Street, 10th floor
New York, NY 10018-2852
e-mail: themilitant@verizon.net
fax: (212) 244-4947

Visit us on the Web: WWW.THEMILITANT.COM and WWW.PERSPECTIVAMUNDIAL.COM

Building a PROLETARIAN PARTY

The Changing Face of U.S. Politics
Working-Class Politics and the Trade Unions

JACK BARNES

Building the kind of party working people need to prepare for coming class battles through which they will revolutionize themselves, their unions, and all society. A handbook for those seeking the road toward effective action to overturn the exploitative system of capitalism and join in reconstructing the world on new, socialist foundations. $23

Their Trotsky and Ours

JACK BARNES

To lead the working class in a successful revolution, a mass proletarian party is needed whose cadres, well beforehand, have absorbed a world communist program, are proletarian in life and work, derive deep satisfaction from doing politics, and have forged a leadership with an acute sense of what to do next. This book is about building such a party. $15

The History of American Trotskyism, 1928–38
Report of a Participant

JAMES P. CANNON

"Trotskyism is not a new movement, a new doctrine," Cannon says, "but the restoration, the revival of genuine Marxism as it was expounded and practiced in the Russian revolution and in the early days of the Communist International." In twelve talks given in 1942, Cannon recounts a decisive period in efforts to build a proletarian party in the United States. $22

What Is To Be Done?

V.I. LENIN

The stakes in creating a disciplined organization of working-class revolutionaries capable of acting as a "tribune of the people, able to react to every manifestation of tyranny and oppression, no matter where it appears, to clarify for all and everyone the world-historic significance of the struggle for the emancipation of the proletariat." Written in 1902. In *Essential Works of Lenin*, $12.95

In Defense of Marxism

The Social and Political Contradictions of the Soviet Union on the Eve of World War II

LEON TROTSKY

Writing in 1939–40, Leon Trotsky replies to those in the revolutionary workers movement beating a retreat from defense of the Soviet Union in face of the looming imperialist assault. Why only a party that fights to bring growing numbers of workers into its ranks and leadership can steer a steady revolutionary course. $24.95

The Struggle for a Proletarian Party

JAMES P. CANNON

"The workers of America have power enough to topple the structure of capitalism at home and to lift the whole world with them when they rise," Cannon asserts. On the eve of World War II, a founder of the communist movement in the U.S. and leader of the Communist International in Lenin's time defends the program and party-building norms of Bolshevism. $21.95

Revolutionary Continuity

Marxist Leadership in the U.S.

FARRELL DOBBS

How successive generations took part in struggles of the U.S. labor movement, seeking to build a leadership that could advance the class interests of workers and small farmers and link up with fellow toilers around the world. Two volumes: *The Early Years, 1848–1917*, $17.95; *Birth of the Communist Movement 1918–1922*, $19

CAPITALISM'S LONG HOT WINTER HAS BEGUN

CAPITALISM'S LONG HOT WINTER

HAS BEGUN

by Jack Barnes

A MASS REVOLUTIONARY party is forged in the heat of great social crises, political upheavals, and wars. Such turmoil unfolds unevenly and extends, with ebbs and flows, over substantial time. But the core of a proletarian party—seasoned in mass work, knowledgeable and disciplined in working-class politics, with cadres spread across several generations—is built *before* such giant class battles and revolutionary explosions erupt. Such a party cannot be built from scratch once decisive class confrontations posing which class shall rule have begun. That is the lesson Lenin and the Bolsheviks taught us in practice. In the affirmative. Lenin also generalized from the history of the revolutionary activity of the toilers under capitalism to explain that lesson in numerous speeches and writings. And over the course of the last century, our class has learned that lesson in the negative as well—in more costly ways than anyone could have foreseen.

Report and summary discussed and adopted by delegates to the Forty-first Constitutional Convention of the Socialist Workers Party, held July 25–27, 2002, in Oberlin, Ohio.

Our organizations strive to act today in such a manner that when revolutionary mass struggles begin, we can build on our already existing internationalist program, proletarian habits, and organizational norms. Only by acting in that manner can parties be built that are capable of leading the toilers to the revolutionary conquest of power, to the establishment of a workers and farmers government.

To remain true to this historic charge, the delegates to this convention face one challenge above all. We must prepare the Socialist Workers Party, Young Socialists, and supporters of the communist movement to understand the unfolding depression and intensified drive toward imperialist wars, and to reorient our activity in face of these realities. Every other political responsibility and opportunity needs to be understood and acted on in this light. In doing so, we will collaborate with communists and young socialists worldwide, as well as with revolutionists in Latin America, Africa, the Middle East, and Asia engaged in uncompromising national struggles against the domestic and international beneficiaries of the imperialist system.

❖

Communists are not prognosticators. No one can make accurate predictions both about *what* will happen in society as well as *when*. Those with a materialist understanding of the laws of the class struggle, including the place of chance in human affairs, know better than to try. But communists can and do have a responsibility to follow the course of capitalist development that is unfolding and to absorb and explain its implications for the class struggle and the twisting line of march of the proletariat toward power. When enough evidence has accumulated about the logic of these developments, there is no other responsible course but to *act* on it. If we do not do so, regardless of what we have accomplished beforehand, *it will be too late*. At that moment, we are not from Missouri; we are from Petrograd.

Many members of the communist movement today have never lived through a ground war launched by the imperialist rulers, one involving large numbers of soldiers from the ranks of the American working class and resulting in many thousands of deaths on all sides. We are going to see wars of that kind not just in the decades ahead, but in the years, possibly even months ahead.

Only a couple of participants at this convention, those close to eighty years old, have lived, as political people, through a world depression. Some of us have experienced two or three deep-going slumps since the mid-1970s. In one or another of these downturns stock prices dropped sharply over a number of years, unemployment shot into double digits in several imperialist countries, and there were sudden bursts of inflation. That's different, however, from a deflation of such magnitude that the financial backbone of world capitalism—its debt structure and dominant financial institutions—buckles, production plummets, long-term joblessness spreads worldwide, and the great mass of humanity is hit by economic contraction or bouts of ruinous price explosions—sometimes both together. Masses of people lose faith in capitalism, but at first they just lose hope. Conditions of that kind, which have stalked the most vulnerable parts of the colonial world over the past decades, will become widespread and devastating. We're not predicting such a world depression; we're living through its very opening stages today.

CORBIS

"Conditions of the kind that have stalked the most vulnerable parts of the colonial world over the past decades will become widespread. We're living through the opening stages of a world depression."

ABOVE: Breadline at 42nd Street and Sixth Avenue in New York City, February 1932, during Great Depression.

ASSOCIATED PRESS

LEFT: LANDOV. RIGHT: MARCOS HAUPTA / REUTERS

TOP: Alexandra township in Johannesburg, South Africa, 2002. Many residents lack electricity, running water, and basic sanitation.
LEFT: Unemployment line in Berlin, January 2003. Jobless rate in eastern Germany remains around 20 percent fifteen years after 1990 unification.
RIGHT: In wake of 2001–02 financial crisis, Argentine peso lost three-quarters of its value against the U.S. dollar. Devaluation devastated millions, sparking bank runs seen here.

To function effectively as communists in the world situation that is developing, we have to internalize an understanding of imperialism—the stage of world capitalism reached early in the last century. Until the contradictions of that exploitative and oppressive social system are resolved—and that can be achieved only by the proletariat taking power from the capitalists and landlords in the imperialist countries and joining in the worldwide struggle for socialism—humanity has no sure future.

As Lenin helped us learn, for the imperialist rulers "there is no such thing as an absolutely hopeless situation," even when capitalism is in profound crisis.[1] There is no hopeless situation for the bourgeoisie so long as state power is not wrested from it by the proletariat, led by a revolutionary movement that will not, at the decisive moment, fear the awesome responsibility of assuming power and shrink from taking it. And holding it.

Without such a revolution—without the insurrection that opens the road to workers power—the capitalist state and the employers will wreak devastating enough defeats on the working class through fascist terror, and will destroy enough agricultural and industrial productive capacity through wars as well as economic means that are "natural" (to capitalism) to restart a miserable but real revival of production and trade. They will continue dominating the earth, exploiting and oppressing the great majority of humanity, and threatening the very survival of

---

1. V.I. Lenin, "Report on the World Political Situation and the Basic Tasks of the Communist International," in *Workers of the World and Oppressed Peoples, Unite!: Proceedings and Documents of the Second Congress, 1920* (New York: Pathfinder, 1991), vol. 1, p. 139. Also in Lenin, *Collected Works*, (Moscow: Progress Publishers, 1966), vol. 31, p. 227.

civilization. So long as they don't lose state power, the law of value guarantees that their system will start back up. They must only endure; we must conquer.

No fear of the rulers

The ruling class in this country, while the wealthiest and most militarily powerful in history, is a bloated giant that is in fact past its zenith. We don't *fear* the propertied rulers; we have contempt for them. We look forward to doing battle with them. Because we know that before the exploiters can impose their ultimate horrors, the working class and its allies among farmers and other toilers will have the opportunity to resolve the crises of imperialism in humanity's favor. We say, speed the day. And act as if we mean it.

Communist workers in the United States enjoy political work. That is, the *politics*, and the *work* together that makes the politics possible, *interest* us. Our confidence in the working class flows from long experience, and is based on facts unfolding in front of our faces. It's not a matter of faith. It's not an "idea" in an individual's head. It's not a "goal" we're "shooting for." And we have a special political obligation to demonstrate this confidence in the way we conduct ourselves.

Around the world today, including among revolutionists, U.S. imperialism is generally portrayed as a virtually omnipotent, "hegemonic" power in a "unipolar" world. We have a duty to make clear that while we never give an inch to adventurism that disregards the U.S. rulers' brutality and monopoly of state power, we also never cower before them. We never ask them for the right to be communists. We present a realistic appreciation of who they are and what they are capable of. We explain that they operate pragmatically, with no idea of the laws of motion of modern society. They don't have to win; they only have to not lose. There are no limits to their self-delusion, and for the same reason there are no limits to the suddenness and extent of the violence and brutality they will lash out with when it becomes stunningly clear that they are wrong.

Above all, we point out how the capitalist rulers keep creating and concentrating within their own borders a larger and larger world proletariat, and how working people—how *we*—can make a revolution to overturn them.

We have a special obligation to help revolutionary-minded toilers around the world understand that there is not "*a*" United States; there is not some socially and politically homogeneous population in North America with that name. "We Americans" is a fabrication of the rulers. There are the tens and tens and tens of millions of workers and farmers in the United States; we are part of a "we" with our class brothers and sisters throughout the world. There is a "they": the tiny handful of propertied families in whose interests the imperialist United States government acts at home and abroad. It is "they," their state, that "we" must overthrow in order to end imperialism's inexorable advance toward deepening crisis, violence, brutality, and devastation—toward fascism and world war.

Proletarian response to September 11

Our movement acquitted itself well last September in face of the attacks on the World Trade Center and Pentagon, and the rulers' subsequent accelerated militarization drive and preparations to push back workers' rights. We spoke out forcefully on September 11 itself, in a statement issued by the party leadership in the name of the Socialist Workers candidate for mayor of New York City, Martín Koppel. We simultaneously began campaigning with that statement across the United States, offered it for posting on the Web sites of the *Militant* and *Perspectiva Mundial,* and for publication in the next issue of those periodicals. We explained the stakes and clarified the political issues for members, supporters, and contacts of our movement, as well as for anyone interested in hearing what communists had to say.

The party's statement got both the content and the tone just right—and tone can be decisive in working-class politics, especially at moments such as September 11, 2001. The attacks in New York and the District of Columbia, we said, were carried out in reaction to and emulation of what the United States government had been countenancing for decades in advancing "its 'right' to launch military assaults on other countries." Now the U.S. rulers would "become even more brazen" in this course.

We called special attention to the fact that during its closing months in the White House, "the Clinton administration established, *for the first time in U.S. history,* a North American command—that is, the command structure for deployment of U.S. armed forces at home, aimed first and foremost at working people in this country." We noted that these "homeland" units of the armed forces, together with various federal police agencies, were being deployed by the Bush administration "in their first domestic military operations."

"The U.S. government and its allies for more than a century have carried out systematic terror to defend their class privilege and interests at home and abroad"—from the slaughter in the Philippines and in the Caribbean and Central America at the turn of the twentieth century and its opening decades, to the firebombing of German and

Japanese cities and the atomic annihilation of more than one hundred thousand at Hiroshima and Nagasaki; from the murderous leveling of Korea at the opening of the 1950s, to the ten-year-long slaughter in Indochina, devastation of Central America, and support to murderous tyrannies across South America in the 1960s and 1970s; from the war against the Iraqi people in 1990–91, to the incineration of eighty people in Waco, Texas, on its own soil, and the murders of many more both at home and abroad.

The party statement echoed a 1940 warning by communist leader Leon Trotsky. As the interimperialist conflict that became World War II was inexorably expanding, Trotsky responded to the mounting efforts of the Zionist movement and its imperialist backers to dispossess the Palestinian people and establish what eight years later would become the colonial-settler state of Israel. What these reactionary forces were doing, Trotsky said, was transforming Palestine into "a bloody trap" for the Jews. "Never was it so clear as it is today," he wrote, "that the salvation of the Jewish people is bound up inseparably with the overthrow of the capitalist system."[2]

More than sixty years later, Trotsky's prognosis has not only been confirmed, but the dangers are even greater, as rightist demagogues once again do as they always will under crisis conditions—whether Israel exists or not—so long as the capitalist system remains. They spew the poison of anti-Semitism and Jew-hatred as an antidote to capitalism's ills. The party's response to September 11 emphasized that "U.S. imperialism is turning North America into a death trap for working people and all who

---

2. Leon Trotsky, *On the Jewish Question* (New York: Pathfinder, 1970), p. 16.

live here." It is doing so "by its systematic superexploitation of the peoples of Asia, Africa, and Latin America; by
its never-ending insults to their national and cultural
dignity"; by its ceaseless collaboration in murderous violence in countless forms. By the very workings of capitalism in its imperialist stage.

The U.S. rulers are adding to the armature of their
mailed fist, we pointed out. They are strengthening their
hand at home and abroad for the battles they know are
coming.

WE FOLLOWED UP THE CAMPAIGN using this statement
less than three weeks later with the mobilization of a large
public meeting in New York City. At that meeting, we
called attention, above all, to the inability of the U.S.
rulers to whip up the kind of patriotic response that
could, for a period of time, cow working people into re-
coiling from fights by appealing for "Americans" to "all
pull together." The day after we met, tens of thousands
of state workers in Minnesota went on strike against
employer efforts to slash their wages and medical benefits. Labor resistance was not halted by patriotic rallying
cries. The aftermath of September 11 did not become the
occasion and rationalization for an attempt to impose no-
strike pledges.

The battle by workers for union recognition against the
Point Blank company in South Florida is proving to be
another example. The fact that workers there produce
armored vests for the police and military hasn't stopped
them from organizing and fighting for better wages and
conditions on the job. At least one delegate who would
otherwise be at the convention here today is in Miami taking his responsibilities in the union organizing drive there.

The post–September 11 realities of the class struggle in the United States were delightfully illustrated at the gathering in New York by an experience we pointed to in opening the meeting. I told the story of how several days earlier, together with another leader of the Socialist Workers Party, I had been on my way to a meeting in mid-Manhattan on what happened to be Mexican Independence Day. Shortly after we came up from the subway, we walked past a young Latina on the street selling American flags. She wasn't saying anything; just holding up the flags, hoping someone would buy one for a buck. Patriotic zeal was not the main motivation of most of those selling flags and colored ribbons on the streets those days (or any other day).

Just at that moment, a big truck rounded the corner, decked out by the boss with two huge American flags, one on the side panel and another flying from the cab. The young driver spotted the woman, shot his fist out the window, and shouted: "Viva Zapata!" as a big smile broke out on both their faces.

I'm glad I was with another comrade at the time who can confirm it really happened! Once you got beyond the professional and middle classes, the patina of petty-bourgeois hysteria and panic in New York City was not even skin deep.

Workers and farmers in the United States were abruptly and violently dragged into the world by the events of September 2001. Before then the rulers had largely convinced working people that at least on U.S. soil, since the "victory" in the Cold War, "we" would never—*never*—face any direct consequences for the murderous violence and misery experienced by toilers worldwide as a result of capitalism's inherent drive toward imperialist domination, superexploitation, and wars of conquest. That illusion began to crack on September 11.

The events in New York and Washington, D.C., gave the U.S. rulers a pretext to *accelerate* the course they have been on for some fifteen years—since the deepening crisis of the world capitalist order signaled by the 1987 stock market crash and the collapse a few years later of Stalinist regimes across Central and Eastern Europe and in the Soviet Union.

But the acceleration, if maintained, brings its own changes. Controlled actions set uncontrolled forces into motion, and thus bring unexpected consequences. The *political and military* evolution of the world's imperialist powers has become more tightly related to their *economic* evolution—with the destabilizing shocks of a more and more violently competitive world finance capital.

These conclusions, to my knowledge shared by no other current in the workers movement, are important for the delegates here to discuss and decide. Because everything the National Committee—which is responsible to act for the party between conventions—has done over the past year has been based on these judgments, and will continue to be based on them if this course is reaffirmed.

U.S. imperialism's march toward war

The big-business press has given a lot of attention over the past two months to Bush's June 1 [2002] address to the graduating class at West Point. That speech marked another step in Washington's drive toward war, toward the aggressive use of its military might, but not for the reasons babbled by the bobbing heads on TV.

The self-styled pundits, parroted by many on "the left," proclaim that Bush said something dangerously new at the military academy when he spoke of being "ready for preemptive action when necessary to defend our liberty

and to defend our lives." But the fact is, *all* military assaults by Washington and other imperialist powers have
been "preemptive."

The U.S. armed forces weren't under attack by Korea
in 1945 when Washington ordered the troops to occupy
the southern half of the peninsula, divide it across the
middle, and when the inevitable result occurred five years
later, launch a murderous war aimed, unsuccessfully, at
conquering the entire country. Cuba did not threaten or
invade the United States in 1961, nor in 1962. Neither
the assault by U.S.-backed mercenaries at the Bay of Pigs
in April 1961, nor the U.S.-provoked "missile crisis" of
October 1962 was an act of "self-defense." Vietnam did
not hurl weapons against American cities or territories,
provoking a massive escalation of U.S. bombing and troop
deployments in the mid- and late 1960s. These actions
that defined the "American Century" were all "preemptive" bipartisan assaults by the U.S. rulers.

So, too, were the bloody twentieth century wars among
the imperialist powers—World War I and World War II.
In the years leading up to both of these slaughters, the
rival powers instigated incidents and provocations they
knew would inevitably hand them a pretext to declare war
and advance their national interests.

At least as early as President Franklin D. Roosevelt's
"Quarantine the Aggressor" speech in October 1937, for
example, the Democratic administration had set a course
toward building up U.S. military power in order to take
on Japan in the Pacific, establish itself as a dominant
imperial power in Europe, and hopefully preside over the
subordination if not the destruction of the Soviet workers state in the process. According to the history we're
taught in school and see in the big-business dailies and
on TV, it was Tokyo's "preemptive" bombardment of Pearl

Harbor on December 7, 1941, that drew the United States into World War II. Since that "unprovoked and dastardly attack by Japan," Roosevelt told Congress the very next day, "a state of war has existed between the United States and the Japanese empire."

What usually goes conveniently unmentioned by apologists for the allied powers is the Roosevelt administration's "preemptive" act against Japan six months earlier imposing a total embargo on Japanese oil imports (as well as an embargo on scrap metal imports and the freezing of all Japanese assets in the United States). Washington knew that act of economic war, designed to starve Japan and stop the wheels of industry from turning, would force Tokyo to respond militarily. The only surprises were the unexpected audacity of the Pearl Harbor attack, the reach of Japan's naval fleet, and the skill and boldness of "the little yellow" pilots from Asia.

IN REALITY, what was noteworthy for class-conscious workers about Bush's West Point talk was not his comment about "preemptive action" but the ease with which he slid back and forth between proposals for strikes against "enemies" at home and "enemies" abroad. "Our security," Bush said, "will require the best intelligence to reveal threats hidden in caves and growing in laboratories. Our security will require modernizing domestic agencies such as the FBI, so they're prepared to act, and act quickly, against danger."

More important than the West Point talk was Bush's "axis of evil" speech to Congress four months earlier— his State of the Union address in late January 2002. We take seriously the threats issued in that talk. The White House did not simply pick Iraq, Iran, and the Democratic People's Republic of Korea out of a hat as a representative sample of Clinton's many "rogue states." And the "axis of evil" is not simply three oppressed countries whose governments the U.S. rulers would like to overturn. They are three such governments that have the economic, engineering, and technical capacities to someday soon place weapons—including nuclear warheads—on ballistic missiles whose range could at least prevent Washington from attacking those countries with impunity. In fact, the most immediate aim of the U.S. rulers' drive for an Anti-Ballistic Missile System, reinitiated during the Reagan administration, resumed during the later Clinton years, and now being pressed forward by Bush, is to restore Washington's ability to use its massive nuclear arsenal to blackmail governments such as these in the colonial world, as well as their "friends," the fickleness of one or two of whom might be revealed in an ever-changing future.[3]

We must act on the assumption that the Pentagon plans for a multifront invasion and war against Iraq "leaked" earlier this month are the initial steps to prepare a massive U.S.-organized military assault. Within days [British prime minister Tony] Blair weighed in, pledging complete support and participation. "Leaked" documents detailed the use of depots for war matériel in Uzbekistan and plans for air, sea, and land operations staged from bases in Kuwait, Qatar, Bahrain, Turkey, Diego Garcia, and elsewhere. There are great hopes among sections of the Turkish bourgeoisie that in return for their cooperation imperialism will

---

3. In July 2004 the U.S. government loaded the first ground-based Anti-Ballistic Missile interceptor into a silo in Alaska, a project begun during the Clinton administration. President Bush hailed the installation as "the beginning of a missile-defense system that was envisioned by Ronald Reagan."

offer some relief from the growing debt burden and economic crisis gripping that country. And the U.S. rulers will make sure their royal highnesses in Saudi Arabia and Jordan also come around before the shooting starts.

Washington is determined to accomplish what it could not try to do as part of the "Free Kuwait" alliance during the 1990–91 war. The U.S. rulers aim to fight a major war to the finish—and are gathering a coalition accordingly. With one foot in Tel Aviv and another in Baghdad—and new military bases to the north, east, and south of Iran—they believe, U.S. imperialism will then be able to recoup some of what it lost with the revolutionary overthrow of the U.S.-backed shah of Iran in 1979. Above all, Washington is confident it can redivide military and political influence over the region at the expense of its rivals in Europe and Japan and assert its domination over oil and other resources. Some 65 percent of the world's oil reserves are in that region—more than 10 percent in Iraq, and a quarter in Saudi Arabia alone.

The United States is bolstering its military presence elsewhere as well. It used the war in Afghanistan to establish bases not only there but across former Soviet Central Asia, in Uzbekistan, Tajikistan, and Kyrgyzstan. Last December Congress approved the so-called Andean Initiative, which builds on the existing "Plan Colombia" to expand the presence of U.S. armed forces across Latin America in the guise of "fighting drug trafficking." The 1,200 U.S. military "trainers" in the Philippines, scheduled to complete their mission there in a few days, may prove to have been just a foot in the door, as indicated by talks already under way between Washington and Manila about reestablishing permanent U.S. military storage facilities there. At least it will be the opening wedge in stepped-up Filipino-American cooperation in the war against "terrorism" and "Islamic extremism" in the Pacific region.

Two processes are taking place unevenly but in tandem: U.S. imperialism's war preparations abroad together with its ongoing militarization on the home front, anticipating increased resistance by workers and farmers down the road. The Bush administration and Congress are advancing along the bipartisan trail blazed by the Clinton administration and Congress during the previous eight years. Reinforcement of the so-called homeland defense command structure; centralization of intelligence operations; use of "secret evidence," "preventive detentions," and curtailment of review and appeal rights, targeting noncitizens and prisoners first and foremost; bolstering of commando and SWAT-style squads on the federal, state, and local levels—none of this began in the closing months of 2001.

The Northern Command will formally stand up later this year. The prototype for this homeland command was established in October 1999, tagged with the Clintonian Pentagonese euphemism "Joint Task Force Civil Support." It is undergoing a slight metamorphosis, to emerge as the (more Rumsfeldian) Northern Command on October 1. Under the banner of combating "terrorism," this new military command will be charged with maintaining "law and order" as needed within the boundaries of the United States when there is a threat of civil disorder.

Currently, the U.S. military command structure consists of nine Unified Combat Commands—the European Command, Pacific Command, Southern Command,

Central Command, and so on. The chain of command goes directly to each of them from the president of the United States, through the secretary of defense. The new Northern Command will be headquartered at Peterson Air Force Base in Colorado and will be headed by Air Force Gen. Ralph Eberhart, currently commander of the U.S. Space Command. NORTHCOM, as it will be called for short, will encompass NORAD—the North American Aerospace Defense Command—whose U.S. commander has the ultimate power by treaty, without prior consultation, to put the Royal Canadian Air Force under his command. When NORTHCOM stands up a few months from now, Mexico, in the eyes of Washington, will for the first time fall under the responsibility of a U.S. combat command.

If you simply add up figures on economic output, arms budgets, and conventional and strategic weaponry, then U.S. imperialism is the strongest power in world history, towering above its closest rivals on every front. But that's a snapshot lifted out of time as well as political and economic context and direction of development. The course we've been describing here is that of an imperialist power that is *weakening* vis-à-vis its ability to stabilize a world in which the lives of hundreds of millions of restive toilers in semicolonial countries are marked by the increasing turmoil, want, and disease produced by the world capitalist system itself. An imperialist power less and less able to handle the political challenges it cannot but create, because it is a power that cannot stabilize the global capitalist economy, the effects of which keep coming down on workers and farmers worldwide. A power that must bear a disproportionate load in policing the planet for imperialism in one crisis of its own making after another, from the Balkans to every corner of the semicolonial

*[margin notes: weakening * ; a strong imp. power ; * KEY political + military consequences. and depression ; Imperialism]*

world. One that has not achieved its goals in a single major war since 1945. One that now, after supposedly winning the cold war "without firing a shot," is no longer exempt from attacks on its home soil.

An imperialist power in its heyday is able to bend regimes to its will. To order "allies" to turn to. To crush resistance by toilers in the colonial world. It has the economic reserves to stabilize its international currency and state finances. That is not the situation of U.S. imperialism today, however, and has been less and less so since the mid-1970s. Instead, the moves we are witnessing are part of the decline of the world's final empire, which today faces the political and military consequences of its imperialist course at the same time it is entering its greatest economic crisis since the 1930s.

The highest stage of capitalism

Our movement will be better armed to respond to these political developments if we organize a winter school to read and study Lenin's *Imperialism, The Highest Stage of Capitalism.* We can do this in the organized, intensive way we've studied *Their Trotsky and Ours, The History of American Trotskyism,* and *The Changing Face of U.S. Politics* during the socialist summer schools over the past several months. We structure these schools into the weekly rhythm of political work by party members, young socialists, and those around us who are seriously considering joining the movement, so we can share and conquer the same material together.

Lenin's description and explanation of imperialism are a foundation stone for everything the communist movement has done for close to a century. And that continues to be the case.

Lenin focused on clarifying two questions:

• First, he presented a concrete and detailed explanation of the more and more parasitic character of capital's operations in the imperialist epoch.

• Second, drawing out the practical implications of that analysis, he rejected the possibility of any form of "super-imperialism," or "ultra-imperialism," that could reduce the sharpening contradictions of capitalism, buffer conflicts among rival national ruling classes, soften class struggle, let alone foster world peace. Instead, Lenin insisted, imperialism opened an epoch of recurring crises, of imperialist wars, of civil wars, of wars for colonial domination, of struggles for national liberation, and of proletarian revolutions.

The imperialist stage of capitalism is marked by the increasing domination around the world of giant monopolies in industry, commerce, and banking. Drawing on what Marx had already explained in *Capital,* Lenin demonstrated that far from reducing competition, increasing monopolization makes the blind operations of rival private capitals *more violent.* And in the face of crises, the violence increasingly involves forces that are not purely economic—from private goon squads and local cops and sheriffs to, above all, the capitalist state and its cops, courts, and armed forces.

The merging of banking capital and industrial capital— "the creation, on the basis of this 'finance capital,' of a financial oligarchy," as Lenin puts it—increases the parasitism of the bourgeoisie. Above all it increases their reliance on multiplying forms of debt in their ruthless competition among themselves to capture the largest shares of surplus value created the world over by the labor of workers and farmers, of miners and fishermen. The debtor-creditor relationship becomes increasingly central to the functioning of international capitalism, outstripping the earlier centrality of the relationship of buyer and seller. "This is the essence of imperialism and imperialist parasitism," he writes.[4] Lenin would not have been surprised by the explosion over the past couple of decades of more and more forms of debt, more and more flavors of fictitious capital: not just traditional bank loans and bonds, but so-called derivatives, options, bundled mortgages and consumer debt, swaps, repos, the bond and gold carry trades, and others too numerous to list. He would not have been surprised by the increasing—and usually camouflaged and denied—state manipulation of the prices of currencies, debt, precious metals, commodities, and insurance, as well as the continuing deployment of various and more open trade barriers. All the above are manifestations of violent interimperialist and intercapitalist competition, as well as semicolonial exploitation, in the form of state conflict.

Finance capital divides, and redivides, the world in new ways. It reorganizes the colonial system—the superexploitation of peasants and workers in "independent" countries across Asia, Africa, and Latin America—in new, "neocolonial" ways. It transforms the banking system and patterns of world trade and finance. It increases the enormity of debt and the leverage of worldwide speculation almost beyond imagination—and beyond control.

THE DIVISION OF THE WORLD described by Lenin between a handful of oppressor nations and the great majority of oppressed nations—between the imperialist powers and the colonial and semicolonial countries—will

---

4. Lenin, *Imperialism, The Highest Stage of Capitalism* (New York: Pathfinder, 2002), p. 38.

be fundamentally the same when Washington embarks on its next military adventure as it was in 1898 during the so-called Spanish-American War, when the U.S. rulers conquered Puerto Rico and the Philippines and put their boot on the neck of the Cuban people. And it will remain ✳ so as long as capitalism dominates the world.

If, as part of a study group, you read, discuss, and absorb Lenin's *Imperialism,* you are better equipped to understand the problem with using the term "emerging," as in, "emerging market countries." You're better equipped to understand why not one of these countries has ever "emerged" as an advanced capitalist power, or ever will. If what the crisis of 1997–98 revealed about the "Asian tigers"—South Korea, Taiwan, and a few others—wasn't proof enough, then what's been happening in Argentina over the past year and is unfolding in Brazil right now certainly should be.[5] With the exception of China, Brazil has the largest economy of any country in the colonial world, measured by gross domestic product. But with $264 billion in debt owed to U.S. and other banks such as Citigroup, J.P. Morgan Chase, and FleetBoston, Brazil remains as firmly lodged among the oppressed nations *✳ debt is key* as it was twenty-five, fifty, or a hundred years ago. So is Argentina, which is also among the largest economies in the colonial world—and on a per capita basis, actually

---

5. In December 2001 the Argentine government defaulted on $100 billion of government bonds, owned largely by capitalists in Western Europe. The peso, which had been pegged to the dollar, was cut loose and its value plummeted by 75 percent, with devastating consequences for working people and broad layers of the middle classes in Argentina. Over the next year, as economic growth fell by 12 percent, joblessness shot up to nearly 25 percent and inflation reached 40 percent. The Argentine crisis sent shockwaves throughout the entire region.

much wealthier than Brazil—and owes some $132 billion to banks and bondholders, largely in imperialist Europe, as well as Japan and the United States. The workers and peasants of Brazil and Argentina are not only directly exploited by domestic and foreign capitalists but also— through the agency of the national bourgeoisies in those countries—are held in debt bondage to international finance capital.

It is in rebellion against the social consequences of the highest stage of capitalism, of imperialism, Lenin pointed out, that resistance grows among workers and rural toilers both in the centers of finance capital themselves and in the oppressed nations. What's more, as he described four years later at the Second Congress of the Communist International, capital's penetration into more and more parts of the globe for the first time makes it possible for the workers movement to become truly international in its composition and its reach.[6] This is true even in the economically least developed parts of the world, Lenin noted. As fighters for national liberation recognized their common interests with the workers and peasants who had conquered power in Soviet Russia—as well as their common class enemies—prospects would grow for the development of leaderships that would fight for

---

6. Lenin, in his opening report to the Second Congress of the Communist International, said that the gathering "merits the title of a World Congress" because "we have here quite a number of representatives of the revolutionary movement in the colonial and backward countries. This is only a small beginning, but the important thing is that a beginning has been made." Lenin, "Report on the World Political Situation and the Basic Tasks of the Communist International," in *Workers of the World and Oppressed Peoples, Unite!*, vol. 1, p. 144. Also in Lenin, *Collected Works*, vol. 31, p. 232.

a popular revolutionary dictatorship, for governments based on soviets of the oppressed and exploited toilers. That had become a realistic world perspective. In recognizing this, the Comintern anticipated by more than half a century a Thomas Sankara of Burkina Faso, a Maurice Bishop of Grenada. In its own way, it anticipated a Malcolm X emerging toward revolutionary socialism from the proletarian ranks of the fighting Black nationality in the United States. And emerging as a leader of world stature and caliber.

Ultra-imperialism?

We also need to discuss and absorb the second major aspect of Lenin's *Imperialism*: the polemic against the assertion by German centrist leader Karl Kautsky of a trend toward the consolidation of what Kautsky called ultra-imperialism. This was not a "theory" or an "idea." It was a *rationalization* for the political course that had led Kautsky and many other leaders of the Second International away from Marxism, in fact, and toward reconciliation with "their own" bourgeoisies—concretized as a horrible reality during the interimperialist slaughter of World War I and its aftermath. It was, and remains, a matter not just of the head but the gut, a matter of political backbone—that is, of class orientation.

Kautsky and other centrist leaders did not challenge the basic facts presented by Lenin about the growing domination of monopolies, of finance capital. Rather, they denied that these tendencies increased the violence of capitalism on a world scale and created the conditions for its overthrow by the toilers led by a proletarian vanguard. In fact, the centrists said, these trends fostered the conditions for the development of a stable order, based on a convergence of interests of the largest capitalist powers, that would transcend contradictions and conflicts and could lay the basis, over time, for peace on earth.

It's only a short distance from such an "analysis," Lenin said, to beginning to worship at the altar of finance capital and its seeming omnipotence. Centrists can be very critical of what they call "ultra-imperialism" and its greedy and downright mean actions. They can speak very harshly about it. They nonetheless ascribe *powers* to the capitalist world order that it does not have—embellish it with fetishes that make it appear more and more impregnable. Much of the talk we have heard the last few years about "globalization," and about "transnational" institutions replacing national states, is simply a retread of the Kautskyist rationalizations Lenin ripped apart in *Imperialism* and elsewhere.

One or another variety of this notion became the banner under which the petty-bourgeois opposition in the Socialist Workers Party, on the eve of World War II, retreated from the working class and from proletarian internationalism under the pressures of the impending imperialist slaughter. Pick up *In Defense of Marxism* by Leon Trotsky, and *The Struggle for a Proletarian Party* by James P. Cannon, and read what these communist leaders had to say about the "theory" of bureaucratic collectivism during the 1939–40 fight with the opposition led by James Burnham and Max Shachtman. Together with Lenin's *Imperialism*, these polemics by Trotsky and Cannon remain our historical benchmarks on these questions. As these renegades from Marxism recoiled from proletarian struggle, they often continued for quite some time writing about, complaining about, and pointing to shortcomings and moral evils of capitalism, its industry, and its agriculture—all the while building up the case that it was pointless for the working class to try to do anything about it—anything revolutionary, that is. Anything that can lead to a workers and farmers government, to the dictatorship of the proletariat.

Today, the self-avowed anarchist, Noam Chomsky, does the same thing. It's why his radicalism is no threat to the powers that be. And why there is an anti-working-class toxin in his radical medicine, especially anti-working-class in the United States.

Every tendency toward the supposed dissolution of state boundaries of the great imperialist powers in our epoch has been, and remains, an illusion. The trade battles among these powers—which manifest themselves, among other forms, as credit and currency conflicts— cannot and will not be overcome. Each seeming success in stemming a crisis postpones and increases the magnitude next time around, sharpening the contradictions.

Compete or die   *125 - 141*

Driven inexorably by the necessity to compete or die, capitalists, without exception, act pragmatically—on the basis that what *has been* happening *will continue* to happen. They seek to maximize profits by moving in directions that currently bring the highest returns. The more they inflate credit to shorten the turnaround time of capital in order to reap massive gains, the more successful any individual capitalist seems to be—the more they guarantee disaster when the inverted pyramid becomes shakier and shakier and the trends begin to play themselves out, and then to reverse. That's when all the talk about "new economies," the "end of cycles," even "the end of history" turns to ashes in their mouths. It's always "different this time." Indeed. And always the same.

Today the propertied families of finance capital, and their hired circles of managers, politicians, technicians, academics, and professionals—the "cognitive elite"—are incapable of believing what's happening to the mountains of paper values they've piled up over the past two decades. What worked so wonderfully well over those years for the well-heeled, what seemed like free money, has today inflated bubbles of debt that—as they overlap and reinforce one another, and before the contraction in stock prices has come anywhere close to running its long, full course—will bring down major banks, brokerage firms, insurance companies, pension and health trusts, and industrial and commercial corporations.

For the first time since the opening of the depression-ridden, war-ridden 1930s, all the evidence in the advanced capitalist countries points to the onset of something more than a deep, international recession such as those in 1974–75, 1980–81, or 1990–91. We're seeing the symptoms of a debt-deflation deadness that only sluggishly responds to the monetary or fiscal prodding that accelerates an upturn in a normal trade cycle. In short, we're in the opening stages of what will come to be recognized as a world depression.

Whenever overall profit rates are under pressure in these ways, each capitalist intensifies competition to corner the greatest possible share of the wealth, the surplus value, produced by the labor of workers and farmers. And it's the biggest banks—Citibank, J.P. Morgan Chase, Bank of America, and a few others—that make the biggest loans. On bank ledgers these giant loans are listed as assets, since they guarantee a steady stream of interest payments, *so long as the debtors are able to pay*. But when bankruptcies and loan defaults begin piling up, then it's also the biggest banks, insurance companies, and brokerages that will take the biggest hit. And when these institutions begin to crack—the ones rated by Wall Street agencies as the most "solid" and "reliable"—that's when a financial catastrophe starts looming.

Let's say, for example, that you or some other worker were allowed by a big company to lease a car for less than 1 percent interest. Not only that, the company also let you sell the car and use the money—so long as you agreed to return a car of comparable value when the lender calls in the loan. What's more, if the price of cars started going up—and the lender became worried you couldn't afford to buy one back to return—the leasing outfit would actually step in behind the scenes to hold down car prices on the market! So you could buy a car back for less than you sold a comparable one, return it to the leasing company, and walk off with a handsome profit. And the leasing company would get their car back, undriven, plus the 1 percent interest.

Quite a deal, isn't it? But workers don't have that option, of course. We're members of the wrong class.

GIANT BANKS do have such an option, however. And that's how it has worked over the past decade, until it started *not* working so well a year or so ago. How is it done?

Central banks, which hold large quantities of gold, lend it to a handful of the largest commercial and investment banks and insurance companies for a nominal interest rate—usually around 1 percent. These financial institutions then turn around and either sell that gold and invest the cash in bonds, or lend it to someone else for a small fee. The world's biggest banks then create a market in what are called gold derivatives—a highfalutin term for bets on the future direction of gold prices (their bet always is that prices will stagnate at worst)—and manipulate that market to help keep the price down. So, when it comes time to give back the gold to the lender, the borrowing institution buys it back at a lower price, pockets the difference, and returns the gold.

That's wonderful for the "bullion bankers," as they are called—so long as capitalism is in an upswing, stock prices are soaring, real interest rates are relatively high, and not too many well-endowed institutions or wealthy individuals around the world are interested in buying gold. But when all that begins to go into reverse, the demand for gold starts increasing and its price begins edging up. All those outstanding bets on a declining future price of gold—amounting to tens of billions of dollars—don't look so good anymore. The derivatives become time bombs. The banks face a tightening squeeze. And they will fight to avoid the destabilizing consequences of violent swings *not only in gold prices but also in all major commodities and the prices of major currencies in the imperialist world.*

What's more, those wagers on the price of gold are themselves only a small fraction of the overall outstanding bets—on the direction of interest rates, of the value of the dollar and other currencies, of the prices of stocks and commodities, and of many others. Worldwide, the nominal value of those bets—those derivatives—more than doubled between 1995 and 2001, to a total of about $120 *trillion.* And in the United States, 60 percent of derivatives are held by only five financial institutions, with J.P. Morgan Chase holding the largest share—some $25 trillion—followed by Bank of America and Citigroup.[7] So, as the direction of interest rates, the dollar, stocks, gold,

---

7. By the end of 2003 the nominal value of derivatives worldwide had reached nearly $200 trillion, with more than a third held by U.S. banks. By the end of the first quarter of 2004, the top five holders among U.S. banks accounted for 94 percent of all U.S.

and other commodities began rapidly shifting over the past two years, those long-term bets started getting shaky. It's a bit as if the undisputed favorite had broken his leg halfway through the Kentucky Derby, when the bets are already down. So much for another "sure thing."

It's worth remembering that we know a certain amount about the credit risk of banks such as J.P. Morgan Chase and Citibank, since they are by law "commercial banks" that must file a substantial amount of information with the federal government for the public record. With large "investment banks" such as Goldman Sachs, Merrill Lynch, Deutsche Bank, or Credit Suisse First Boston, however, the debt load may well be much the same, even while public knowledge is much less.

I N 1933, AS PART of the U.S. rulers' efforts to stabilize and salvage the capitalist system during the Great Depression, the U.S. Congress adopted a law called the Glass-Steagall Act. Under this reform, banks were supposed to separate out "commercial" banking—that is, holding checking and savings deposits, as well as issuing mortgages and business loans—from "investment" banking—that is, serving as a middleman for big corporations in peddling their stocks and bonds. Commercial banks are supposed to derive most of their profits from interest payments on business, home, and personal loans, backed up by the banks' highly leveraged deposits. Investment banks, on the other hand, grow wealthy off the fees they make from brokering deals for big business, including their own participation in these deals. Under Glass-

---

derivatives, with J.P. Morgan Chase alone holding just over 50 percent (almost $40 trillion).

Derivatives held by U.S. commercial banks (1992–2004)

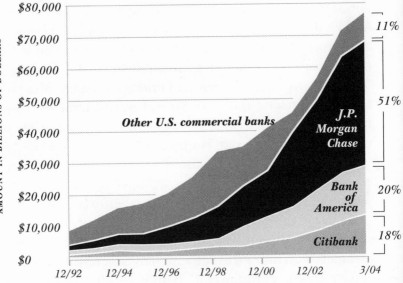

SOURCE: FEDERAL DEPOSIT INSURANCE CORPORATION

Steagall no institution was supposed to engage in both kinds of activity, which involve contradictory obligations and conflicts of interest. That was supposed to forestall bankers' temptation to pour all the money at the bank's disposal—including the checking accounts of workers and the middle class—into unsound loans to corporations they had a stake in (for example, Enron or WorldCom today), or into highly risky "financial products" (of which there are many, many more varieties at the opening of the twenty-first century than were dreamt of in 1933).

Over the years, banks found more and more ways to get around the Glass-Steagall restrictions. And in 1995—at the initiative of the Clinton administration and its Treasury Department head, the liberal Democrat bleeding-heart Wall Street bond-trader Robert Rubin—the act was repealed altogether. So the sluice gates were opened even wider.

Debt pyramid begins wobbling

When the giant debt pyramid finally begins to tumble, some of the world's largest financial institutions—banks, mutual funds, insurance companies, pension funds—will be on the losing end. The collapse and writing down of debt eventually fells those who are owed the money. The rolling collapse of a number of these massive entities can paralyze the functioning of international finance. And the "wisest" central bank in the world will stand helpless—at best—or else, in a panic, make the global crisis worse and more widespread.

It's not complicated: whenever any of us hears about the gigantic derivative deals we've been discussing, we should always remember that there are two sides to such agreements, and when one side makes money, the other side loses—and sometimes a much bigger amount.

Household debt in U.S. (1976–2004)

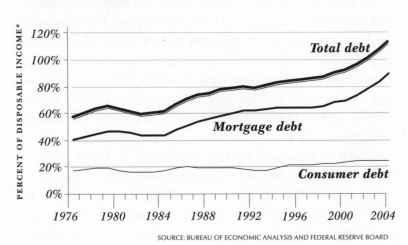

SOURCE: BUREAU OF ECONOMIC ANALYSIS AND FEDERAL RESERVE BOARD

Household debt payments in U.S. (1980–2004)

Mortgage and consumer debt payments

* *Disposable income is defined by the U.S. government as personal income minus taxes, fees, and fines.*

SOURCE: FEDERAL RESERVE BOARD

The "long" side—those betting on rising prices of a security or commodity, who've paid for the option to buy a certain amount for a certain price on a certain date—can lose everything they've "invested" if prices fall, but only that much; there's a known limit beforehand.

The risks are much greater, however, for those on the "short" side, who borrow massively from banks ("margin," as it's called on Wall Street) to cover their commitments to the other party in the transaction. If the bet starts going sour—if stock prices, interest rates, currencies, or commodities prices start moving in a direction opposite of that anticipated—then their losses can for all practical purposes be unlimited, as the banks begin calling in their loans (a "margin call").

THAT TYPE of "naked" or "uncovered" bet is part of the psychology of capital during a boom, when confidence becomes nearly absolute that it's "a sure thing" the prices of most securities can only keep going up or that interest rates and the prices of most commodities (including gold and oil) can only keep going down. But when those rates and prices "unexpectedly" reverse direction, that leveraged pyramid of speculative debt—the piling up of loans at an ever-growing ratio to the underlying capital—begins to wobble. While they can, the banks extend massive lines of credit to help insurance companies, brokerage houses, hedge funds, pension schemes, mutual funds, heavily hedged gold producers, and other financial entities "trade their way out" of the crisis. At some point, however, these massive institutions begin defaulting on their loans, and in the worst-case scenario—one that has occurred more than once in history—they catastrophically start bringing down the banks themselves.

When the stock market began declining in 2000, many of the financial publications and commentators initially tried to pass it off as nothing more than a volatile patch for technology stocks. "Don't worry," we were told. "Things will never get as rocky here as in Japan. Japan has a massive bubble in real estate and banking. In the United States it's only in computers, dot-coms and their ilk."

But that's worse than wishful thinking. It's true, of course, that the stock prices of many so-called hi-tech companies—the internet dot-coms, telecommunications outfits like WorldCom and Global Crossing, and many others—skyrocketed in the late 1990s to levels wildly out of whack with their assets, revenues, profits, or prospects. Many more computers and computer-related commodities were produced than were needed by businesses or could be sold at prices individuals and corporations could afford or were willing to pay. There was massive overcapacity that will take years and years of economic growth to unwind, as factories are shut down, equipment is scrapped, capital goods deteriorate, inventories are devalued—and prices keep going down. Less than 3 percent of the 39 million miles of fiber-optic cable laid in the United States over the past decade, for example, is currently even in use![8]

But it's not the hi-tech mania, multiple bankruptcies, or massive accounting frauds such as WorldCom or Enron that lie at the root of the current capitalist crisis. These are merely diversionary symptoms of the giant debt bubble built up by finance capital over nearly two decades

---

8. According to telegeography.com, publisher of *International Bandwidth 2004*, "overcapacity continue[s] to plague the industry." At the end of 2003, they say, "just 3–5 percent of upgradeable capacity" of installed undersea and underground fiber optic cable was in use in Europe and the United States.

to counteract growing global overproduction and downward pressure on profit rates. World capitalism's greatest vulnerability doesn't have to do with what WorldCom or Enron is worth today. The debt bubble is centered in "old money" institutions and respectability. The real question is: What is Goldman Sachs worth? Or J.P. Morgan Chase? Or Citibank? What is the viability of the banks and financial institutions that issued the debt, even "capitalizing"—what Wall Street calls "securitizing"—all of your credit card debt? (Believe it, brothers and sisters! For them, your credit card debts are listed as an asset!) How sound are the institutions that stood behind all the forms of fictitious capital that allowed the owners of many companies to rake in profits from all over the world totally out of proportion to any lasting expansion of socially necessary productive capacity?

AT THE RISK OF OVERSIMPLIFYING, we could put it this way: When Microsoft stock goes down, some people in Washington State are sad. When Apple stock goes down, a different set of people in California are sad. When IBM stock goes down, some people in New York are sad. When Enron goes under, a lot of people in Texas are sad. And Ole Miss weeps for WorldCom. But when J.P. Morgan Chase stock heads south, it will be the leading families of U.S. finance capital who shudder.

That's why world capitalism was shaken by the financial crisis in Asia and the debt-payment default in Russia in 1997–98. That's why finance capital is worried right now about trying to make sure that Argentina and Brazil pay up on their giant debts to banks such as J.P. Morgan and Citibank. Morgan had to write off $350 million in bad loans in Argentina in 2001, and has more than $2 billion at risk in Brazil today.

The most misnamed institution in the world must have been "Long-Term Capital Management." It was a giant U.S. hedge fund—sort of an exclusive unregulated mutual fund for the very rich. In 1998 LTCM went with a begging bowl to Federal Reserve Bank officials, saying it faced massive losses on its "investments"—actually derivatives gambles. (Try going yourself to knock on the Fed's door and say *you* finally put everything you could beg, borrow, or steal on one too many sure things, and are in big trouble. See if they bail you out—or whether your nearest and dearest have to post bond.) LTCM had been dealing in bets on minute-by-minute moves of interest rates, currency rates, and perhaps gold—derivatives, once again—that had mounted up to some $1.25 trillion and turned sharply sour. So it couldn't meet loan payments to many of the world's largest banks. (That was the real rub, of course. Officials at the Fed couldn't have cared less about LTCM.)

Just the previous year, by the way, two of the principal founders of "Long-Term Capital Management," which quickly became Short-Term Speculative Plunging, had won the Nobel Prize in economics for developing a mathematical formula demonstrating how to minimize risk in derivatives markets! Looking back on the fund's collapse, one of those prizewinners later remarked, "In a strict sense, there wasn't any risk—if the world had behaved as it did in the past." Brilliant! So much for mathematical "certainties"—and Nobel Prize winners! Dumber than a rock. And greedier than Scrooge McDuck.

T HE HEAD OF THE Federal Reserve Bank of New York stepped in during September 1998 and organized some fifteen major banks and brokerage houses—mostly from

Wall Street, but also from London and Paris—to put up $3.5 billion to bail out LTCM. Federal Reserve chairman Alan Greenspan later said he didn't think it had been prudent for a branch of the U.S. central bank to have intervened quite so openly, but his own take on the situation could hardly have been too comforting to the capitalist class he serves. Greenspan said he thought the "probability that LTCM's collapse would unravel the entire world financial system was significantly less than 50 per cent." The entire world financial system! Just a few days ago, Greenspan told Congress that "an infectious greed seemed to grip much of our business community." Hard to disagree with that, except for the qualifier "much," and the past tense for "seems." Contrary to Greenspan's unctuous scolding, however, greed under capitalism is not a character flaw, much less an attitude alien to business. As a decades-long acolyte to Ayn Rand, the Federal Reserve chairman knows better. Greed is inherent to capitalist competition. Capitalism truly is a dog-eat-dog system, as Cuban president Fidel Castro often says. That is the engine of market relations. It is the foundation of the bourgeoisie's values and the contempt for human solidarity they so blithely display. Their "family values" stop with America's Sixty Families.

The bubble that hasn't yet been touched in the United States is the housing bubble; it too will burst. It may not start with a collapse in real estate like that in Japan, where commercial property prices have dropped by more than 80 percent over the past decade and the cost of homes has fallen too, if less. But those of you who follow the local papers where you live know how home prices have shot up over the past half-decade or more. Part of the ballooning in paper values has involved home mortgages taken on by workers and the middle class—not so

much to buy houses as to secure refinancing to go deeper
into debt to meet other expenses. Since 1995 home prices
have risen much faster—30 percent faster—than the rate
of inflation, while equity in these homes—the percentage of its current market value that has actually been paid
off to the bank or finance company—is at its lowest point
since World War II.[9] Even a 10 percent drop in housing
prices would wipe out well over a trillion dollars in assets
corresponding to paper values of homes. There's already
a rise in bank foreclosures on families that can't keep up
with the payments.

What's more, when home equity plummets, all the
other debts facing workers and the middle class become
all that more ruinous, since the ability to borrow against
that home drops as well. Average personal household
debt is already at record levels.[10]

The pricking of the housing bubble will have substantial consequences for the entire capitalist financial system.
Banks and other lenders slice up mortgages they've is-

---

9. In mid-2004, even with interest rates rising, the housing bubble
was still inflating. Home prices rose 40 percent faster than the
overall rate of inflation over the previous eight years. As of May
2004, home equity loans doubled to $326 billion in just over three
years. Homeowners' equity in their houses was at an all-time low,
having fallen to 55 percent of the market value of the home in
mid-2004 from a high of 84 percent in 1945; the average over
those six decades was 67 percent.

10. As of the end of 2003, household debt had risen to 83 percent of the U.S. gross domestic product (GDP) from 70 percent
in 1999. More than 13 percent of household income went toward
paying interest and principal on those debts. Under the combined
pressures of mortgage and other personal debt, 1.6 million individuals in the United States filed for bankruptcy in 2003, nearly
twice the number ten years earlier.

sued, package them according to risk, and then sell them to big, government-backed financial institutions such as the Federal National Mortgage Association and Federal Home Loan Mortgage Corporation—popularly known by their "NASCAR names" Fannie Mae and Freddie Mac. Between them, they control about 40 percent of the home mortgage market—some $3 trillion in mortgages—so a collapse of the housing bubble is an additional threat hanging over the U.S. banking system.[11]

Fannie Mae and Freddie Mac are themselves big holders of risky interest-rate derivatives. And no one can say how risky! That's not due to a lack of information, but due to the "short" character of so much of their derivative holdings—with potential losses, as noted earlier, that have no preestablished cap.[12]

T HE ACCELERATION of the world capitalist crisis today is also bringing an intensification of economic conflict among the rival imperialist powers. These can result over

---

11. By early 2004, the two agencies' share of all U.S. residential mortgages outstanding ($7.8 trillion) had risen to 50 percent.

12. In 2003 it was revealed that Fannie Mae had covered up $7 billion in derivatives losses in 2003 and $12.1 billion in 2002. That same year Freddie Mac was exposed as having used derivatives between 2000 and 2002 to cook its books. No one in their management went to jail. Don't try to emulate them! By September 2004 the federal agency charged with "overseeing" Fannie Mae had little choice but to issue a report confirming growing evidence that management was manipulating financial records to make its earnings look good, make its derivative holdings look less risky, and—naturally—justify massive executive bonuses. Two weeks later a House of Representatives subcommittee began public hearings. Stay tuned.

time in catastrophic trade and currency wars, not just protectionist skirmishes of the kinds we've become increasingly accustomed to over the past quarter century. And just as it did at the very opening of the Great Depression in 1930, global trade could plummet rapidly, accelerating the devastation of production, employment, productivity, and wages not only in the United States but also worldwide.

Posturing as the champion of "free trade," the U.S. imperialist government ravages the toilers of Africa, Latin America, and Asia by slapping both tariff and nontariff barriers of all kinds on textiles, shoes, and agricultural commodities such as sugar, cotton, fruits, vegetables, and others. Washington's 2002 Farm Bill—a gigantic giveaway to capitalist farmers—is the latest dagger in the stomach of billions worldwide who barely get by on less than $2 a day. That comes on top of the tariffs on steel and timber imports also imposed by the U.S. government this year.

To the U.S. rulers, starvation across Africa is a small price to pay to boost the profits of a handful of bullion banks such as J.P. Morgan Chase and wealthy farmers and agricultural trading monopolies such as Cargill and Archer Daniels Midland. Certainly one of the most gratuitous acts of cruelty in recent memory has to have been the tour in May by U.S. treasury secretary Paul O'Neill and rock star Bono across sub-Saharan Africa. In a region whose already meager share in world trade has been slashed by two-thirds over the past twenty years by the workings of the laws of capital—*to 2 percent*—one of the top spokespersons for finance capital in the wealthiest country on earth traipsed across the continent saying how upset he was by the deaths from hunger, poisoned water, AIDS, and other infectious diseases, wagging his finger at the "corruption" and "mismanagement" of African governments. But O'Neill's class is the architect of this devastation! It's the architect of what is, in fact, mass murder!

Imperialism is not a 'policy'

Lenin said that one of Kautsky's central illusions was that imperialism was "a policy, a definite policy 'preferred' by finance capital,"[13] rather than an inevitable product of the development at an initial stage of monopolization of the economic system that will be with us until capitalism is overthrown on a world scale. To this day, this pretense still serves to rationalize the course of centrist and other middle-class currents within the workers movement. They act as if a different administration—Wellstone or Gore, instead of Bush, a "third party," a social-democratic-"valued" party—or even a different Senate, a different defense or treasury secretary, a different head of the Federal Reserve Bank would fundamentally alter the course of the imperialist state.

But neither the class structure nor the instability of the economic structure of imperialism, nor what drives it toward fascism and war, are policy matters. These are a product of the laws of motion of capital working along a constantly shifting historic curve of capitalist development. They are molded in concrete ways by the accelerating unevenness of the development of capitalist social relations in different parts of the world.

The development of giant monopolies at the end of the nineteenth century and opening of the twentieth didn't diminish let alone eliminate competition, but instead raised it to a more violent level. All its consequences became more severe, including the world reach and depth

---

13. Lenin, *Imperialism, The Highest Stage of Capitalism*, p. 34.

of financial panics, economic depressions, and wars.

Lenin's "theoretical" contribution to "economics" is one no bourgeois economist will admit to and that petty-bourgeois radicals recoil from. Lenin's main point, more true today than when he wrote it eighty-five years ago, is that this monopoly stage of capitalism is one in which state-organized violence, imperialist wars, national rebellions, civil wars, and proletarian revolutions are just as much an inevitable, lawful consequence of that mode of production as business cycles, inflation, and depressions. All these social and political phenomena are built into the laws of capital in the imperialist epoch.

On the "purely" economic level, a big expansion of loans or bond issues by major banks and corporations, a temporary lowering of nominal interest rates, a big increase in government deficit spending, legislation of various sorts, even giant war spending—such policies may be able to *postpone* a crisis, but they cannot and will not *prevent* a crisis.

All the newly packaged and ever more leveraged forms of debt have made credit relations today even more explosive. New forms of insurance (that's what derivatives were supposed to be when they were "invented") are turned into new forms of gambling. The underlying relationship between the credit system and capitalist production explained by Marx in *Capital* has not changed. While credit greases the wheels during prosperity, Marx wrote, in a "period of overproduction and swindle, it strains the productive forces to the utmost, even beyond the capitalistic limits of the production process. . . . In a system of production, where the entire continuity of the reproduction process rests upon credit, a crisis must obviously occur—a tremendous rush for means of payment—when credit suddenly ceases and only cash payments"—that is, payments redeemable in gold—"have validity."

And while "ignorant and mistaken" legislation and government policy "can intensify [such a] money crisis," Marx adds, none of it "can eliminate a crisis."

In a footnote to this passage in *Capital*, written a decade after Marx's death, Frederick Engels, Marx's closest collaborator, added a point that anticipates the evolution of capitalism in the 1980s and 1990s. "Thus every factor, which works against a repetition of the old crises," Engels wrote, "carries within itself the germ of a far more powerful future crisis."

LAST YEAR, IN 2001, the Federal Reserve Bank lowered the short-term interest rate eleven times—from 6.5 percent, down to its current level of 1.75 percent, and they will drop it further. But the U.S. economy continues to weaken, and Greenspan and Co. know they can only take it down a little bit further. Most importantly, they are acutely aware that the central bank of Japan lowered short-term interest rates on the cost of funds to industry to virtually zero without sparking an economic turnaround. Already in the U.S. today, real short-term rates— once we account for inflation, that is—are not just low, they are *negative!*

Never forget, capitalists don't borrow money because banks are offering low interest rates. Nor do banks offer low interest rates to encourage borrowers to put the funds to use. Businesses borrow money because they're convinced they can do something with it to turn a profit. And bankers lend at a particular interest rate because they think that's the best they can do and still cover the risk of not getting paid back. When the odds on defaults start rising, banks begin making fewer and fewer loans regardless of their liquidity, that is, regardless of the reserves they command. And when capitalists become convinced there's no money to be made, they won't take out a loan no matter how low the rates go. There comes a point, as bourgeois economists sometimes put it, when it's like pushing on a string. The economy becomes a giant "liquidity trap" into which the central bank can keep pouring more and more money at lower rates, but the commercial bankers won't lend it and corporations won't borrow it.

THERE WILL BE UPS AND DOWNS in the long-term bear market the stock exchanges entered in mid-2000. At some point, however, there will be a panic, with massive selling that liquidates share prices to lows we find impossible today to imagine. Enormous quantities of paper values will be destroyed, with no seeming link to anything happening to actual facts of production and trade. Marx wrote in *Capital* that to the capitalist, "The production process appears simply as an unavoidable middle term, a necessary evil for the purpose of money-making." That's why, Engels explained in a note to this passage by Marx, "all nations characterized by the capitalist mode of production are periodically seized by fits of giddiness in which they try to accomplish the money-making without the mediation of the production process."[14]

Such giddiness—which led to the stock and credit bubbles of the past two decades that are now contracting—is a manifestation of what Marx called commodity fetishism, the illusion that commodities and capital somehow have a social meaning in their own right, independent of the social labor that went into creating them, a

---

14. Karl Marx, *Capital* (London: Penguin, 1978), vol. 2, p. 137.

life of their own, independent of the character of the social relations that determine their use. "In interest-bearing capital, the capital relationship reaches its most superficial and fetishized form," Marx writes in *Capital*. Even in the case of giant trading companies, he says, profit "presents itself as the product of a social *relation*"—buying and selling—"not the product of a mere thing." But in banking and finance, profit seems to appear "unmediated by the production and circulation processes. . . . The social relation is consummated in the relationship of a thing, of money, to itself."[15]

Credit, paper money, stock prices—all these can lift off from underlying real values. Nobody knows the limits—except that they always become greater than we guess possible—until the "giddiness" turns to panic, as the entire structure starts crashing. When everyone rushes to the exit at the same time, no one gets out.

More than one hundred and fifty years ago, a book was published called *Extraordinary Popular Delusions and the Madness of Crowds*. It describes various manias and panics in the early history of capitalism—when tulips, for example, began selling for more than gold in the early 1600s—and the social and political chaos that ensued when those fictitious values collapsed. Marxists don't deny "the madness of crowds" under capitalism. To the contrary, it is a necessary by-product of commodity fetishism. We simply insist that the "madness" we already have on Wall Street, and will see much more of, is not that of the average person, even the "average" investor. The majority of shares on stock markets in the United States are owned by so-called institutional investors—insurance

---

15. Marx, *Capital* (London: Penguin, 1981), vol. 3, pp. 515–16.

companies, mutual funds, investment houses, pension and health funds, hedge funds, banks, and so on. What's more, fully 90 percent of the transactions on stock and bond markets today are made by these institutions (up from just 10 percent as recently as the early 1970s); half of all such transactions are made by the fifty largest institutional investors.[16] In times like today, more of these outfits start going belly up. And more and more, the prices are held hostage to loans, futures, options, and other astronomically leveraged, sliced and diced, bets on the direction of motion of different aspects of the stock itself! In a real stock market panic, in fact, many thousands of mutual funds will go bankrupt, as will tens of thousands of pensions and medical funds.

Many smaller investors in the middle class, and even some better-off workers, hold on to their stock when it begins going down in the belief they can weather the storm and, if not, they can sell before things really start going bad. But that assumes someone wants to buy their stock at that point. When everyone panics, however, including those giant capitalist institutions, small investors can wake up one morning and find that there are days— many days—when there are no buyers at any price. That is when fear finally trumps the greed of the greediest, and the final collapse occurs.

Sea change in working-class resistance

We're in the very opening stages of what will be decades of economic, financial, and social convulsions and class

---

16. The figures are from *Winning the Loser's Game* by Charles D. Ellis (New York: McGraw Hill, 1998). Ellis, a Wall Street investment manager, is a director of the Vanguard Group and chairs the Yale University investment committee.

battles. Insecurity will mount. At some stage, confidence in the capitalist order will begin to be shaken. And openness to radical solutions will grow—including "anti-imperialist" and "anticapitalist" solutions of the radical right, which will be attractive to layers of the ruined, bitter, or threatened middle classes. We'll see the rotten fruit of the bourgeois politics of resentment and its pornographication. We'll see the bloody fruit of the increasing political factionalization not only of the cops but of the officer corps and "intelligence professionals."

Like most other workers, communists participating in this convention must internalize the fact that this world— the likes of which none of us have known before in our political lives—is not only the world that must be faced today, but the one we will be living and fighting in for some time. By *acting* on this reality today, we will not be caught short politically as wars erupt, deeper social crises explode, pogroms are organized and attempted, and union conflicts become life-and-death battles. The proletarian party that exists tomorrow can only grow out of the proletarian party we put together *today*.

The evidence before us is that the communist movement can strengthen itself politically if we stay the course that is described under the title "A Sea Change in Working-Class Politics," the opening chapter of *Capitalism's World Disorder*. Our progress in advancing along that road lays the basis for the cadres of our branches, organizing committees, and union fractions to reconquer the proletarian norms we hammered out during the opening years of our turn to the industrial working class and unions. It's the course that we drew together as a handbook and published under the title *The Changing Face of U.S. Politics*. As the Socialist Workers Party has done throughout its history, we capture this kind of disciplined

functioning in the term *worker-bolshevik*, "a political designa-
tion that originated in admiration among the fighting
toilers of the October 1917 Russian Revolution and was
used not infrequently by Lenin," as the preface by Mary-
Alice Waters to the 2002 edition of *The Changing Face of
U.S. Politics* explains. When we talk about worker-bolsheviks, we're talking about forging "a communist cadre
whose integrity and discipline, organizational functioning, class training, milieu, and political habits are proletarian to the core."

THE KIND OF SHIFT in resistance among working people
such as we've been living through over the past half decade can initially be difficult to see. It's impossible to see
from outside the vanguard of the working class and labor
movement. But we are not outside, and our movement *did*
recognize it. Even more important, we responded, starting with the lines of labor resistance as they were given to
us and with the communist parties we had. We adjusted
our organizational forms to meet the new conditions. We
began following those lines of resistance among workers
and farmers. Instead of hunkering down in larger branch
units in a few cities, we've extended our geographical
spread and our political reach, deepening our integration
among vanguard layers of labor who are resisting the brunt
of the mounting assaults by the employing class. The comrades shouldering responsibility for this effort in party units
across the United States have increasing weight in the leadership of the Socialist Workers Party.

The collective and cumulative political work of our
branches and organizing committees is decisive to party
building and recruitment. They are the basic units of a
communist party. Their activity is combined with the

trade union activity of our union fractions—among garment workers in UNITE, the United Food and Commercial Workers (UFCW), and the United Mine Workers (UMWA)—which function in a narrower arena of working-class politics than the branches and organizing committees. Together these are the instruments through which we are deepening our integration into what will be decades-long class battles from within a developing vanguard of workers who are using the space they have carved out on the job, in the labor movement, and through other forms of proletarian social resistance. We are transforming ourselves and our institutions in the process. We are attracting young people who not only are repelled by the evils of imperialism but much more importantly are drawn to the battles of workers and farmers. And, whether they initially understand it or not, attracted away from a radical, fighting right wing in the only way possible—through involvement in the working-class struggle. In this way, we are strengthening our collaboration with revolutionary-minded youth and others around the world.

In hawking our papers, periodicals, and books, communists are always testing the wide seas of the working class. That is, we are permanent practitioners of reaching out as broadly as possible to working people with our literature. That is the only way to carry out consistent, proletarian propaganda activity—to learn as well as to sell. A small revolutionary party is always ignorant of slowly changing trends in broad layers of the working class. It couldn't be otherwise. When we're systematically reaching out in our propaganda work, we sense these shifts a little earlier and have a better feel for them.

"Pissing in the wind" was the epithet applied to this political activity in the opening years of the 1950s by the

Cochran faction that was preparing to split from the party, blaming the working class for their own decline. Some of you will remember the Cochranites from reading Jim Cannon's *Speeches to the Party.* We took their epithet as a tribute rather than a smear. The working class *is* our milieu, not "the left," not "radicals." That *is* where we concentrate sales of the *Militant, Perspectiva Mundial,* and our books and pamphlets that orient readers toward the revolutionary course of the proletariat. We're always working to extend our reach, to learn more, and to find fellow working people who are interested in arming themselves with a concrete analysis of the unfolding class struggle, as well as the lessons from a century and a half of struggles by the modern working-class movement.

This convention, and the meetings here yesterday of our union fractions, registered steps forward for the party in carrying out what we have called the third campaign for the turn. Since we launched that campaign four years ago at a conference in Pittsburgh, we have established fractions where we need to be—in sewing jobs in garment and in textile factories to build a UNITE fraction; in cut-and-kill operations of UFCW-organized packinghouses; and in UMWA-organized coal mines. We'll continue helping comrades conquer—and improve—skills we need to get and hold such jobs. We'll confront layoffs. We'll transfer comrades. We'll work to get into garment shops, meatpacking plants, and mines that haven't hired us so far, mines that are ripe for organizing, and find others in new regions where we want to build fractions. Above all, however, we can now reap the fruits of this ongoing effort by *using* our fractions to engage in communist trade union work and carry out propaganda activity on the job and in the labor movement. We can concentrate on building politically strong units of the party in areas where we've established organizing committees, as well as in workers districts in many places where we have existing branches. We can continue working with comrades in Communist Leagues in other countries to deepen the convergence in this regard that has accelerated over the past year.

We can act more effectively as a nucleus of worker-bolsheviks who are cadres and leaders of a communist political organization. Branches and organizing committees are beginning to carry out systematic plant-gate sales again, boldly acting to involve comrades working in those plants so we can reach larger numbers of coworkers with our press, our candidates and socialist campaign literature, and our books and pamphlets. We're making progress toward our norm that every fraction member takes part in a plant-gate sale at another factory or mine where comrades are working.

Leveraging our political arsenal

These advances provide a foundation upon which we are restructuring the work of comrades assigned full time to editorial responsibilities preparing the books and pamphlets that make up our political arsenal and organizing to keep them in print. We're simplifying the structure of our publishing operation, bringing it in line with the character of the party units we've been building, in order to place ourselves on the best possible footing to maintain the worldwide political leverage that our books give the communist movement. There are no more important weapons produced by the working class than the written record of the political lessons earned in sweat and blood and generalized from the struggles by labor and our allies over the past century and a half. The lessons contained in that record are the foundation of effective proletarian politics and a precondition to advances in strategic understanding and in Marxist theory. Without accurate and truthful history there is neither Marxist strategy nor theory. Both will wither away, supplanted by abstract counterfeits to rationalize the lives—and thus the political course—of the radical petty bourgeoisie and opportunist misleaders of the workers movement. The political curiosity and then hunger for these historic lessons of the working class will grow among workers and farmers, as well as among youth attracted to their struggles in this country and around the world. And no one other than the communist movement is either willing to do the work to keep making these lessons available or, more accurately, even interested in doing so—that is, feel they are necessary to its very existence.

OUR MOVEMENT not only keeps this basic communist arsenal in print but we keep adding to it. We publish the political analysis and orientation working people need *today* to build an effective revolutionary movement—books, pamphlets, and magazines such as *The Changing Face of U.S. Politics, Capitalism's World Disorder, Cuba and the Coming American Revolution, The Working Class and the Transformation of Learning*, the issues of *New International*, and more. And we root our politics, piece by piece, in one hundred and fifty years of battles and lessons drawn from the toilers' class-struggle and revolutionary resistance. In doing so, we are meeting an obligation, one that all of us—members and supporters alike—gain political satisfaction from working to accomplish. We will be able to sustain this effort, however, only if we can organize it in line with our movement's current size, resources, and needs. That's the precondition for the auxiliary organization of supporters we are building to gain the confidence to keep raising the bar and taking on new challenges in the production—and now increasingly the distribution— of these books and pamphlets.

It's important to absorb the political leverage the communist movement gains from the effort we put into the prefaces and introductions we prepare for new books and new editions. One of the displays at the back of this conference hall, I believe, features a copy of a letter Mary-Alice [Waters] received about a week ago from Ramón Labañino Salazar, one of the five Cuban revolutionists being held under long sentences in federal prison here in the United States. He was convicted on frame-up charges of conspiring to act as an unregistered agent of a foreign power and carry out espionage, and sentenced to life imprisonment.

Ramón had received a package of books Mary-Alice sent him, including *Playa Girón/Bay of Pigs: Washington's First Military Defeat in the Americas* by Fidel Castro and José Ramón Fernández. He wrote Mary-Alice saying how much he had enjoyed reading it, and called special attention to what he described as "a great virtue of the book" that he—as a Cuban revolutionist who already knew quite a bit about the defeat of the U.S. mercenary invasion at Playa Girón—"had never read in any other book on this subject." The foreword we had prepared, Ramón said, gave him a feel for the first time of "the direct influence of the Cuban Revolution, its example and impact, on the people of the U.S., and on the education of the revolutionary left movement and the movement in solidarity with our country." The foreword, he noted, recounted the impact among youth and others in the United States "first of the battle, then of the defeat of the mercenary force at Playa Girón." In doing so, he concluded, it "shows us, once again, that our peoples are fraternal and invincible."

That's precisely one of the goals we've had in writing prefaces and introductions to translations of books by leaders of the Cuban Revolution and about the political lessons and example of that revolution. We add something that communists in this country know a great deal about—the U.S. class struggle, its real history, and how it is intertwined with revolutionary political developments around the world. We can explain what revolutionary-minded workers and young people in this country were doing at the time, what they were responding to, and the political consequences of their actions. The accurate political picture we draw of the contending class forces in the United States is always quite different—much richer, more complete and contradictory—from that others, including revolutionaries, have heard before.

These prefaces and introductions are even more necessary here—for workers, farmers, and youth in the United States. They underline the class reality that there is no "we" in the United States that includes both working people, and the propertied rulers and their government and political parties. Whether the reader is living here or abroad, it's always a wonderful thing when they discover the truth that the U.S. rulers work hard to keep secret from workers here—that there is no such thing as a homogeneous, classless "United States."

The cadres of the Socialist Workers Party live, work, and carry out politics among fellow workers. We understand the radical political divisions and deep social stratifications within our class. We know both the militancy and solidarity among workers in this country, as well as the low political level and absence of any living heritage of mass revolutionary class combat. We're becoming more integrated into the stepped-up resistance by vanguard workers and farmers, and we know the openness we find among them to writings that offer a revolutionary perspective. We understand the attraction of radicalizing youth to this working-class resistance, and the ways it can lead them to the communist movement, to the Young Socialists, and toward the party—and open the door to winning them away from petty-bourgeois radicalism. For all these reasons, it's too easy for us to take for granted the production, reproduction, and worldwide circulation of the written record of the fighting vanguard of our class and its anti-imperialist allies.

B UT WE MUSTN'T DO SO, either in our political work here in the United States, or in our relations with revolutionists in other countries. Because these realities can be seen accurately, in all their richness, only through participation in the militant resistance of the working class, and even then can be understood and explained in clear class terms only by communists. Rectifying the false or distorted picture that is so often painted by various groupings on "the left" is a precondition for rebuilding a genuinely world communist movement. Workers, farmers, and youth around the world need to recognize the U.S. working class not as potential helpers of other people's revolutions (at best), but as the social force that can and will lead a successful revolutionary struggle for workers power—state power—in the United States. That is the vantage point from which vanguard workers and farmers in this country draw political strength from the class struggle on a world scale, including that engaged in by the communist vanguard in Cuba.

This is not the starting point for most "friends" of the

Cuban Revolution in the United States, to say the least. If ever they once gave lip service to such a perspective, it has been many moons since they were willing to act in a way that was consistent with it. They may "admire" the resoluteness of the Cubans they know. But they have no interest whatsoever in sharing a common condition with those who—as Enrique Carreras explains in *Making History*—get up each morning, kiss their loved ones goodbye, and then do what needs to be done, never knowing for sure whether or not they'll get home again that night, or ever.

It is a tremendous conquest that today the substantial majority of the new books we publish come out, often almost simultaneously, in English and Spanish, and sometimes, soon, in French as well. Plus we've improved our use of the "universal language," working-class Esperanto we might call it—the photo section. The pictures tell fellow workers a great deal about the book, whatever language they might speak, whatever political experience they may have had. They can see themselves and others like them in those photographs.

Many of the delegates and observers at this convention have read the reports in the *Militant* and *Perspectiva Mundial* about recent trips comrades have taken to Paraguay, Argentina, and Venezuela to report for our press and collaborate with militant workers, women, and youth in those countries. We don't just bring with us newspapers, magazines, and books that provide a communist view of the world class struggle. This literature is produced and distributed by us, by cadres of a workers party, often in the midst of action, not literary repose. That combination makes a political impact.

When the reporting team visited an occupied garment factory in Argentina a few weeks ago, for example, the workers there were, of course, happy to receive some solidarity and coverage from supporters of an English-language newspaper and Spanish-language monthly based in New York. And they were pleased to get hold of some books, pamphlets, and papers that could help them situate their fight in a broader world political context. But they were also surprised, very pleasantly so, that one of those bringing them this solidarity and these valuable written materials was a garment worker from the United States who operated a sewing machine exactly like the one they used and could explain things about wages, the pace of speed-up, and other conditions on the job that were utterly familiar to these Argentine workers. This is the process of workers everywhere beginning to see ourselves as part of a world working class—one that doesn't recognize just the "familiars" of our common exploitation, but also the possibility of a class politically fighting for itself and for a future for humanity.

Boldness and simplification

Later in the convention we will discuss and vote on a report presented by Mary-Alice that we called "Boldness and Simplification." Those twin challenges—both boldness and simplification—are decisive right now. Because we must continue advancing in the production and sales of books and pamphlets increasingly demanded by workers and youth, while we simultaneously lead a retreat from aspects of our publishing operations that are outsized, that are outmoded technologically and in relation to our size and skill possibilities, and thus have become an obstacle to accomplishing our political goals. Thanks to the "digital revolution" in printing and publishing, we can now radically simplify our apparatuses, including our publishing apparatus, at the same time we organize to use our books and pamphlets with greater political boldness.

At the same conference in Pittsburgh four years ago where we launched the third campaign for the turn, Peggy Brundy, a member of the steering committee of the newly constituted Reprint Project, made the first public presentation of the international effort by supporters of the communist movement to organize the scanning, formatting, and reconstruction of the graphics, photographs, and covers for each of our then-existing 350-some titles. By the fall of 2000 party supporters had already taken on not only the initial digital preparation of all those titles, but the work of correcting and updating the electronic files for each subsequent reprint, as well. They also began formatting and proofreading all *new* books, as well as organizing quality control on graphics, covers, and photographs of both reprints and new books. This international effort made it possible for us to establish a labor-saving digital workflow and to substantially reduce the size of the shop where the books and pamphlets are printed.

At this party convention, we are registering a number of new steps forward along this course:

• The first week in September, party supporters in Atlanta will be taking on the day-to-day organizing of warehousing and maintaining our book inventory, doing credit checks and filling orders, maintaining our Web site, convincing customers to order online, packing and shipping the books, billing and collecting on those bills, and helping customers with glitches.

• Beginning this month, the steering committee that oversees what has become known, because of its history, as the Reprint Project—even though it already involves much more than that name denotes—will start supervising the work of supporters in upgrading the promotion of books and organizing the systematic and sustained work necessary to expand accounts with bookstores and libraries that carry our titles in the United States and around the world.

• The party branches in New York City have taken on the weekly effort to mail the bundles and the subscriptions of the *Militant*, as well as the monthly *Perspectiva Mundial.* This is another step in the simplification of our publishing efforts that has made it possible to reduce to eight the number of party members volunteering full time in the printshop, down from some forty-five prior to the Pittsburgh conference in mid-1998.[17]

In a letter to a supporter that we published for our entire movement in 2000, I pointed to the longer-term significance of what they and the cadres assigned to the party's publishing operation are accomplishing:

> In addition to meeting the goals of putting in digital form every book, pamphlet, and education bulletin produced by our movement, a much bigger accomplishment is being prepared. Together with the shop, the supporters are helping put in place, for the first time in history, an irreplaceable, Web-

---

17. Based on this experience, another step in streamlining the production of books and pamphlets was taken in early 2003. With the advances in digital printing, what could only have become a more and more inefficient offset printshop dedicated to producing books and pamphlets could no longer be anything but an unnecessary drain on cadres and financial resources. Since that time volunteers in the project have organized the production not only of reprints, but new editions, and editorially completed new titles from start to finish, working with several businesses in the United States and elsewhere that do digital printing. Volunteers have accordingly renamed themselves the Printing Project.

based infrastructure of digital propaganda
production, decentralized so that no matter what
financial, security, or other conditions may confront
the communist party in the decades ahead, the
program and legacy of the modern revolutionary
workers movement can be prepared outside any
physical "brick and mortar" apparatus and then
printed on presses wherever they can be found and
whenever they can be paid for. What the Bolsheviks
would have given for that!

As we've explained many times, the supporters movement is an auxiliary organization not of any particular
local branch but of the *Socialist Workers Party* (or of one
of our sister communist leagues in other countries). The
relationship of supporters to the party is a *political* one,
based on their agreement with and attraction to our international program, our strategy and course of conduct
in the class struggle, and the activity of party cadres in
advancing that proletarian orientation. As John Benson
put it, succinctly and accurately, a couple of years ago,
"A supporter is someone who sees their political activity
through the eyes of the party, not as an independent
political activist. A supporter sees the party as essential—
as their vehicle for carrying out politics."

The advances we're registering at this convention now
make possible the next step in the simplification of our
structure and the transformation of the organization of
our work: to move the party full-timers on the periodicals staff and national office to a central Manhattan loca-
tion that they can share with a workers district branch in
New York City. We can begin organizing the party's national center and the editorial offices of the *Militant* and
Perspectiva Mundial into a headquarters of the size and

character we need. It will be a center whose physical layout is built around a workers' hall featuring a weekly Militant Labor Forum, a hall that the New York Headquarters branch of the party can afford, maintain, and *use* to advance the party. Having the cadres assigned to these national responsibilities operating out of a common headquarters with a workers district branch that most of them are members of and are helping to lead will mark an advance both in building a proletarian organization in New York and in meeting the party's national and international responsibilities. We will start looking like who we are. What you see is what you get.[18]

We are closing in on a historic accomplishment that every party member, Young Socialist, and supporter of the communist movement, here and around the world, has had a hand in realizing over the four years since we set out on this course, together with the third campaign for the turn, at the Pittsburgh conference.

A cadre of worker-bolsheviks

At the close of this convention, the delegates will elect the National Committee, the most authoritative component of the party leadership. Equipped with this picture of the world we've entered and our movement's tasks, it's useful to say a few words about what we're looking for in electing a leadership of the party, since this is also what we're looking for in the cadre of the party as a whole.

I was asked to speak at a meeting in St. Paul, Minnesota, a little over a week ago to celebrate the sixty-five years

---

18. In March 2004 the communist movement celebrated the opening of a new combined headquarters of this kind at 306 W. 37th Street, 10th floor, a building filled with garment shops located in the middle of New York City's Garment District.

of communist political activity of Charlie Scheer, a friend and a charter member of the Socialist Workers Party who died last month. At that meeting, we discussed what it is that makes somebody a communist. How do we explain what leads a person to make this lifelong decision?

There is no such thing as a "communist type." If we recognize that fact, it makes recruitment a lot easier. There is a glorious variety of "types," alas all manufactured in the bourgeois world, who find their way to the communist movement. Those who can and do become deeply political people are not shaped by a cookie cutter, let alone a common cookie cutter. What communists share is not our personalities, our genetic backgrounds, our range of interests, and so on. In fact, communists are more uneasy than anybody with "social engineers" who try to homogenize, "improve," and channel working people—whether of the Hillary Clinton bourgeois liberal flavor, the Swedish social-democratic variety, the Stalinist thug-love type, or the Ashcroftian "do-it-the-Jesus-way" cops. We're deadly enemies of the concept of the perfectibility of humanity. We know the reactionary consequences of such notions, from Hitler's Germany, to Mao Zedong's Cultural Revolution, to Pol Pot's Kampuchea, to Gerry Healy's Workers Revolutionary Party. These are the notions of middle-class intellectuals and bureaucrats and their goons, not revolutionary-minded workers. We don't trust people who peddle such notions, whether bureaucrats, saviors, or saviors on their way to becoming savior-bureaucrats.

What we *do* trust is the power of *political* people working together, as an organized part of the proletarian vanguard, with neither capital nor coercion to bind us. Proletarian revolutionists work together by conviction, not by force. We do so as we discover that is the only way possible for workers to put together a combat party—a *political* instrument able to withstand the most difficult pressures, embrace new challenges, and carry out its revolutionary tasks. We operate together on the basis of politics and mutual respect, not authority, and that's a very different thing. We are confident in our class. Our confidence is born of experience—becoming citizens of time, of the world, of history. "We are heirs of the world's revolutions," as Thomas Sankara so eloquently explained it.[19]

W E DON'T HAVE "faith" in socialism. We have no revelations. We impose no bright ideas. We don't create a new world out of our heads. In practice, we advance the line of march of the working class as it unfolds through complex and permanent class struggle toward the dictatorship of the proletariat. In practice, we transform the conditions that shape our lives, and are in turn transformed by that struggle. And we do it all voluntarily.

As we gain more experience in the communist movement, we don't change our personalities, our "type." We do, however, strive to develop proletarian habits. We come to understand better the centrality of human solidarity to the line of march of the working class. How alien solidarity is to the social relations of capitalist society—to all the norms, values, attitudes, and fetishes it creates. Above all, the employers depend on a workforce that lacks confidence in the working class itself and in each other.

---

19. See Sankara's October 1984 talk before the United Nations General Assembly, in *Thomas Sankara Speaks: The Burkina Faso Revolution 1983–87* (New York: Pathfinder, 1988), p. 124; and in *We Are Heirs of the World's Revolutions* (New York: Pathfinder, 2002), p. 45.

Communists are not "determinists," contrary to what most of us are told before joining the movement. "Men make their own history," Marx taught us in *The Eighteenth Brumaire of Louis Bonaparte*, "but they do not make it just as they please; they do not make it under circumstances chosen by themselves."[20] We're believers in the reality of chance, in the interplay of causality and accident, even in luck (although we try to affect the odds). What is luck? Luck is being ready. That's what the communist movement organizes to do. We build a disciplined proletarian party, so we're politically prepared to respond to openings for intensified class combat and revolutionary activity when they rapidly or unexpectedly occur. Jim Cannon was fond of saying: if you live right, you get some breaks.[21] Be ready.

We don't pretend to predict the twists and turns through which the working class will march. No one can chart *both* direction and timing; both *what* and *when*. We carefully and honestly analyze the logic of the class struggle, as well as the concrete channels through which the current course of capitalist development is flowing and the lines of resistance among workers and farmers to stepped-up assaults by the exploiters. We organize and

---

20. Karl Marx, *The Eighteenth Brumaire of Louis Bonaparte*, in Marx and Engels, *Collected Works*, vol. 11 (Moscow: Progress Publishers, 1979), p. 103.

21. "If you live right and conduct yourself properly, you get a lucky break now and then," Cannon said in one of the twelve public talks he gave in 1942 on the effort to build a communist party in the United States. "And when an accident comes your way—a good one—you should grab it and make the most of it." James P. Cannon, *The History of American Trotskyism, 1928–38: Report of a Participant* (New York: Pathfinder, 1944, 2002), p. 178.

act in a centralized way on the basis of those judgments, weighing those facts, discussing them together with those militants.

Charlie Scheer and Helen Scheer, also a longtime party cadre who died a few years before Charlie, were companions for fifty years. Each of them was quite a different "type." At the same time, each was a communist, each was a worker, and each was a very political person. When Charlie or Helen wrote you a letter about one or another thing, their letters would be very different in tone and style. But almost without exception, somewhere toward the end of the note each of them would throw in the sentence: "What are you reading?" And they expected an answer. Each would have been an active participant in the socialist summer schools we just completed, and an enthusiastic partisan of organizing a school to dig into Lenin's *Imperialism* in the same serious and systematic way.

COMMUNISTS LIVE IN THE PRESENT, not in the future. We do so in practice, as well as "in our heads." To us, nothing is more alien than the notion of a utopia. Real utopians are dangerous, ultimately antihuman people. They have a "plan," a "vision," a "blueprint" for the society of the future, and they move toward imposing it on others. See the light? Whack! Now see the light? The modern revolutionary workers movement was in fact born in breaking with all the early petty-bourgeois utopian socialist movements.

Communists, by contrast, understand the present; we understand it not as a clump of episodes but as part of history. The *Minneapolis Star-Tribune* ran an obituary article about Charlie that said he "was convinced that in the long-haul his views would prevail." But if you knew

Charlie, you know that he—like every communist, like every revolutionary—didn't do what he did with his life out of faith that his "views" would someday prevail. To the contrary, Charlie knew that our program *prevails every day.* It guides us to effective communist action, action that maximizes the fruits of our joint efforts. Communists weave a web of class-struggle experience over generations, so that everything that happens in the present, and everything we do about it, is informed by the sweep of history.

Another newspaper article about Charlie commented on the big library, the many filled bookshelves he had had, calling him a "worker intellectual." But that writer got Charlie wrong, too. (A little projection can be a dangerous thing.) Communists like Charlie know that worker-bolsheviks are better informed, and better equipped to make political judgments and decisions, than so-called "worker-intellectuals." Worker-bolsheviks internalize what they've read, along with what they've learned *with others* in class-struggle experience. They enjoy reading and studying *together* with others fighting for common goals. They read more, not less, as the pace of the class struggle and political activity picks up. They are convinced that centralized revolutionary activity, as cadres of a revolutionary party to whose discipline they gladly submit, opens the road to a fulfilling life's work. That's what it means to be political.

Setting a revolutionary example

In the months and years ahead, communist workers and youth will come to appreciate more and more the benefits of the fact that an upturn in resistance among our class and its allies—both here and in many other parts of the world—began before the harshest initial shocks of the period of depression and wars we've now entered. We'll understand more concretely the importance of the political space workers carve out in struggle, and the stakes involved in using that space if it's not to be lost. We'll see more examples of how experience gained from any single battle—even battles that end in a stalemate with the class enemy, or a temporary setback—doesn't just dissipate; how individual workers absorb lessons and a little later turn up again, either on that same battlefront or another one. How they don't forget militants, organizations, or newspapers they learn through experience can be trusted for their proletarian integrity and for being in the front ranks of a just battle.

One of the most important political contributions our movement makes through our propaganda work today— in the *Militant*, in *Perspectiva Mundial*, in the books and pamphlets we choose to print—is pointing to the magnificent examples of toilers who stand tall and fight without fear, who display contempt for the rulers and are confident of victory. We shine a spotlight on the more than forty-year record of Cuba's working people and their revolutionary leadership being ready for whatever comes along that threatens their sovereignty and their socialist revolution. That intransigent revolutionary attitude is captured in the words of Fidel Castro and Osvaldo Dorticós in a statement that closes Pathfinder's forthcoming book, *October 1962: The 'Missile' Crisis as Seen from Cuba.* Responding to renewed provocations by the new Democratic administration toward the end of that crisis in late November 1962, the two Cuban leaders spoke for the big majority of Cuban toilers in saying: "We have as little faith in President Kennedy's words as we have fear of his veiled threats."

We glory in the combativity and resilience of the Palestinians. On the cover of one of its booklets, Pathfinder proudly displays a photograph of determined young Palestinians against the background of the slogan emblazoned on a wall: "We fight Israel because it occupies our land!"

This determination to fight, this absence of cowering fear, this class hatred for the oppressors and exploiters, is the necessary stuff that precedes any renewed international revolutionary movement. As we integrate ourselves in the fight of militants imbued with this spirit both here in the United States and the world over, our movement has the capacity to simultaneously discuss a communist political perspective rooted in the experience and lessons of more than one hundred and fifty years of revolutionary struggle.

With the irreversible disintegration of the world Stalinist movement, the obstacles within the workers movement to talking with revolutionary-minded workers, farmers, and youth—and getting communist literature into their hands—are smaller than at any time since the closing years of the 1920s. They'll be attracted to the revolutionary political fiber of worker-bolsheviks like Charlie Scheer.

Charlie was already living in a nursing home when the September 11 attacks took place, and his health had declined to the point that he sometimes had a difficult time following things. His son Bill sat down with Charlie that day and began telling him about the attack on the World Trade Center in New York. Charlie seemed to be listening, to understand, but he didn't respond. Then Bill added that another plane had smashed into the Pentagon.

At that point, Charlie turned his head, looked straight at Bill, smiled, and said in a very loud voice, so he could be heard by all his fellow patients, "That's good, isn't it!"

CONVENTION SUMMARY

I T IS IMPORTANT to be concrete about where we find ourselves today along the long-term curve of capitalist development worldwide, as well as in class politics in the United States. Otherwise, we will speak in formulas, instead of presenting a sharp, clear analysis, a communist program. We won't be able to accurately explain what we need to do now to build a proletarian party in this country. This dialectic between the international program and national terrain of communists' march toward state power applies to party building everywhere in the world. But nowhere are the consequences of failing to act on that class reality more damaging to revolutionary prospects and proletarian integrity than in the strongest bastion of world imperialism, the U.S.A.

In the closing paragraphs of the draft political report before this convention, we address this question directly. Thinking and acting along proletarian internationalist lines, we say, is and will remain not only a special responsibility but a special challenge for revolutionists who live and work in the United States:

[We] carry out our political activity not only in the wealthiest country on earth, but in one that has not experienced war on its own soil since 1865. It is a country in which there have been bloody class battles and proletarian social movements, but there has never been a revolutionary situation or workers' insurrection. It is a country that has seen genocidal treatment of native populations and organized murderous violence over decades by reactionary outfits such as the Ku Klux Klan, as well as systematic brutality by cops, National Guardsmen, and employer goons—but has experienced only limited combat in the streets and on the picket lines between fascist gangs and defense guards of labor and the oppressed.[22]

Along the road to a revolutionary situation, the working class in the United States, together with its broad political vanguard, will go through all these combat experiences. Each of them will take concrete forms, not identical to what has happened anywhere else or ever before in history. There will be unique combinations. Certain stages of class politics will be truncated and combined, others extended. Some will be accelerated, "with a truly American speed," to use Trotsky's phrase.[23] But communist workers in the United States will experience all these forms of political struggle before the revolutionary battle for power is posed.

The working class in this country will face efforts by the capitalist rulers, their government, and ultrarightist

---

22. Jack Barnes, "Our Politics Start with the World," in *New International* no. 13 (New York, 2005).

23. Trotsky, *Europe and America* (New York: Pathfinder, 1971), p. 82.

forces to smash the labor movement. Bonapartist regimes, whether installed with electoral cover or through
open military coups, will use the power of the imperialist state and heightened levels of demagogy against organizations of workers and farmers. In order to maintain
capitalist rule, the propertied families of the bourgeoisie will accept methods they themselves fear and seek to
avoid in more tranquil times. They will promote the rise
of fascist demagogues and movements, including their
most virulent form: national socialist organizations that
seek a mass base among the insecure middle classes and
layers of demoralized workers by combining radical, anticapitalist verbiage with appeals to the most reactionary—and deadly—nationalist, racist, anti-Semitic, and
antiwoman prejudices and superstitions.

In *Capitalism's World Disorder* we deal quite a bit with
what the working class has learned over the past century
about fascism and how to fight it, including the various
forms we've just noted, as well as the ways they can and
will manifest themselves in the class struggle in the United States. We note what veteran SWP leader Farrell Dobbs
often said: if anybody thinks that as class battles heat up
in the United States we are not going to see all these forms
of reaction, "then they are dead wrong and will never
build a revolutionary workers party in this country. We
will see every one of those [ruling-class] alternatives
tried"—from a repressive state, to military regimes, to
efforts by radical anticapitalist, fascist mass movements
to save capitalist rule.[24]

This underlines why it's so important that communist
during the convention discussion yesterday a delegate

24. Jack Barnes, *Capitalism's World Disorder: Working-Class Politics
at the Millennium* (New York: Pathfinder, 1999), p. 296.

proposed that, together with *Imperialism, The Highest Stage of Capitalism,* we put at the center of the winter school a number of Lenin's other political works from the same period. But that would get us off track politically. Our reason for choosing this topic has nothing to do with any similarity between the political conditions we currently face, and those Lenin was preparing the cadres of the Bolshevik Party to confront when he wrote *Imperialism* in the first half of 1916, in the midst of World War I.

At roughly the same time Lenin was completing *Imperialism,* he wrote that "[r]evolution was on the order of the day in the 1914–16 period"—not just in Russia but in Germany and elsewhere in Europe. It was "hidden in the depths of the war, was *emerging* out of the war. This should have been '*proclaimed*' in the name of the revolutionary class, and *its* programme should have been fearlessly and fully announced; socialism is impossible in time of war without civil war against the arch-reactionary, criminal bourgeoisie, which condemns the people to untold disaster."25 The Bolsheviks placed front and center the perspective of turning the war the imperialists were dragooning the workers and peasants to fight into a civil war to overthrow the propertied classes.

It's important to read and discuss these political writings, of course. We did so during the intensive study of Lenin our movement organized in the early 1980s, for example, and we'll do so in times to come. But Lenin did not derive the analysis of the highest stage of capitalism he presented in *Imperialism* from the conjuncture the toilers were living through, as important as he considered

25. Lenin, "The Junius Pamphlet," in *Lenin's Struggle for a Revolutionary International* (New York: Pathfinder, 1986), p. 589, and in *Rosa Luxemburg Speaks* (New York: Pathfinder, 1970), p. 578.

those political questions—and he considered *nothing* more important at the time, since those were the questions of revolution versus counterrevolution.

What Lenin presented in *Imperialism* was based on an objective analysis of the structure and evolution of the world capitalist economy over several decades. "I trust that this pamphlet will help the reader to understand the fundamental economic question, that of the economic essence of imperialism," he wrote in April 1917 at the conclusion of his preface to the first edition, "for unless this is studied, it will be impossible to understand and appraise modern war and modern politics."[26]

WHAT MEMBERS of the Socialist Workers Party, the Young Socialists, and our contacts need to study right now is not the period during which Lenin wrote *Imperialism*— a period when the party he was leading already had somewhere over twenty thousand members and was within a little more than a year of taking power. Those are nothing like the political conditions we are functioning in today, either in the United States or anywhere else.

Instead, we need to challenge ourselves to read and study *Imperialism* in order to understand and explain to others why Lenin's presentation of the tendencies inherent in the world system of capitalist exploitation and oppression still holds in its fundamentals today—*regardless* of the very different conditions, the different stage, prevailing in world politics in 1916–17 from those in the opening years of the twenty-first century. The enormous international expansion and spread of the market system since *Imperialism* was first written; the ongoing transfor-

26. Lenin, *Imperialism, The Highest Stage of Capitalism*, p. 3.

mations in techniques of production and circulation; the
Stalinist counterrevolution that betrayed the Soviet workers state and destroyed the Communist International as
a revolutionary instrument; the rise of fascism and a second world war; the victories for national liberation movements across the Caribbean, Africa, the Middle East, Asia,
and the Pacific; the revolutionary overturn of capitalist
property relations in Yugoslavia, China, Korea, Vietnam,
and Cuba; the worldwide flood of American fiat money
as the first international reserve currency redeemable in
neither gold nor silver; and countless other momentous
developments. All these are concrete manifestations of
the stage of capitalism explained in *Imperialism*; all exac-
erbate the tensions that Lenin's analysis underscores.

We will read *Imperialism* today for the same reasons
Lenin explained in April 1917: "for unless this is studied,
it will be impossible to understand and appraise modern
war and modern politics." The central contradictions of
imperialism will not be outgrown. That system will either
be overthrown, or it will create a hell on earth. Don't get
used to it. Get used to facing and fighting it.

Rulers not 'running with 9/11'

A couple of delegates made remarks to the effect that the
U.S. rulers, as they press forward their war drive and assaults on workers' rights, are still "running with September 11." That they're still fighting with "9/11" inscribed
on their banners.

That's not the case; the assessment we're placing before the convention is a different one. Since the opening months of 2002, the events of last September 11 have
had less to do with the rulers' pretexts for their policies
and stated goals. The rulers are not rationalizing these
policies—whether ditching the Anti-Ballistic Missile Trea-

ty, preparing an assault against Iraq, setting up the North-ern ("homeland defense") Command, rejecting the In-ternational Criminal Court, or chipping away at habeas corpus rights—primarily, or sometimes even at all, by harking back to the World Trade Center attacks. That's less and less the focus of their "global war on terrorism." It's more of a periodic patriotic rallying yelp—one part sentiment, two parts imperialist nationalism, all parts demagogy.

Instead, they say that "we"—a "we" that encompasses British prime minister Tony Blair and other imperialist allies of Washington—must go after the "axis of evil" and stop "them" while "we" still can. Bush's assertion in his State of the Union address to Congress at the end of Janu-ary 2002 that Iraq, Iran, and north Korea constitute three points along an "axis of evil" was not a continuation of the 9/11 demagogy from last fall. In fact, the "axis of evil" speech marked a break from using "9/11" to rationalize Washington's imperialist course. Why has Osama Bin Laden faded in the U.S. rulers' propaganda? Why the downgrading of attention to Afghanistan?

First, as we said in the report, Washington has shifted to *naming* and preparing to go after the countries that have demonstrated they can build the defensive military capacity to deal devastating blows in response to assaults by U.S. imperialism: Iraq, Iran, and north Korea. That's independent of whether they do in fact possess that ca-pacity today. Washington is not limiting the rationaliza-tions for its current preparations for a war against Iraq to the necessity of stopping further terrorist acts. It is organizing a classical imperialist war to tighten its domi-nation over that region—and its oil—and to strengthen its military force posture vis-à-vis its imperialist rivals.

The rulers recognize that they can't wait for "another

9/11," which they have no way of predicting. It could be a long wait. And we don't need any conspiracy theories that they're planning one themselves. The U.S. rulers very much need what they failed to get during their assault on Afghanistan: a self-feeding surge of patriotism in response to the blood of U.S. soldiers shed *on the battlefield of war*. They need that to put the initiative in their hands. To put the patriotic mobilizations under their control. That's what they're after. And they have the illusion they can fire an initial, quick salvo in the Middle East in order to better prepare a long struggle on a world scale.

Simultaneously, the U.S. government is moving to institutionalize the option of using federal forces at home, under a centralized military command, sometime in the future. This goes hand in hand with stepped-up probes today to legitimize the option of using "preventive" detentions with no charges (and even without the right to see a lawyer), secret courts, and increased wiretapping and other forms of spying and harassment. While there are divisions within the ruling class over how far and how fast to go, and while they will have to retreat on one or another aspect of their course, there is backing on both sides of the aisle in Congress for laying the groundwork to allow any administration to move in this direction, at its discretion.

The Homeland Security Act is getting coverage in the bourgeois press right now. And what will anchor even Homeland Security, as we noted in the opening report, is the Pentagon's Northern Command that will stand up in October, aimed at further legitimizing, in extremis, the use of U.S. military forces against working people in the United States—in all of North America!—with the U.S. military as the force of last resort when it's decided that rapidly putting down civil disorder is needed to prevent "terrorists" from taking advantage of "openings."

"All military assaults by Washington and other imperialist powers have been 'preemptive.' Cuba didn't threaten or invade the United States in 1961 or 1962. Vietnam didn't hurl weapons against U.S. cities."

TOP: Captured members of U.S.-organized mercenary brigade that invaded Cuba at Playa Girón (Bay of Pigs), April 1961. Invaders were defeated by revolutionary army and militia in less than 72 hours.
BOTTOM: Armored Troop Carrier and U.S. Army helicopter carry out operations against liberation forces in Vietnam, 1968.

BELOW: TIME LIFE / GETTY IMAGES. RIGHT: GRANMA

"To boost profits, employers are pressing down wages and benefits, lengthening hours, and intensifying labor. This stretch-out and speedup is the 'secret' of the productivity gains the bosses brag about."

TOP: Meatpacking plant in Plainview, Texas, 2003. Since early 1980s, owners have often more than doubled line speeds, slashed wages and benefits, and stepped up union-busting. **BOTTOM**: Some 1,000 coal miners and families join protest organized by United Mine Workers in Lexington, Ky., July 20, 2004, demanding that Horizon Natural Resources honor union contracts. Two weeks later the company eliminated medical coverage for 1,000 miners and 2,300 retirees.

UFCW NEWS SERVICE

ASSOCIATED PRESS

Curve of capitalist development

The underlying contradictions of world capitalism push-ing toward depression and war did not begin on Septem-ber 11, 2001. Some were accelerated by those events, but all have their roots in the downward turn in the curve of capitalist development a quarter century ago, followed by the interrelated weakening and then collapse of the Stalinist apparatuses in the Soviet Union and across East-ern and Central Europe at the opening of the 1990s. We have followed these trends over that entire period: in *The Changing Face of U.S. Politics,* in feature articles in several issues of *New International* magazine—"What the 1987 Stock Market Crash Foretold," "The Opening Guns of World War III," "Imperialism's March toward Fascism and War," and "U.S. Imperialism Has Lost the Cold War"—in *Capitalism's World Disorder,* and in *Cuba and the Coming American Revolution.*

It's useful now to go back to *Capitalism's World Disorder* and reread "So Far From God, So Close to Orange County: The Deflationary Drag of Finance Capital," a talk given to a regional socialist conference in Los Angeles at the opening of 1995. The rudiments of the unexpected and violent credit contraction we are threatened with once again today could be seen in late 1994 in the col-lapse of the Mexican peso and in the bond default—cho-sen in preference to raising taxes—by the government of a wealthy county in southern California. We said at the time:

> With returns on investments in capacity-expanding plant and equipment under pressure since the mid-1970s, owners of capital have not only been cost cutting; the holders of paper have been borrowing larger and larger amounts to buy and sell various

forms of paper securities at a profit. They blew up a giant balloon of debt in Orange County over a period of years [betting that interest rates would surely continue to go down in the early '90s. This was a nearly metaphysical "insight" only greedy county administrators and Merrill Lynch bond salesmen were given by God; going massively short and uncovered was protected by the alignment of the stars!] The bondholders thought they had died and gone to heaven. . . . When the balloon international bankers had inflated in Mexico in the 1980s began to collapse, the bondholders stepped in and blew it back up for a while. But in Orange County, the more local officials borrowed to make a killing using public funds to gamble [in collusion with] bond merchants, the greater their vulnerability became. . . .

Now the capitalists and their public representatives —and not just in Mexico or Orange County—have been given another warning of the long-run possibilities of an uncontrollable deflation. Over the past couple of decades, upturns in the business cycle have relied on floating large amounts of fictitious capital—ballooning debt and other paper values. The capitalists are now paying the piper for the lack of sufficient economic growth during that period to keep rolling over the loans.[27]

The capitalists pushed off the crisis for another half decade after the mid-1990s by inventing and inflating more credit instruments and paper assets. The stock market, as measured by the Dow Jones Industrial Average and

---

27. Barnes, *Capitalism's World Disorder*, pp. 60–61.

the S&P 500, more than tripled. Corporate borrowing more than quadrupled in the United States over that five-year period—not to expand productive capacity, but often to buy back their own bloated shares, bloat them further, and sit on what more and more becomes a cash hoard.[28] Between 1995 and 2000 in the United States, corporations were the biggest net buyers of shares—often the bloated stocks of the very same corporations that had issued them. And we've already discussed the explosion in Wall Street leveraging of casino chips called derivatives.

That's why, at this early stage in the onset of a world depression, we need to keep our eyes on the unfolding *financial* crisis of the bourgeoisie. We need to keep our eyes on the growing imbalances in state finances, incipient currency runs, the threat of capital controls, the deflationary ogre lurking behind every rise in interest rates, the increasing monetization of precious metals and the additional pressures this brings to bear on the relative strength of rival "international reserve currencies." In the history of modern capitalism, and in the

---

28. Government figures showed declining capital investment throughout 2001 and 2002. Even the modest upswing beginning in mid-2003 focused on replacing worn-out equipment, driving labor costs down by intensifying the pace of work and lengthening the workday, not by expanding capacity and output. An article in the July 19, 2004, *Business Week* magazine, headlined "Corporate Coffers Are Stuffed With Dough," pointed out that "so far at least, instead of putting all this firepower to work—by pumping up capital budgets, upping the pace of hiring, restocking inventories, or passing out bigger dividends—companies are keeping much of their powder dry." Companies, *Business Week* said, are putting their cash into money market funds and stock buybacks of their own shares.

imperialist epoch above all, the first giant shocks that begin shattering the confidence of sections of the rulers themselves are centered in financial institutions— in the banks and markets for currencies, debt, and equity—not in factories, mines, and mills. The devastation of production and employment follows afterwards, and with a lag.

D URING THE GREAT DEPRESSION the stock market crashed in October 1929 and continued downward—with numerous large and sharp upward rallies—until it had lost more than 85 percent of its value by mid-1932. (More money was almost certainly lost by individuals acting on an almost religious belief during the 1930 "suckers' rally"—greed still trumping fear—than had been lost in the 1929 crash itself.) The first banking panic and rash of bank failures hit in late 1930, with ten thousand institutions closed by 1932—40 percent of the 1929 total. Unemployment climbed more slowly, with government figures rising to 8.7 percent in 1930, 16 percent in 1931, to fully one-quarter of the labor force by 1933. By then a widespread, quasi-mass despair had begun to take hold, reflected in the assumption that the economy—and capitalist America itself—could never recover.

Sometime in the mid-1970s we entered a downward segment in the curve of capitalist development, and that's the period we're still living through today. Lenin and Trotsky provided us with the necessary political tools to analyze these long-range trends in the history of capitalism and their consequences for communist strategy and party building. Some of the most useful were their reports and writings around the time of the third and fourth congresses of the Communist International in

1921–22.[29] Trotsky summarized these conclusions in a brief 1923 letter that we published in *New International* magazine under the title, "The Curve of Capitalist Development."[30]

Unlike capitalist business cycles of recession and recovery with their chartable, and recurring, patterns, Trotsky said, there is no "rigidly lawful rhythm" to the long-term development of world capitalism. In the 1923 letter, Trotsky contrasted this conclusion to that of a Soviet academic named Nikolai Kondratiev. Pretending to formalize what could not be formalized—the materialist dialectic of modern history—Kondratiev bourgeoisified the work Lenin and Trotsky had presented at the third and fourth Comintern congresses. He argued that in addition to shorter trade and inventory cycles, there were also regular cycles of roughly fifty years that could be charted over the history of capitalism since at least the opening of the industrial revolution in the latter half of the 1700s.

Kondratiev's empirical chart itself was a roughly accurate sketch of trends that had occurred in capitalist development over the previous century and a half, Trotsky said. But if you looked carefully at its turning points— and at the duration and steepness of its various upward, downward, and flatter segments—it was clear that these corresponded to major events in politics and the class struggle, not solely "economic" factors as normally un-

---

29. These reports can be found in the two-volume collection of Leon Trotsky's writings entitled *The First Five Years of the Communist International* (New York: Pathfinder, 1972) and in Lenin, *Collected Works*, vols. 32 and 33. Major portions of two of those reports are reprinted in this issue on pp. 211–294.

30. Trotsky, "The Curve of Capitalist Development," in *New International* no. 10 (New York, 1994), pp. 209–10.

derstood. There was nothing "automatic" or "cyclical" about an *upturn* in this longer curve, as there is at a certain point in the destruction of value and drawing down of inventories during a capitalist recession.

"As regards the large segments of the capitalist curve of development," Trotsky wrote, "their character and duration are determined not by the internal interplay of capitalist forces but by those external conditions through whose channel capitalist development flows. The acquisition by capitalism of new countries and continents, the discovery of new natural resources, and, in the wake of these, such major facts of 'superstructural' order as wars and revolutions, determine the character and the replacement of ascending, stagnating, or declining epochs of capitalist development."[31]

KONDRATIEV DID EMPLOY a useful metaphor in describing this long-term curve, whose character and dynamics he did not understand. He, and his rediscoverers and vulgarizers today, speak of the slow beginnings of recovery as "spring"; sharply rising segments as "summer"; the stagnant opening of a downward segment as "autumn"; and the more sharply downward segment as "winter." We've been in autumn since the mid-1970s; now one of capitalism's infrequent long winters has begun. With no seeming limits on the Federal Reserve and Treasury Department's blowing up every balloon they can find, and now the accompanying acceleration of imperialism's drive toward war, it's going to be a long, hot winter. Even more important, slowly but surely and explosively, it will

31. Ibid., p. 210.

be one that breeds a scope and depth of resistance not previously seen by revolutionary-minded militants throughout today's world.

During world capitalism's quarter-century-long "autumn," the business cycle continued oscillating, including two long capitalist upswings: one for nearly eight years after 1982 in virtually all imperialist countries except New Zealand; the second stretching an entire decade from 1991 to 2001—the longest cyclical upturn in U.S. history, with relatively steady growth throughout that period in most other imperialist countries with the important exception of Japan. Both upturns, however, were limited to the majority of imperialist countries and a minority of the relatively economically developed semicolonial countries. Both were fueled by a massive inflation of debt and paper values, adding little to productive capacity in comparison to the post–World War II expansions in the United States and later in Europe and Japan. In seeking to boost their profit margins, more and more employers have been unable to count on anything other than pressing to drive down wages and benefits, lengthening hours, and intensifying labor. This stretch-out and speedup is the "secret" to the productivity growth that Greenspan exaggerates and brags about in order to reassure the capitalist class that something more is happening than a further expansion of the massive government debt and its private counterpart in corporate paper, mortgages, and credit cards. By the U.S. government's own figures, however, including those of the Federal Reserve, neither economic output nor labor productivity during these two most recent booms came anywhere close to increasing at the rates logged from the late 1940s through the early 1970s.

At the same time, it's worth repeating what a delegate

from Washington, D.C., Sam Manuel, reminded us of during the discussion. It's never enough just to look at government statistics, or even at how the average or median sector of the working class might be faring for a few years. We have to keep our eyes on various layers of the working class, and the differential social *consequences* of "booms" such as these. Over the past quarter century, not only did wage inequality *increase* within the working class, but above all the income gap widened explosively between all workers and better-off middle-class and professional layers, not to mention the wealthiest propertied families (whose astronomical annual incomes, let alone their accumulated wealth, are not even counted in government statistics). Real wages, medical and pension coverage, the value and duration of jobless benefits, the availability and real worth of workers' comp, the affordability of housing, food, and college education—all these declined, often sharply, for the majority of workers and working farmers. If, during the late 1990s, take-home pay rose for certain layers for several years, even that relief has reversed engines once again today.[32]

As long as the capitalist economy is heading up, as long as real interest rates are stable or coming down, as long as the dollar remains strong relative to the currencies of Washington's imperialist rivals, this debt-ridden house of cards keeps standing—and standing taller (in dollar terms!). But as all this begins to change, as it has since sometime late in 2000, the entire structure becomes increasingly unstable. Marx's observation that "interest-

---

32. In late 2003, according to the Wall Street investment bank Goldman Sachs, the annual growth rate of hourly earnings in the United States fell to "the slowest pace ever recorded." Through the middle of 2004, real weekly earnings actually fell.

bearing capital always [is] the mother of every insane form" of capital is once again being demonstrated in spades.[33]

Neither we nor anybody else has any way of predicting exactly how long it will take for these gigantic balloons—stock prices, consumer debt, real estate costs, the relative "value" of the dollar—to deflate. But since everyone can see it coming, it can seem natural to say: "Surely the capitalists will do something to stop it!"

But that's not how the law of value works. That's not how a market system driven by the competition of capitals—and, in the imperialist epoch, on the more and more violent competition of bigger and bigger capitals, and more and more leveraged speculation—operates. Finance capital since the mid-1970s has postponed the crisis and moderated the frequency and volatility of the swings of the trade cycle. But it did so only at the expense of inflating the debt balloons more and more, increasing their variety as they debase the purchasing power of the currency, thus making the eventual bursting of the bubble even more destructive to imperialist stability, self-confidence, and alliances.

Middle classes shaken first

Class-conscious workers recognize that history teaches that the most direct impact of a capitalist *financial* crisis at the opening of a depression period can be on the middle classes, more so initially than on the working class.

It took a long time in the United States to develop what Marx and Engels called a "hereditary proletariat," a class whose members in their great majority remain, from one

---

33. Marx, *Capital*, vol. 3, 596.

generation to the next, propertyless proletarians. No land, no tools, no capital. Those of us who survive only by selling for a wage our ability to use muscle and mind to labor for another—our laboring power. Marx and Engels followed this development closely over the second half of the nineteenth century and wrote about it extensively. Until chattel slavery was abolished, they pointed out, and until the free land to be had as U.S. capitalism expanded westward was exhausted, there could be no hereditary working class nationwide in the United States. And until this hereditary proletariat came into being, there were limited possibilities to organize either working-class resistance to the rising industrial bourgeoisie or a mass class-conscious party that could speak and act decisively in the interests of workers, other exploited producers, and brothers and sisters subjected to bonded labor of any kind.

For much of the nineteenth century, what became the United States remained a huge, largely undeveloped landmass, stretching from the Atlantic to the Pacific. On behalf of wealthy landowners, traders, canal developers, and later big railroad and mining interests, the U.S. government carried out brutal mass population transfers and genocidal assaults against Native Americans.

But working people migrated, too, in growing numbers. When living and working conditions in eastern cities became too onerous, workers could and did "go west, young man," to a new life. Workers escaped workshops and factories to become dirt farmers. Following the U.S. Civil War, hundreds of thousands took advantage of the Homestead Act to get a little plot of land. Even now the dream persists among many American workers of saving up a little money and starting their own business. Even more, they dream of doing something so their children can rise into the middle class. Reality for the vast majority of workers, however, long ago became a proletarian condition that is hereditary.

Workers accumulate no net wealth over the course of a lifetime. You often see reference to the "fact" that a majority of Americans are stockholders. But such assertions simply camouflage the harsh class reality that a growing number of companies are dumping employer-financed defined benefit pension funds—themselves anything but "guaranteed," as millions of workers with such "vested" pensions are now learning—and replacing them with defined contribution "retirement plans" entirely dependent on the fortunes of stocks, bonds, and mutual funds. Although workers have no control over such plans, the fact that we may "have" a so-called 401k supposedly makes us players in the stock market. In fact, these plans make us *victims* of the stock market. The truth is that individuals in only one-third of households in the United States hold even a single stock outside a retirement plan, and that figure has dropped, not increased, in the last half decade. Some 85 percent of the value of stocks is held by those in the top 10 percent income bracket in the United States. Ownership of government and corporate bonds is even more highly concentrated in the hands of the propertied ruling families and very well compensated professionals, who put much more of their wealth into bonds than into stocks. The ruling families of the final empire consider ownership of a piece of the returns on worldwide debt-slavery to be their parasitic birthright.

Whatever small savings, including equity in their homes, most workers manage to scrape together by middle age, are usually more than offset by mounting indebtedness and by the ruinous expenses of advancing age. So when stock and bond markets plunge, most workers experience little or no direct, immediate impact on their living standards.

Less so for millions in the middle classes—at first. So long as the capitalist crisis continues to unfold more sharply in banking and finance than in production and employment, it will not be the working class that first begins to radicalize in response to these developments. It will be the growing numbers whose families had escaped the proletarian condition over the last generation or so—they hoped forever—only to see their illusions of security and stability begin to shatter.

During the opening few years of the millennium, many in the middle classes feel they are being nibbled to death by ducks, with no relief in sight. As stock prices started going down in 2000, they were "advised" to just sit tight and wait for the market to rebound, as it had done in 1987 and again in 1991. Most of them did so—watching a substantial portion of their holdings melt away, until it dawned on them that nobody knows how long it may be before stock indexes regain past levels, or if they or their heirs will be solvent by then, or even alive! So, what do they do now? Sell at a big loss, or wait for a brighter day? The market goes down. Then it rallies for a few days, or a few weeks, or a few months, or a year. Hope! More than simple greed, hope, fueled by desperation and transforming fear, springs anew. The sheep buy as it goes up, and are mercilessly sheared when it drops still further. Each new high is lower than the previous high; each new low is lower than the previous low. But it's still a long way down—years and years down—to "the bottom."

Among growing middle-class layers, as well as layers of better-off workers who've bought into the myth that they've made it into the middle class, the fear accompanying the anticipation of further drops is palpable. In the absence of any independent working-class voice that can polarize and attract sections of the petty bourgeoisie, those most panicked by what's happening will become more open to the radicalism and violence of radical rightist appeals. Propaganda promoting conspiracy theories will win a wider hearing. Crank notions will proliferate, preaching the exact opposite of class realities explained by Lenin in *Imperialism.* So-called populist "theories" will spread, seeking to distinguish the "productive" working and entrepreneurial classes from the "usurers" and "speculators" (the simpler and quieter terms soon to be replaced by "the Jews"). And these nostrums will often come dressed up in anti-imperialist, antiwar, and even anticapitalist rhetoric. More and more often we'll run into echoes of such views among farmers fighting to hold off foreclosures, as well as among some coworkers, their friends and families—working people who have no explanation for what is beginning to happen to them and all around them. They just see it collapsing like something in a slow-motion movie.

COMMUNIST WORKERS need to be politically prepared to answer the radical demagogy of ultrarightist and incipient fascist forces. We will explain to the toilers: No! There need be no conspiracy. For at least a century, the monopolized banking, industrial, and commercial capitals have been fused in the United States and other imperialist countries under the ownership and control of a handful of parasitic propertied ruling families, the families of finance capital. The names of America's ruling families are no secret. They are the owners of these monopolies: the banks, brokerages, insurance businesses, industrial corporations, wholesale and retail distributors, real estate trusts, the largest newspapers, magazines, radio and TV stations, and entertainment companies. They are the bondholders. They dominate the market in stocks, commodities, and every form of debt under the sun. They own the professional sports franchises, and finance the opera houses, largest museums, libraries, foundations, and think tanks of all persuasions. They finance and control the Democratic and Republican parties. They run the capitalist government at the federal, state, and local levels. They are served and protected by the courts, cops, and armed forces. We can name the clubs they belong to, the boards they serve on, the universities they attend and endow, and the schools their children go to. The task is to lead the vanguard of the working class to overthrow the rulers and bring to power a government of the workers and farmers, thus establishing solidarity at the center of society.

A communist program

As the capitalist depression deepens, a downturn in production will lead to growing unemployment, sharply declining wages, more and more brutal conditions on the job, and ruinous bursts of inflation as the capitalists churn out money to try to get their engines running again.

Vanguard workers will start becoming more receptive to a communist program. As they go through more and more intense struggle, they will look for ways to fight effectively and win. They will be drawn to the ideas explained by fellow militants who are communists about how to strengthen the solidarity and combat capacity of the working class and our allies and, above all, our unions. We will win a broad hearing for the need to transform social security to encompass universal health care, universal lifetime education, universal workers' compensation, and universal guaranteed retirement pensions. These, we explain, are not benefits "given" to the working class by the employers and their government; the new wealth produced by the labor of working people must be used to guarantee the conditions of a productive life— throughout life—for the working classes. We will find more success in countering efforts by the employing class to pit generations of working people against each other, or to divide and conquer on the basis of job status, skin color, sex, language, resident status, or national origin.

Much of our program makes sense to many working people when we explain it, but it doesn't seem to flow out of a struggle they are engaged in that is central to their lives. It hasn't seemed urgent or practical. And it won't, so long as illusions persist about the long-term stability of the capitalist system, or, even more important, about the political incapacities and permanent acquiescence of toilers worldwide, of us. Many initially see our program as just a set of ideas, even a utopian projection, not a line of march through class combat toward the organized fight for the dictatorship of the proletariat. They haven't gone through enough political combat under a proletarian leadership to develop confidence in their own and their class's ability to organize and manage the economy and "guide the ship of state."

We've all heard the same kinds of things for many years from many fellow workers and family members: "I'll be taken care of by the VA." "I've got a railroad pension, and it's even 'vested' by a federal agency." "I've been here twenty years. This is my retirement job." Over the past decade or so, these old saws have been joined by: "I couldn't live off my social security and company pension, but now we've made the company set us up a 401k and I'm putting aside a little more each month." All these comfortable—and temporary—myths are encouraged by the class-collaborationist union officialdom, a petty-bourgeois layer with bourgeois values and aspirations, and ultimately thuggish self-centeredness.

Today, it's not just the workweek and the work year that are being extended for the working class (paid vacation time and holidays are dwindling for millions of workers)—it's the *work life*.[34] The number of years the average worker in the United States spends as part of the labor force, which had been declining until the mid-1980s, has begun rising again over the past fifteen years.[35] The official retirement age to receive full benefits under Social Security will be upped in stages starting in 2003, going from 65 to 67. And this is just for starters, as the rulers in coming years press their assaults against the social

---

34. The average work year in the United States was longer in 2003 than half a century earlier. The average workweek in mining and manufacturing is above forty hours, and both average hours and overtime have increased sharply since 1955. Production workers putting in overtime have an average workweek of more than fifty hours—nearly sixty hours for miners. According to U.S. government figures, the percentage of workers with no paid vacation time jumped from 3 percent in the early 1990s to 13 percent in 2003 in medium- or large-sized workplaces (more than 100 employees), and from 12 percent to 27 percent in small workplaces.

35. According to the U.S. Bureau of Labor Statistics, the percentage of workers between the ages of 65 and 74 still in the labor force rose from 16.7 percent in 1990 to 19.1 percent in 2000, and is projected to grow to 22.1 percent by 2010. The percentage of men in that age group in the labor force grew from 21.4 percent in 1990 to 24.4 percent in 2000, and is projected to reach 27.7 percent by 2010.

wage. This has nothing to do with bridging the generations and ensuring a lifetime of education and productive social labor for every human being, as we discuss in
The Working Class and the Transformation of Learning. It has
to do, instead, with a longer lifetime of *exploitation* to swell
the profits of a boss. And with it come increased job-re-
lated injuries and workplace deaths. This would be the
case even without speedup. And, as everyone here knows
and feels, there *is* speedup, *brutal* speedup.

We presented central aspects of our program last year
in a popular way in *Cuba and the Coming American Revolution.* We can use that book effectively as we talk socialism
with young people and workers. Some of our clearest and
more extensive presentations are to be found in the pio-
neering documents from the party's turn to industry in
the late 1970s and early 1980s, contained in *The Changing Face of U.S. Politics,* as well as throughout *Capitalism's
World Disorder.* In "Leading the Party into Industry," for
example—the February 1978 report that launched the
turn—we explained how far the employing class, with
help from the union officialdom, had gone during the
post–World War II "summer," a long upward segment in
the curve of capitalist development, toward gutting the
very foundations of working-class solidarity.

More and more "so-called general fringe benefits—
pensions, health-care plans, supplemental unemployment benefits—all [became] contingent on the continuing profits of the boss you work for," the 1978 report said.
"We see this growing in industries like coal, steel, and
auto. These benefits are not won for the class as a whole,
or even a section of the class." The report continued:

> These fringes are good in good times—for workers
> who have them—because they're a substantial

addition to everything else industrial workers can count on. But when the squeeze comes, this all begins to fall apart. Your pension funds are threatened. Your health-care plans are dismantled. The supplemental unemployment benefits run out. . . .

This is the payoff when the debt of business unionism comes due. This is the price paid for the class-collaborationist policy of refusing to fight for the real needs of the class—the social security of the class, national health care, for national unemployment insurance that's real and high enough, for a shorter workweek at no cut in pay, for protection against inflation, and for independent working-class political action. This is the price paid for a bureaucracy that says independent social and political struggles are secondary, and says the employers' promises in the contract are decisive.

This is the payoff for the refusal of the bureaucracy to lead the labor movement to fight for the broad social needs of the working class and to build a political instrument to fight for them.[36]

Learning to speak concretely

When we speak of the depression conditions we are entering, that very word itself—*depression*—can easily become an empty abstraction if we're not careful, if we are not concrete. Trotsky warned of such dangers in the 1923 letter on the curve of capitalist development we quoted from earlier. During a long period of capitalist stability, Trotsky said, it's natural to reduce various political phenomena and

---

36. Barnes, *The Changing Face of U.S. Politics: Working-Class Politics and the Trade Unions* (New York: Pathfinder, 2002), p. 147.

economic trends "to a familiar social type," since doing so makes it possible to communicate and act. "But when a serious change occurs in the situation," he said, "such general explanations reveal their complete inadequacy, and become wholly transformed into empty truisms."[37]

If you go back and take a look at the Teamsters series, for example, you'll notice that Farrell [Dobbs] always talks about discrete, concrete periods within the depression and their political consequences, not simply about the "Great Depression."

Farrell describes the four years following 1929, when production dropped by one-third and joblessness eventually rose to 25 percent. "At first the workers accepted these blows in a more or less passive manner," he says. "They had been stunned by the economic debacle and it took time to recover from the shock effect."[38]

Then Farrell points out what started happening in the working class and labor movement in 1933, when production began a four-year climb, regaining more than a third and unemployment fell almost by half to about 14 percent. During that year, he says, "strikes broke out here and there in industry," and continued through 1934—when labor struggles of a new kind erupted in Minneapolis, San Francisco, and Toledo—and continued through the sit-down strikes and other battles of 1935–37 in auto, steel, and other industries: strikes and organizing drives that built the industrial unions, the CIO. "These walkouts," Farrell writes, "resulted from the interaction of two basic factors: the workers' determination to regain ground they

---

37. Trotsky, "The Curve of Capitalist Development," in *New International* no. 10, p. 207.

38. Farrell Dobbs, *Teamster Politics* (New York: Pathfinder, 1975), p. 56.

had lost in the depression and their rising confidence—stimulated by partial economic recovery under the New Deal—that their objectives could be obtained."

Finally, Farrell recounts the impact of the renewed capitalist downturn in 1937–38, including a slowing of the CIO battles and the beginning of the Democratic administration's accelerating drive toward the second world imperialist war. "When the national economy again began to slump in mid-1937," Farrell writes, "the employers sought to use the changed situation as the basis for an offensive against organized labor. . . . They felt emboldened in that course because the downturn in production tended to blunt somewhat the combativity of the trade-union ranks."[39] During this period, the very real political momentum to advance toward an independent labor party—which had gained ground among vanguard workers engaged in battles to build the industrial union movement—was pushed back. Instead, the Stalinist misleadership of the Communist Party won an increasing hearing among workers for its popular front course of hitching the labor movement ever more tightly to the Democratic Party, and to the course of the big majority of the CIO and a substantial number of the AFL tops.

We'd never see revolutionary developments anywhere in the world if economic activity, political life, and the class struggle all moved in a straight line. If production just kept going down during a depression, the working class would finally be so devastated that effective class combat, let alone revolutionary struggle, would founder. It's the sharp ups and downs, the increasing violence of the fluctuations, the promises and dashed expectations that transform work-

---

39. Ibid., p. 141.

ers' consciousness. That is what allows the determination to fight to build up among many. And that's what leads many others to look to those fighters, until or unless it's shown they can't match words with deeds.

Our five Cuban comrades

This convention should not close without reminding ourselves that our movement has new obligations to work politically with five communists from Cuba who are serving time in federal prisons across the United States. These compañeros, of course, look to Cuba for the fundamental strategic lines of their work and their worldview, as they should. But they are now engaged, for however long, in an arena of the class struggle where the leadership of the Cuban Revolution has little direct or even indirect experience. That is inside the United States itself. Although their engagement on this front is involuntary, while they are so deployed they are determined to deepen their scientific understanding of class politics here and carry out a disciplined course of action. And we welcome them as a reinforcement brigade of the revolutionary workers movement in this country.

Incarcerated in the dehumanizing U.S. prison system, among their many experiences, these five comrades are running up against the ways in which rightist and fascist ideas gain a toehold among layers of toilers in the United States.[40] They're actually learning why it's not accu-

---

40. Ramón Labañino, in a letter to Mary-Alice Waters, had expressed his interest in getting a copy of the book *Behold a Pale Horse*, by William Cooper, which had been recommended to him by fellow inmates. The book is an ultrarightist presentation of conspiracy theories about everything from UFOs to the assassination of President John F. Kennedy. It includes the full text of

rate to say that because of this country's democratic traditions substantial numbers in the United States can never be won to a fascist movement. Those traditions are *bourgeois-democratic* traditions, we should always remember. And they will be shredded like scraps of paper if the working class in this country fails to forge a leadership capable of organizing workers, farmers, and our allies in a successful revolution when sharply accelerating class combat poses the question of which class shall rule.

Our Cuban compañeros are not only observing but also learning in practice the place and weight of workers who are Black in forging a social and political vanguard of the working class in the United States. They are learning why reading and absorbing the speeches of Malcolm X from his last year opens a road to revolutionary politics and organization. They're learning about the usefulness of the *Militant, Perspectiva Mundial,* and Pathfinder literature—including books and pamphlets on the Cuban Revolution—in the class struggle in this country.

A deeply political cadre

For the back cover of *Their Trotsky and Ours,* we prepared a brief description of what that book is about. "History shows that small revolutionary organizations will face not only the stern test of wars and repression," it begins, "but also the potentially shattering opportunities that emerge unexpectedly when strikes and social struggles explode."

That's where not only chance but the preparedness that can help turn the unexpected into good luck become decisive.

---

the notorious Russian tsarist anti-Semitic forgery, *The Protocols of the Elders of Zion.* Cooper was shot and killed by a sheriff's deputy in Arizona in November 2002.

"As that happens," the text continues, "communist parties not only recruit many new members." And they do recruit under those conditions, more rapidly and in larger numbers than almost anybody in this room can imagine from our own experience in the revolutionary workers movement. In addition to direct individual recruitment, we say, communist parties under those conditions also converge *politically* with other fighting forces. They "politically fuse with other workers organizations moving in the same direction and grow into mass proletarian parties contesting to lead workers and farmers to power."

Then we come to the part that's of the greatest practical importance for communist workers right now.

This assumes, first of all, "that well beforehand" the cadres of such parties "have absorbed and grown comfortable with a world communist program." That an international communist perspective has become a political habit; has been internalized; has become a matter of seeming reflex.

Second, it assumes that the revolutionary political orientation of such parties is built on the daily activity of cadres who "are proletarian in life and work." Both are equally important—in *life*, and in *work*. That's what our turn to industry and the industrial trade unions a quarter century ago, and our ongoing efforts to strengthen that course ever since, is about. That's what makes revolutionary centralism possible. It is not an organizational caricature of proletarian habits. It's about being where we need to be, among a vanguard of our class, and being there in a structured, disciplined manner.

Third, the nuclei of communist parties need to be made up of those who "derive deep satisfaction from doing politics." That might seem to be a stretch. But it's not. Yes, revolutionists can and will have a bad month, a bad three-month period, even a bad year. That's part of the human condition under capitalism. Anyone who claims they haven't ever had a bad patch is scary; they must never blink. None of us would want an angel on our flank. But if over the medium and long haul, a party cadre does not derive deep satisfaction from engaging in communist political work, then they can't live up to the founding rules of the Communist League drafted by Marx and Engels in 1847. One of the "conditions of membership" stated in those rules was "revolutionary energy and zeal in propaganda."[41] Those were the words Marx and Engels chose for a document placed for vote before delegates to the same congress that assigned them to draft the Communist Manifesto. To be a member meant to conduct propaganda work with *"revolutionary energy and zeal."*

And fourth, we say that well before a rise in revolutionary struggles, a communist party needs to have forged a "leadership with an acute sense of what to do next." What to do now. *Today.* Not the day after tomorrow. And always *concrete.*

That's what we expect of leadership in the communist movement.

I thought about that summary of what kind of movement we are building as we were preparing the meeting to celebrate the political life and work of Charlie Scheer. I've spoken at more than one memorial meeting over the past year or so, and many others before that, to honor the lives and contributions of comrades who have died. What struck me most as I was thinking about Charlie, and discussing his life with others, was that what all these com-

---

41. "Rules of the Communist League," in Marx and Engels, *Collected Works*, vol. 6, p. 633.

rades—each of them gloriously different from the others in many ways—had in common was the fact that they were deeply *political* people. Not just people who were interested in politics. But people who organized their lives within the proletarian movement, and for whom politics provided the practical axis of their lives—the foundation of the enjoyment and satisfaction they derived from living. It was the wellspring of their accomplishments.

Their Trotsky and Ours is about the lifetime work of such cadres.

Stay the course

Over the past several days of this convention, we have come to a common understanding of the political importance of the example communists in the United States can and do set for fellow working people and revolutionists. The class politics we have conquered, and the steps we are taking through our branches, organizing committees, and union fractions, make up the foundation on which we pledge to the world never to show fear in face of a single deed by American imperialism. The might of the U.S. rulers is matched only by their pretense. The uncontrolled, the unintended consequences of their economic and military power undo the very conditions they seek to use to stabilize, to buttress their crises-ridden system of exploitation and oppression.

The Socialist Workers Party's response to the events of September 11 and to the reaction of the U.S. rulers was not bravado. Nor is our determination to stand firm in face of U.S. imperialism's drive toward war and in face of the hard rain that's begun to fall across the length and breadth of the world market system. What worker-bolsheviks do in the United States gives added confidence to every worker, farmer, or young person anywhere in the world who refuses to bend their knee. It gives added confidence to militants who discover from an issue of the *Militant* or *Perspectiva Mundial*, from a Pathfinder book or pamphlet—or from watching vanguard workers in a plant, in a neighborhood, in the course of a common struggle—that there are others like them doing the same thing.

We have no pumped-up view of ourselves, or of what the working people of the United States can and will accomplish. It simply happens to be the fact that while the world's final empire will never fall of its own dead weight, it *will* be brought down by a revolutionary struggle of workers and farmers in this country, fighting shoulder to shoulder with internationalist toilers the world over.

The deep satisfaction we derive from doing politics stems from the knowledge born of history and the concrete experiences of the working classes that such a goal is palpable and real. And when the deed is done, the revolutionary energy and zeal that will spring from toilers worldwide is something we can barely begin to imagine.

Here we have taken one more step along that road.

Join the
PATHFINDER READERS CLUB

BUILD A MARXIST LIBRARY!

15% OFF ALL PATHFINDER BOOKS AND PAMPHLETS

25% DISCOUNT ON MONTHLY SPECIALS

Get your annual card for only *US$10*. Available at pathfinderpress.com or at any of more than 30 Pathfinder book centers around the world.

The Curve of Capitalist Development

Capitalism's World Disorder
Working-Class Politics at the Millennium

Jack Barnes

The opening of the 21st century, says the author, is marked by a sea change in working-class politics, "defined by the actions of a vanguard resisting indignity and isolation, whose ranks increase with every single worker or farmer who reaches out to others with the hand of solidarity and offers to fight together." $24

Capital

Karl Marx

Marx explains the workings of the capitalist system and how it produces the insoluble contradictions that breed class struggle. He demonstrates the inevitability of the fight for the revolutionary transformation of society into one ruled for the first time by the producing majority: the working class.
Volume 1, $14.95
Volume 2, $13.95
Volume 3, $14.95

Imperialism, the Highest Stage of Capitalism

V.I. Lenin

Imperialism increases not only the weight of debt bondage and parasitism in capitalist social relations, writes Lenin, but above all makes the competition of rival capitals—domestic and foreign—more violent and explosive. Amid capitalism's growing world disorder, this 1916 booklet remains a foundation stone of the communist movement's program and activity. $10

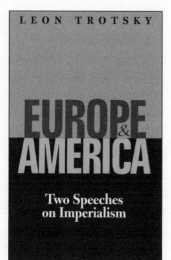

Europe and America
Two Speeches on Imperialism
Leon Trotsky

In two speeches from the mid-1920s, Russian Bolshevik leader Leon Trotsky explains why the emergence of the United States as imperialism's dominant economic and financial power became the decisive factor in international politics following World War I. He describes the sharpening conflicts between Washington and its European rivals and highlights the revolutionary prospects for the workers of the world. $6

The Curve of Capitalist Development
Leon Trotsky

Turning points in the long-term trends of capitalist development, wrote Trotsky in this 1923 article, are a product of factors outside the realm of "economics" as normally understood. Periods of advance, stagnation, and decline, the Bolshevik leader explained, are shaped by major developments in politics and the class struggle such as wars, uprisings, and revolutions.
In *New International* no. 10. $14

Imperialism's March toward Fascism and War
Jack Barnes

"There will be new Hitlers, new Mussolinis. That is inevitable. What is not inevitable is that they will triumph. The working-class vanguard will organize our class to fight back against the devastating toll we are made to pay for the capitalist crisis. The future of humanity will be decided in the contest between these contending class forces." In *New International* no. 10. $14

Basic works of Marxism

The Communist Manifesto

KARL MARX AND FREDERICK ENGELS

Founding document of the modern working-class movement, published in 1848. Explains why communism is derived not from preconceived principles but from *facts* and from proletarian movements springing from the actual class struggle. $4

The Origin of the Family, Private Property, and the State

FREDERICK ENGELS,
INTRODUCTION BY EVELYN REED

How the emergence of class-divided society gave rise to repressive state bodies and family structures that protect the property of the ruling layers and enable them to pass along wealth and privilege. Engels discusses the consequences for working people of these class institutions — from their original forms to their modern versions. $18

Socialism: Utopian and Scientific

FREDERICK ENGELS

Modern socialism is not a doctrine, Engels explains, but a working-class movement growing out of the establishment of large-scale capitalist industry and its social consequences. $4

Questions of National Policy and Proletarian Internationalism

V.I. LENIN

Why the fight of nations oppressed by imperialism for self-determination is decisive in the worldwide proletarian struggle to take and hold power. Why workers and farmers in imperialist countries have a deep class interest in championing this right. $16

WWW.PATHFINDERPRESS.COM

The Working Class & the Transformation of Learning

The Fraud of Education Reform under Capitalism

JACK BARNES

"Until society is reorganized so that education is a human activity from the time we are very young until the time we die, there will be no education worthy of working, creating humanity." $3

Pathfinder Was Born with the October Revolution

MARY-ALICE WATERS

From the writings of Marx, Engels, Lenin, and Trotsky, to the speeches of Malcolm X, Fidel Castro, and Che Guevara, to the words of James P. Cannon, Farrell Dobbs, and leaders of the communist movement in the U.S. today, Pathfinder books aim to "advance the understanding, confidence, and combativity of working people." $3

WWW.PATHFINDERPRESS.COM

New International articles *in Farsi*

Opening Guns of World War III: Washington's Assault on Iraq
by Jack Barnes. $10

Also

Imperialism's March toward Fascism and War
by Jack Barnes. $10

U.S. Imperialism Has Lost the Cold War
by Jack Barnes. $14

Published by Talaye Porsoo, Tehran.
These and more available from Pathfinder at www.pathfinderpress.com.

CRISIS, BOOM, AND REVOLUTION

1921 REPORTS BY V.I. LENIN AND LEON TROTSKY

This appendix to "Capitalism's Long Hot Winter Has Begun" includes reports by Bolshevik leaders V.I. Lenin and Leon Trotsky debated and approved by the Third Congress of the Communist International, held in Moscow in 1921. In "In This Issue" at the opening of the magazine, Jack Barnes explains the reasons the editors of *New International* considered it useful to include these as an appendix.

Major excerpts from Trotsky's 1921 report are printed here. The full text was translated into English by John G. Wright and first published at the close of World War II in Pathfinder's *The First Five Years of the Communist International*; it has been checked against the original Russian and corrected. The English translation of Lenin's report, available in volume 32 of his *Collected Works*, was also checked against the Russian and corrected.

The publication of these two 1921 reports fills out a package of related materials now available from Pathfinder Press, especially Trotsky's 1923 letter, "The Curve of Capitalist Development," available in issue 10 of *New International*. In addition, two talks by Trotsky from 1924 and 1926 are published together in the pamphlet *Europe and America: Two Speeches on Imperialism*.

THE WORLD ECONOMIC CRISIS

AND THE TASKS OF COMMUNISTS

by Leon Trotsky

June 23, 1921

1917–1921

WITH THE IMPERIALIST WAR we entered the epoch of revolution, that is, the epoch when the very mainstays of capitalist equilibrium are shaking and collapsing. Capitalist equilibrium is an extremely complex phenomenon. Capitalism produces this equilibrium, disrupts it, restores it anew in order to disrupt it anew, concurrently extending the limits of its domination. In the economic sphere these constant disruptions and restorations of the equilibrium take the shape of crises and booms. In the sphere of interclass relations the disruption of equilibrium assumes the form of strikes, lockouts, revolutionary struggle. In the sphere of interstate relations the disruption of equilibrium means war or—in a weaker form—tariff war, economic war, or blockade. Capitalism thus possesses a dynamic equilibrium, one that is always in the process of either disruption or restoration. But at the same time this equilibrium has great resilience, the best proof of which is the fact that the capitalist world has not toppled to this day.

The last imperialist war was an event that we rightfully appraised as a colossal blow, unequaled in history, to the equilibrium of the capitalist world. Out of the war has actually risen the epoch of the greatest mass movements and revolutionary battles. Russia, the weakest link in the capitalist chain, was the first to lose its equilibrium and the first to enter the road of revolution—in 1917, in the month of February.

OUR FEBRUARY REVOLUTION had great repercussions among the working masses of England. In England 1917 was the year of the greatest strike struggles, through which the English proletariat succeeded in checking the war-produced process of declining living conditions among the toiling masses.[1] In October 1917 the working class of Russia took power. Strike struggles extended throughout the entire capitalist world, beginning with the neutral countries. In the autumn of 1918 Japan passed through a zone of tumultuous "rice" riots, which according to some figures involved upwards of 25 percent of the population and which were met with cruel repressions on the part of the Mikado's government.[2] In January 1918, mass strikes took place in Germany. Toward the end

1. In May 1917 metal workers and other workers in Britain launched a wave of strikes protesting rising food prices and other worsening economic and social conditions exacerbated by the war. Failing to defeat the strikes through arrests, the employers and their government made some concessions to strikers' demands. Some 872,000 workers joined strikes in Britain in 1917, and well over 1,100,000 the following year.

2. In the summer of 1918, rebellions against the skyrocketing price of rice spread across Japan. The regime of the Mikado, the emperor, responded with brutal repression, killing more than one hundred working people and jailing thousands. The emperor's cabinet fell in the wake of the rebellion.

of 1918, following the collapse of German militarism, revolutions took place in Germany and Austria-Hungary.[3] The revolutionary movement keeps expanding.

The most critical year for capitalism—at any rate for European capitalism—arrives: the year 1919. In March 1919 a Soviet Republic is formed in Hungary.[4] In January and March 1919 fierce battles between the revolutionary workers and the bourgeois republic break out in Germany. In France there is tension in the atmosphere during the period of demobilization, but the illusions of victory and the hopes for its golden fruits still remain too

---

3. A revolt by sailors in October 1918 initiated a wave of revolutionary action across Germany that toppled the Hohenzollern monarchy and led to the establishment of workers and soldiers councils. The Social Democratic Party, which had supported the war effort of the German imperialist regime, stepped in to form a government together with the centrist Independent Social Democratic Party; the regime was headed by Friedrich Ebert. While formally recognizing the workers and soldiers councils as the basis of governmental power, the Social Democrats in fact ruled through the state apparatus inherited from the monarchy, aiming to stabilize bourgeois rule. In January 1919 the new government unleashed rightist-led military units, the "Freikorps," against the rising workers movement in a reign of terror during which hundreds were slaughtered, including revolutionary leaders Rosa Luxemburg and Karl Liebknecht. The Social Democrats then openly joined with bourgeois parties to form a coalition regime.

Workers' uprisings across the Austro-Hungarian empire in 1918 led to the collapse of the monarchy in November of that year, the establishment of independent governments in Czechoslovakia, Hungary, and the Balkans, and the formation of a Social Democratic–dominated regime in Austria itself.

4. The inexperienced Communist Party leadership of the revolutionary government in newly independent Hungary made the fatal decision to fuse as a single party with the reformist and centrist Social Democratic organizations there. The government also

strong; the struggle does not even begin to approximate here the proportions it assumes in the conquered countries. In the United States toward the end of 1919 the strikes acquire a mighty sweep, embracing the railway workers, the miners, the steel workers, etc. [President Woodrow] Wilson's government unleashes wild repressions against the working class.[5]

In the spring of 1920 in Germany an attempt to install counterrevolution through the Kapp putsch mobilizes

---

tried to move rapidly toward the establishment of collectivized state farms, ignoring the aspiration of poor and middle peasants for a plot of land to till. Its ultraleft leadership refused to carry out a sweeping agrarian reform such as the Bolsheviks had done in Russia. Faced with rebellion in the countryside and open sabotage by the new party's center and right wing, the revolutionary government was overturned after 133 days. Thousands across Hungary, including many Jews, were killed in the subsequent counterrevolutionary White Terror.

5. A wave of strikes in 1919 by textile workers, copper miners, shipyard workers, and others culminated in a walkout by 365,000 steelworkers in ten states in late September and by half a million coal miners in early November. The steel bosses, backed by federal and state governments, organized to break the strikes, killing eighteen workers and wounding many others. The coal miners returned to work in mid-November, having gained some of their wage demands but failing to win reduced hours. Misled by officials in several craft unions in steel, and double-crossed by officers of the railroad crafts, the steelworkers' fight went down to defeat in January 1920.

During 1919 and 1920 in the United States, the U.S. government carried out a wave of raids, arresting thousands of workers on charges of carrying out communist activity and deporting hundreds of them. These assaults became known as the Palmer Raids, since they were organized by U.S. Attorney General A. Mitchell Palmer. For several years following these raids, communist organizations in the United States were forced into clandestinity.

and drives the working class to struggle. The intense but formless movement of the German workers is again mercilessly crushed by Ebert's republic, which they had saved.[6] In France the political situation reaches the pitch of intensity in May of last year during the proclamation of the general strike, which, incidentally, proved to be far from general and which was poorly prepared and betrayed by the opportunist leaders who did not want the strike but didn't dare admit it. . . .[7]

In August the Red Army's advance on Warsaw—likewise a part of the international revolutionary struggle—meets with failure.[8] In September the Italian workers,

---

6. In March 1920 workers in Germany organized a massive general strike to block a coup led by the right-wing politician Wolfgang Kapp. In the aftermath of the failed coup, the Social Democratic–led regime saved by the action of the workers stepped up its assaults on the working class and revolutionary labor movement.

7. In May 1920 the class-collaborationist officials of the General Confederation of Labor (CGT) in France, fearing rising militancy in the ranks, issued a half-hearted call for a general strike and rolling solidarity walkouts to support striking railroad workers demanding the reinstatement of fired unionists. In face of arrests of union leaders and government threats to take legal action against the CGT, the officials called off the strike in late May, resulting in a demoralizing blow to the labor movement. Union membership fell from 2.5 million at the opening of 1920 to less than one million by the spring of 1921.

8. In April 1920 the capitalist regime in Poland, after rejecting a peace offer from the Soviet government that included significant territorial concessions by the workers and peasants regime, launched an invasion of Soviet Russia. The attack was carried out with direct participation by French officers and military support from British and U.S. finance capital. As the Red Army responded to this assault, the Soviet government issued a call for Polish workers and peasants to join in a common struggle against that

taking seriously the verbalistic-revolutionary agitation of the Socialist Party, seize plants and factories, but are shamefully betrayed by the party, suffer defeat all along the line, and are then subjected to a ruthless counterof-

---

country's landlords, capitalists, and their imperialist backers. By July, as Soviet troops crossed into Poland and began marching on Warsaw, Polish communists established a revolutionary committee behind Red Army lines.

The Red Army's advance alarmed the bourgeois rulers across Europe. It gave impetus to stirrings of resistance among peasants and workers in Germany suffering the consequences of the debt bondage imposed as "reparations" under the terms of the Treaty of Versailles by the imperialist victors of World War I. When the British rulers threatened military action against Soviet Russia, workers in the United Kingdom formed nationwide Councils of Action that stayed London's hand. By late summer, however, Red Army troops had been turned back by the Polish army.

Assessing the situation in October 1920, Lenin said: "We lacked the strength to take Warsaw and finish off the Polish landowners, white guards and capitalists, but our army showed the whole world that the Treaty of Versailles is not the force it is made out to be, that hundreds of millions of people are condemned to repay loans for many years to come . . . in order that the French, British and other imperialists may be enriched. [When London sent a communiqué to the Soviet government threatening to send its fleet to attack Petrograd], on the day following the dispatch of this telegram, mass meetings were held throughout Britain, and Councils of Action sprang up. The workers united. . . . That is why the Polish war has ended in a manner no imperialist state had bargained for." ("Speech Delivered at a Conference of Chairmen of *Uyezd* [County], *Volost* [Rural District] and Village Executive Committees of Moscow *Gubernia* [Province]," in Lenin, *Collected Works*, vol. 31, pp. 318–33.)

In March 1921 the Soviet and Polish governments signed a peace agreement—on terms more favorable to the workers and peasants republic than those it had offered Warsaw the previous year.

fensive by the unified reaction.[9] In December a revolutionary mass strike unfolds in Czechoslovakia. Finally, at the beginning of the current year, revolutionary battles with their massive toll of victims erupt in Central Germany; England witnesses the resumption of the stubborn miners' strike,[10] which hasn't ended to this very day; and a general strike breaks out in Norway.

W<small>HEN IN THE INITIAL</small> postwar period we observed the unfolding revolutionary movement, it might have

---

9. In September 1920 some six hundred thousand workers across Italy occupied factories in response to an attempted employer lockout. The wave of occupations coincided with a rise of struggles by peasants and farm workers that year. Instead of using this pre-revolutionary situation to organize the workers and peasants to take power, however, the class-collaborationist leadership of the Socialist Party and SP-led trade unions in Italy demobilized the struggle, opening the door to savage reprisals by the employers and the rising fascist gangs led by Benito Mussolini. In the wake of this defeat, Mussolini's movement seized power in 1922 and crushed the working-class movement in Italy over the next few years.

10. In 1920 union coal miners in Britain organized a brief strike that won higher wages. In March 1921 the government announced that it was returning the mines, which had been state-run since World War I, to their capitalist owners. The owners proposed a contract that not only slashed wages but dumped industry-wide pay levels and tied miners' wages to the profits of the employer they worked for. When miners rejected this proposal, the coal operators began a lockout on April 1. The miners were dealt a heavy blow when the officialdoms of the railway workers and transport workers unions called off a solidarity strike scheduled for April 15 and turned their backs on the struggle. The miners were forced back to work in July 1921 on terms that chopped their wages nearly in half.

seemed to many of us—and with ample historical justification—that this ever-growing and ever-strengthening
movement must terminate directly in the conquest of
power by the working class. But now almost three years
have already elapsed since the war. Throughout the
world, with the single exception of Russia, power continues to remain in the hands of the bourgeoisie. In the
interim the capitalist world did not, of course, remain
standing still. It has been undergoing change. Europe
and the entire world have lived through a period of postwar demobilization, an extremely acute and dangerous
period for the bourgeoisie—the demobilization of people
and the demobilization of things, that is, industry—the
period of wild postwar commercial boom followed by a
crisis that has yet to end.

And now we are confronted in its full scope by these
questions: Does development actually proceed even now
in the direction of revolution? Or is it necessary to recognize that capitalism has succeeded in coping with the
difficulties arising from the war? And if it has not already
restored capitalist equilibrium upon new postwar foundations, is it now either restoring or close to restoring that
equilibrium?

The bourgeoisie gains confidence

If, before analyzing the economic roots of this question,
we approach it purely politically, we shall have to set
down a whole number of symptoms, facts and statements
that attest to this, that the bourgeoisie has become stronger and more stable as the ruling class, or in any case
feels that way. In 1919 the European bourgeoisie was in
a state of extreme confusion. Those were the days of
panic, the days of a truly insane fear of Bolshevism,
which then loomed as an extremely misty and therefore

all the more terrifying apparition and which used to be portrayed on Parisian posters as a killer clenching a knife in his teeth, and so on. As a matter of fact, incarnated in this specter of Bolshevism with a knife was the European bourgeoisie's fear of retribution for its war crimes. The bourgeoisie at any rate was aware how little the results of the war corresponded with the promises it had made. It knew the exact cost in lives and wealth. It feared an accounting.

The year 1919 was, without doubt, the most critical year for the bourgeoisie. In 1920 and 1921 we observe a gradual influx of self-confidence among the bourgeoisie and along with this an undeniable consolidation of its state apparatus, which immediately following the war was actually on the verge of disintegration in various countries, for example, Italy. The bourgeoisie's recovery of its self-confidence took on especially graphic forms in Italy after the cowardly treachery of the Socialist Party in September. The bourgeoisie had imagined itself to be confronted with horrible bandits and assassins; it found instead—cowards. . . .

The objective situation of the Social-Democratic parties in relation to the state and to the bourgeois parties has likewise correspondingly altered. Social Democrats are everywhere being pushed out of the government. If they are again drawn into the government, it is only temporarily and owing to outside pressure, as was the case in Germany. The Independent [Social Democratic] Party [of Germany] has made a complete turn to the right, likewise under the direct or indirect influence of the new situation, whose meaning it tends greatly to exaggerate. The Independents of all countries and the Social Democrats of all countries, who seemed to differ so much a year or a year and a half ago, have been brought closer together today, with the cooperation of Amsterdam.[11]

Thus the enhancement of the bourgeoisie's self-confidence as a class is absolutely undeniable; and equally undeniable is the actual consolidation of the police-state apparatus after the war. But in and of itself this fact—important though it is—does not by far settle the question; and, in any case, our enemies are over-hasty in trying to draw from it the conclusion that our program is bankrupt. We had, of course, hoped that the bourgeoisie would be overthrown in 1919. But we were not sure of it, nor did we build and rest our program of action upon this date. When Herr Otto Bauer[12] and other theoreticians of the Second and Two-and-a-Half Internationals say that our predictions have been proved bankrupt, one might think that involved here were predictions concerning some astronomical event. It is as if we were mistaken in our mathematical calculations that a solar eclipse would occur on such and such a day, and were consequently proved to be poor astronomers.

But that is not at all how the matter stands in reality. We had not predicted a solar eclipse, that is, an event beyond our will and entirely independent of our actions. Involved is a historical event that can and will occur with

---

11. The Social Democratic–led International Federation of Trade Unions was known as the Amsterdam International because of where it was headquartered.

12. Otto Bauer, the author of a number of anti-Marxist works on the national question, was a leader of the Austrian Social Democratic Party. At the end of World War I, with the fall of the Hapsburg monarchy, Bauer was appointed foreign minister of Austria's capitalist government, resigning in 1919. In 1921 he helped form the centrist "Two-and-a-Half" International based in Vienna, which reunited with the Second International two years later in 1923.

our participation. When we spoke of the revolution resulting from the world war, it meant that we were and are
striving to utilize the consequences of the world war in
order to speed the revolution in every way possible. That
the revolution hasn't taken place to this very day throughout the world, or at least in Europe, does not at all signify "the bankruptcy of the Communist International,"
for the program of the Comintern is not based on astronomical data. Every Communist who has to any extent
thought out his ideas understands this. But inasmuch as
the revolution has not come hot on the tracks of war, it is
absolutely self-evident that the bourgeoisie has utilized
the breathing space afforded it, if not to surmount and
eliminate the most frightful and terrible consequences
of the war, then at least to camouflage them, to patch
them up.

Has it succeeded in accomplishing this? In part, yes. To
what extent? It is here that we touch the essence of the
question, which involves the restoration of capitalist equilibrium.

Has world equilibrium been restored?

What is the meaning of capitalist equilibrium, about
which international Menshevism[13] speaks nowadays with

---

13. At the 1903 congress of the Russian Social Democratic Labor
Party, the movement divided into two wings: the Bolsheviks ("majority" in the Russian language), led by V.I. Lenin, and the Mensheviks ("minority" in Russian). During World War I the Mensheviks rejected the proletarian internationalist course charted by
Lenin, and they opposed the Bolshevik-led conquest of power by
the workers and peasants in October 1917. Following the October Revolution, the Menshevik leadership in its majority joined
with Russia's landlords and capitalists, and with imperialist governments across Europe and in the United States, in the civil war

such complete assurance? For their part, the Social Democrats provide no analysis of this concept of equilibrium. They neither separate out its component parts nor give any clear exposition. The equilibrium of capitalism contains a great many factors, events, and facts—some basic, others secondary, and still others tertiary. Capitalism is a world phenomenon. Capitalism has succeeded in embracing the entire terrestrial globe. This manifested itself most acutely during the war and during the blockade, as one country, bereft of a market, was producing surpluses, while another, in need of commodities, lacked access to them. And today this interdependence of the dismembered world market manifests itself here and everywhere.

Capitalism, at the stage attained before the war, is based on a world division of labor and a world exchange of products. America has to produce a certain quantity of grain for Europe. France has to produce a certain quantity of luxury goods for America. Germany has to produce a certain quantity of cheap consumer goods for France. This division of labor is, in its turn, not something constant, something given once and for all. It takes shape historically; it is constantly disrupted by crises and competition—let alone tariff wars. And it is restored over and over again, only to be again and again disrupted. But the world economy on the whole rests on a lesser or greater division among the respective countries of the production of corresponding necessities. It is this world division of labor that has now been severed at its roots by the war. Has it been

---

and other counterrevolutionary efforts to overturn the Soviet republic. In doing so, they were joined by the leadership of the Second International, which Bolsheviks came to refer to as "international Menshevism."

restored or not? This is one aspect of the question.

In each country agriculture supplies industry with prime necessities for the workers and with goods for productive use (raw materials), whereas industry supplies the village with household goods, consumer goods, and the means of agricultural production. Here, too, certain reciprocal relations become established. Finally, within industry itself there is the production of the means of production and the production of the means of consumption, and between these two main branches of industry a certain interrelationship is established, which undergoes constant disruption in order to be regenerated over and over again on new foundations. The war has drastically disrupted all these interrelations and proportions, if only by virtue of this single fact: that during the war Europe's industry, and to a large measure also that of America and Japan, produced not consumer goods and the means of production so much as the means of destruction. To the extent that consumer goods continued to be produced, they were utilized not so much by the workers who produce as by those who destroy—the soldiers of imperialist armies. Now, has this disrupted harmonious relationship between city and country, between the various branches of industry within each country—has this been restored or not?

Next follows the class equilibrium that rests upon the economic equilibrium. In the prewar period a state of so-called armed truce prevailed in international relations. But not alone there, for between the bourgeoisie and the proletariat we also had by and large a reign of armed truce, maintained by a system of collective wage agreements concluded between the centralized unions and the ever more centralized industrial capital. This equilibrium has likewise been wholly disrupted by the war—and it was this that led to the colossal strike movement throughout the world. The relative class equilibrium of bourgeois society without which production is unthinkable—has this been restored or not? And if it has, upon what foundation?

Class equilibrium is closely bound up with political equilibrium. During the war and even prior to the war the bourgeoisie kept its mechanism in balance—although this escaped our notice at the time—through the medium of the Social Democrats, the social-patriots, who were the bourgeoisie's most important agency and who kept the working class within the bounds of bourgeois equilibrium. Only thanks to this was the bourgeoisie enabled to venture into the war. Has it restored anew the equilibrium of its political system today? And to what extent have the Social Democrats preserved or squandered their influence over the masses, and how much longer can they play their part as guardians of the bourgeoisie?

Next in order is the question of the international equilibrium, that is, the world coexistence of capitalist states separate and apart from which the restoration of the capitalist economy is, of course, impossible. Has equilibrium in this sphere been reached or not? . . .

Boom and crisis

Bourgeois and reformist economists who have an ideological interest in embellishing the plight of capitalism say: in and of itself the current crisis proves nothing whatever; on the contrary, it is a normal phenomenon. Following the war we witnessed an industrial boom, and now—a crisis; it follows that capitalism is alive and thriving.

As a matter of fact, capitalism does live by crises and

booms, just as a human being lives by inhaling and exhaling. First there is a boom in industry, then a stoppage, next a crisis, followed by a stoppage in the crisis, then an improvement, another boom, another stoppage, and so on.

Crisis and boom blend with all the transitional phases to constitute a cycle or one of the great circles of industrial development. Each cycle lasts from eight to nine or ten to eleven years. By force of its internal contradictions capitalism thus develops not along a straight line but in a zigzag manner, through ups and downs. This is what provides the ground for the following claim of the apologists of capitalism, namely: since we observe after the war a succession of boom and crisis, it follows that all things are working together for the best in this best of all capitalist worlds.

It is otherwise in reality. The fact that capitalism continues to oscillate cyclically after the war merely signifies that capitalism is not yet dead, that we are not dealing with a corpse. So long as capitalism is not overthrown by the proletarian revolution, it will continue to live in cycles, swinging up and down. Crises and booms were inherent in capitalism at its very birth; they will accompany it to its grave. But to determine capitalism's age and its general condition—to establish whether it is still developing or whether it has matured or whether it is in decline— one must diagnose the character of the cycles. In much the same manner the state of the human organism can be diagnosed by whether the breathing is regular or spasmodic, deep or superficial, and so on.

The gist of the matter, comrades, may be depicted as follows: Let us take the development of capitalism—the growth of coal production, textiles, pig iron, steel, foreign trade, etc.—and draw a curve delineating this development. If in the deflections of this curve we have expressed

the true course of economic development, we shall find
that this curve does not *swing upwards* in an unbroken arc
but in zigzags, looping up and down—up and down in cor-
respondence with the respective booms and crises. Thus
the curve of economic development is a composite of two
movements: a primary movement that expresses the general upward rise of capitalism, and a secondary movement
that consists of the constant periodic oscillations corresponding to the various industrial cycles.

In January of this year the London *Times* published a
table covering a period of 138 years—from the war of the
thirteen American colonies for independence to our own
day. In this interval there have been sixteen cycles, that
is, sixteen crises and sixteen phases of prosperity. . . . If
we analyze the curve of development more closely, we
shall find that it falls into five segments, five different and
distinct periods. From 1781 to 1851 the development is
very slow; there is scarcely any movement observable.
We find that in the course of seventy years foreign trade
rises only from £2 to £5 per capita. After the revolution
of 1848, which acted to extend the framework of the
European market, there comes a breaking point. From
1851 to 1873 the curve of development rises steeply. In
twenty-two years foreign trade climbs from £5 to £21 per
capita, while the quantity of iron rises in the same period
from 4.5kg to 13kg per capita. Then from 1873 on there
follows an epoch of depression. From 1873 till approximately 1894 we notice stagnation in English trade (even
if we take into account the interest on capital invested in
foreign enterprises); there is a per capita drop from £21
to £17.4—in the course of twenty-two years. Then comes
another boom, lasting till the year 1913—foreign trade
rises from £17 to £30 per capita. Then, finally, with the
year 1914, the fifth period begins—the period of the de-

struction of the capitalist economy.

How are the cyclical fluctuations blended with the primary movement of the curve of capitalist development? Very simply. In periods of rapid capitalist development the crises are brief and superficial in character, while the booms are long-lasting and far-reaching. In periods of capitalist decline, the crises are of a prolonged character while the booms are fleeting, superficial, and speculative. In periods of stagnation the fluctuations occur upon one and the same level.

This means nothing else but that it is necessary to determine the general condition of the capitalist organism by the specific way in which it breathes, and the rate at which its pulse beats.

The postwar boom

Immediately following the war, an indeterminate economic situation arose. But by the spring of 1919 a boom set in; stock markets became active—prices bounded upward like a column of mercury plunged into boiling water, speculation swirled in seething whirlpools. And industry? In Central, Eastern, and Southern Europe the slump continued. . . . In France there was a certain improvement, primarily due to the looting of Germany. In England—partly stagnation, partly slump, with the sole exception of the commercial fleet whose tonnage has risen proportionately to the decline in actual trade. Thus on the whole the boom in Europe assumed a semifictitious and speculative character; and it does not signify progress, but a further decline of the economy.

In the United States, following the war, industry slowed down its military production and began reconversion to a peacetime basis. There was a noticeable upswing in the petroleum, automobile, and shipbuilding industries.

Year	Oil in millions of barrels	Automobiles in units	Shipbuilding in thousand tons
1918	356	1,153,000	3,033
1919	378	1,974,000	4,075
1920	442	2,350,000	2,746

In his valuable pamphlet, Comrade Varga[14] quite correctly says:

> The fact that the postwar boom was speculative in character is most clearly revealed by the example of Germany. At the time when prices had increased sevenfold over the course of eighteen months, Germany's industry kept regressing. . . . Its economic conjuncture was the conjuncture of clearance sales: the remainders of existing commodity reserves on the domestic market were dumped abroad at fabulously cheap prices.

Prices rose to their highest levels in Germany, where industry slumped lower and lower. Prices rose the least in the United States where industry continues to rise. France and England stand in between Germany and the United States.

How to explain these facts and the boom itself? In the first place, by economic causes: after the war international connections were resumed, even though in an extremely abridged form, and there was a universal demand for every type of merchandise. Secondly, by political-

---

14. Eugen Varga was a Hungarian communist who had served in the workers and farmers government there in 1919 and subsequently wrote on economic questions for publications of the Communist International.

financial causes: the European governments were in mortal fear of the crisis that had to follow the war and they resorted to any and all measures to sustain during the period of demobilization the artificial boom created by the war. The governments continued to put in circulation great quantities of paper currency, floated new loans, regulated profits, wages, and bread prices, thus subsidizing the earnings of demobilized workers by dipping into the basic national funds, and thus creating an artificial economic revival in the country. Thus, throughout this interval, fictitious capital continued to expand, especially in those countries where industry continued to slump.

The fictitious postwar boom had, however, great political consequences. There is some justification for saying that it saved the bourgeoisie. Had the demobilized workers from the very beginning run up against unemployment, against living standards lower even than those before the war, it might have led to consequences fatal to the bourgeoisie. In this connection an English professor, Edwin Cannan, wrote in the Manchester *Guardian*'s New Year's review that "the impatience of men returning from the battlefields is a very dangerous thing." And he goes on quite correctly to explain the favorable transition through the gravest postwar period—the year 1919—by the fact that the government and the bourgeoisie had through their joint efforts postponed and delayed the crisis, by creating an artificial prosperity through the further destruction of Europe's basic capital. Says Cannan: "Had the economic situation in January 1919 been the same as in 1921, chaos might have descended upon Western Europe."

The violent fever of the war was prolonged for another year and a half, and the crisis erupted only after the de-

mobilized masses of workers and peasants had already
been more or less pigeonholed in their little cells.

The current crisis

Having coped with the demobilization and having with-
stood the first onslaught of the working masses, the bourgeoisie emerged from its state of confusion, alarm, and
even panic, and regained its self-confidence. It became
subject to the hallucination that an epoch had finally arrived of the greatest prosperity, one that would never end.
Eminent English political and financial figures proposed
to float an international loan of two billion pounds for
the work of reconstruction. It seemed as if a shower of
gold would drench Europe, creating universal welfare. In
this way Europe's devastation, the ruination of its cities
and villages, was transmuted into riches by fantastic loan
figures, which actually were in themselves only destitu-
tion's gigantic shadow. Reality, however, quickly shook the
bourgeoisie out of its dream world. I have already described how the crisis began in Japan (in March) and in
the United States (in April), and then leaped over to England, France, Italy, and by the latter part of the year had
spread throughout the world. My entire previous presentation makes it quite self-evident that we are not dealing
with mere fluctuations in the course of a recurrent industrial cycle, but with a period of retribution for the
havoc and waste of the entire war and postwar epoch.

In 1913 the net import of all the states totaled 65–70
billion gold marks. Of this sum Russia purchased 2.5 billion; Austria-Hungary—3 billion; the Balkans—1 billion;
Germany—11 billion gold marks. Central and Eastern
Europe's share thus came to a little more than one-fourth
of the world's total imports. At the present time all these
countries import less than one-fifth of their previous

amount. This last figure alone sufficiently characterizes Europe's current purchasing capacity.

Europe has declined, its productive apparatus has considerably shriveled since before the war. The economic center of gravity has shifted to America, not through gradual evolution, but through America's exploitation of Europe's war market and Europe's exclusion from world trade.

Thereby America obtained the opportunity to experience a short-lived period of the greatest flowering. This phenomenon is an unrepeatable one, however, since Europe by its retrogression created an absolutely artificial market for America that cannot be replaced by any other today. Having fulfilled this role, Europe has since completely lost its capacity to repeat anything like it. Before the war the European market used to absorb more than half, almost 60 percent of all the exports of American industry; in the course of the war Europe became even more important for America, inasmuch as Europe's imports almost tripled those of the prewar days. But Europe emerged from the war as a greatly impoverished continent and is completely deprived of the possibility of obtaining goods from America for lack of equivalents in the shape of gold or other goods. The explanation for the crisis that started in Japan and America is to be found in just this circumstance.

After a brief and highly favorable conjuncture of almost two years' duration, there has arrived a completely genuine crisis, whose meaning for Europe is as follows: "You're poor, you must cut your coat according to your cloth; you're no longer in a position to import the goods you need from America." For America this selfsame crisis means the following: "You've enriched yourself because you were placed in a position to siphon off Europe's wealth. This lasted four or five or six years, as long as the war continued. But now an end has come to this affluent state of affairs."

SOME COUNTRIES are completely ruined, their productive apparatus must be rebuilt anew. Within each people the division of labor must be resumed. The French and German economies still continue to function mechanically owing to the impetus prior to and during the war. Germany, however, must fall back in order to introduce concord and order into its economic apparatus; and just as it was necessary to organize the economy during the war in order to mitigate the privations resulting from it, just so Germany must continue the selfsame policy today, unless the revolution intervenes. Should developments proceed along present lines, it will be necessary to introduce organization into the country's economic life and to establish, first and foremost, the necessary proportion between the means of production and the means of consumption. In other words, the necessary and correct reciprocal relation will be created through the medium of new wars and all sorts of palliative measures, unless the revolution erupts.

The very same thing applies to France and to Europe as a whole so long as this period of regression in economic life continues, a period in which the capitalist countries tend to sink to the level of those that have suffered the most and have become the poorest. During this leveling-out process America will have to forget about maintaining its greatest and most important markets on their former scale. And this means that the foregoing crisis is not a transitory normal crisis for America but the beginning of a prolonged epoch of depression.

Let us refer back to our table in which the various periods are delineated: first, the epoch of stagnation, which lasted seventy years, followed by the epoch of boom from 1851 to 1873. These twenty-two years of turbulent expansion were marked by two crises and two favorable conjunctural periods, and therewith these conjunctures were genuinely favorable, while the crises were of very weak character. Next, from 1873 up to the middle of 1890, stagnation sets in again, or at any rate the development slows down exceedingly. Then, there is unprecedented expansion once again. All this is a process of adaptation, a process of leveling out. Whenever capitalism in any one country runs up against a saturation of this or that market, it is compelled to seek other markets. Major historical events—economic crises, revolutions, and so on—will determine whether we observe stagnation, booms, or regressions in such periods. These are the main features of capitalist development.

At the given moment capitalism has entered a period of prolonged and profound depression. Strictly speaking, this epoch should have set in—insofar as one can prophesy about the past—as far back as 1913 when the world market, as a result of twenty years of turbulent development, had already become inadequate for the development of German, English, and North American capitalism. These giants of capitalist development took it fully into account. They said to themselves: in order to avoid this depression, which will linger for many years, we shall create an acute war crisis, destroy our rival, and gain unchallenged domination over the world market that has become too constricted. But the war lasted far too long, provoking not only an acute crisis but a protracted one; it destroyed completely Europe's capitalist economic apparatus, thereby facilitating America's feverish development. But after exhausting Europe, the war led in the long run to a great crisis in America, too. Once again we are witnessing that selfsame depression they had sought to escape, but that has been intensified many-fold owing to Europe's impoverishment.

And so, what are the immediate economic perspectives?

It is quite obvious that America will have to suffer curtailment, since the European war market is gone beyond recall. On the other hand, Europe will likewise have to reduce herself to the level of the most backward, that is, the most ruined areas and branches of industry. This will mean an economic leveling out in reverse, and, consequently, a prolonged crisis: in some branches of the economy and some countries—stagnation; in others—a weak development. Cyclical fluctuations will continue to take place but, in general, the curve of capitalist development will slope not upwards but downwards.

Crisis, boom, and revolution

The reciprocal relation between boom and crisis in the economy and the development of revolution is of great interest to us not only from the point of theory but above all practically. Many of you will recall that Marx and Engels wrote in 1851—when the boom was at its peak—that it was necessary at that time to recognize that the revolution of 1848 had ended, or, at any rate, had been interrupted until the next crisis. Engels wrote that while the crisis of 1847 was the mother of revolution, the boom of 1849–51 was the mother of triumphant counterrevolution.[15] It would, however, be very one-sided and utterly

---

15. Trotsky is referring to Frederick Engels's 1895 introduction to *The Class Struggles in France, 1848–1850*, written by Karl Marx in 1850. Marx explained that "the world trade crisis of 1847 had

false to interpret these judgments in the sense that a crisis invariably engenders revolutionary action while a boom, on the contrary, pacifies the working class. The revolution of 1848 was not born out of the crisis. The latter merely provided the last impetus. Essentially the revolution grew out of the contradictions between the needs of capitalist development and the fetters of the semifeudal social and state system. The irresolute and halfway revolution of 1848 did, however, sweep away the remnants of the regime of guilds and serfdom and thereby extended the framework of capitalist development. Under these conditions and these conditions alone, the boom of 1851 marked the beginning of an entire epoch of capitalist prosperity that lasted until 1873.

In citing Engels it is very dangerous to overlook these basic facts. For it was precisely after 1850, when Marx and Engels made their observations, that there set in not a normal or regular situation, but an era of capitalist Sturm und Drang for which the soil had been cleared by the revolution of 1848. This is of decisive importance here. This era of "storm and stress," during which prosperity and the favorable conjuncture were very strong, while the crisis was merely superficial and short-lived—it was precisely this period that ended with the revolution. At is-

---

been the true mother of the February and March revolutions [in France and Germany]," Engels said, "and that the industrial prosperity which had been returning gradually since the middle of 1848 and attained full bloom in 1849 and 1850 was the revitalizing force of a regenerated European reaction." Drawing the political conclusions from this shift, Engels said, Marx had written at the time: "A new revolution is possible only in consequence of a new crisis. It is, however, just as certain as this crisis." ("Introduction to Karl Marx's *The Class Struggle in France*," Marx and Engels, *Collected Works*, vol. 27, pp. 507–8.)

sue here is not whether an improvement in the conjuncture is possible, but whether the fluctuations of the conjuncture are proceeding along an ascending or descending curve. This is the most important aspect of the whole question.

CAN WE EXPECT THE SAME effects to follow the economic upswing of 1919–20? Under no circumstances. The extension of the framework of capitalist development was not even involved here. Does this mean that a new commercial-industrial upswing is excluded in the future, and even in the more or less near future? Not at all! I have already said that so long as capitalism remains alive it continues to inhale and exhale. But in the epoch that we have entered—the epoch of retribution for the drain and destruction of wartime, the epoch of leveling out *in reverse*—upswings can be only of a superficial and primarily speculatory character, while the crises become more and more prolonged and deeper-going.

Historical development has not led to the victorious proletarian dictatorship in Central and Western Europe. But it is the most brazen and at the same time the most stupid lie to attempt to conclude from this, as do the reformists, that the economic equilibrium of the capitalist world has been surreptitiously restored. . . .

This movement in reverse will not, of course, continue interminably at one and the same tempo. That is absolutely excluded. There must come a breathing spell for the capitalist organism. But from the fact that it will inhale a little fresh air and that a certain improvement will come about, it is still too early to conclude prosperity. A new phase will set in, when they will try to eliminate the contradiction between the overproduction of fictitious wealth and the underlying impoverishment. After which the paroxysms of the economic organism will continue. All this gives us, as has been said, a picture of profound economic depression.

On the basis of this economic depression the bourgeoisie will be compelled to exert stronger and stronger pressure upon the working class. This is already to be seen in the cutting of wages that has started in the full-blooded capitalist countries: in America and in England, and then throughout all of Europe. This leads to great struggles over wages. Our task is to extend these struggles, by basing ourselves on a clear understanding of the economic situation. This is quite obvious. It might be asked whether the great struggles over wages, a classic example of which is the miners' strike in England, will lead automatically to the world revolution, to the final civil war and the struggle for the conquest of political power. It is not Marxist to pose the question in such a way, however. We have no automatic guarantees of development. But when the crisis is replaced by a transitory favorable conjuncture, what will this signify for our development? Many comrades say that if an improvement takes place in this epoch it would be fatal for our revolution. No, under no circumstances. In general, there is no automatic dependence of the proletarian revolutionary movement upon a crisis. There is only a dialectical interaction. It is essential to understand this.

Let us look at the conditions in Russia. The 1905 revolution was defeated. The workers bore great sacrifices. In 1906 and 1907 the last revolutionary flare-ups occurred and by the autumn of 1907 a great world crisis broke out. The signal for it was given by Wall Street's Black Friday. Throughout 1907 and 1908 and 1909 the most terrible crisis reigned in Russia too. It killed the movement completely, because the workers had suffered so greatly during the struggle that this depression could act only to dishearten them. There were many disputes among us over what would lead to the revolution: a crisis or a favorable conjuncture?

At that time many of us defended the viewpoint that the Russian revolutionary movement could be regenerated only by a favorable economic conjuncture. And that is what took place. In 1910, 1911, and 1912, there was an improvement in our economic situation and a favorable conjuncture that acted to reassemble the demoralized and devitalized workers who had lost their courage. They realized again how important they were in production; and they passed over to an offensive, first in the economic field and later in the political field as well.

On the eve of the war the working class had become so consolidated, thanks to this period of prosperity, that it was able to pass to a direct assault. And should we today, in the period of the greatest exhaustion of the working class resulting from the crisis and the continual struggle, fail to gain victory, which is possible, then a change in the conjuncture and a rise in living standards would not have a harmful effect upon the revolution, but would be on the contrary highly propitious. Such a change could prove harmful only in the event that the favorable conjuncture marked the beginning of a long epoch of prosperity. But a long period of prosperity would signify that an expansion of the market had been attained, which is absolutely excluded. For after all, the capitalist economy already embraces the earth. Europe's impoverishment and America's sumptuous renascence on the huge war market corroborate the conclusion that this prosperity cannot be restored through the capitalist development of China, Siberia, South America, and other countries, where American capitalism is of course seeking and creating outlet markets but on a scale in no way commensurate to Europe. It follows that we are on the eve of a period of depression; and this is incontestable.

With such a perspective, a mitigation of the crisis would not signify a mortal blow to the revolution but would only enable the working class to gain a breathing spell during which it could undertake to reorganize its ranks in order subsequently to pass over to attack on a firmer basis. This is one of the possibilities. The content of the other possibility is this: that the crisis may turn from acute into chronic, become intensified and endure for many years. All this is not excluded. The possibility remains open in such a situation that the working class would gather its last forces and, having learned from experience, conquer state power in the most important capitalist countries. The only thing excluded is the automatic restoration of capitalist equilibrium on a new foundation and a capitalist upswing in the next few years. This is absolutely impossible under the conditions of modern economic stagnation. . . .

I F WE GRANT—and let us grant it for the moment—that the working class fails to rise in revolutionary struggle, but allows the bourgeoisie the opportunity to rule the world's destiny for a long number of years, say, two or three decades, then assuredly some sort of new equilibrium will be established. Europe will be thrown violently into reverse gear. Millions of European workers will die from unemployment and malnutrition. The United States will be compelled to reorient itself on the world market, reconvert its industry, *and suffer curtailment for a considerable period.* Afterwards, after a new world division of labor is thus established in agony for fifteen or twenty or twenty-five years, a new epoch of capitalist upswing might perhaps ensue.

But this entire conception is exceedingly abstract and one-sided. Matters are pictured here as if the proletariat had ceased to struggle. *Meanwhile, there cannot even be talk of this if only for the reason that the class contradictions have become aggravated in the extreme precisely during the recent years. . . .*

Each measure to which capitalism is constrained in order to make a step forward in restoring equilibrium, each and all of this immediately acquires a decisive significance for the social equilibrium, tends more and more to undermine it, and ever more powerfully impels the working class to struggle. The first task in achieving equilibrium is to set the productive apparatus in order, but to do so it is indispensable to accumulate capital. But to make accumulation possible it is necessary to raise the productivity of labor. How? Through an augmented and intensified exploitation of the working class, inasmuch as the decline in the productivity of labor power during these three postwar years is a widely known fact.

To reestablish the world economy on capitalist foundations, it is indispensable to again establish a world equivalent—the gold standard. Without it the capitalist economy cannot exist, inasmuch as there cannot be any production while prices dance their dance of death, increasing 100 percent in the course of a single month as happens in Germany, contingent upon the fluctuations of German currency. A capitalist is not interested in production. For he is being lured from afar by speculation, which tempts him by much greater profits than can be gained from slowly developing industry. What does the stabilization of currency signify? For France and Germany it signifies a declaration of state bankruptcy. But to declare a state insolvent is to incur a vast shift of property relations within the nation. And those states that have declared themselves insolvent have become the arena for a new struggle over the distribution of the new national wealth, which is a giant step toward the sharpening of the class struggle. At the same time all this signifies a renunciation of social and political equilibrium, that is, a revolutionary flux.

The declaration of state bankruptcy, however, does not make it possible immediately to pass to the restoration of equilibrium. This must likewise be followed by the lengthening of the working week, the repeal of the eight-hour day, and more intensive exploitation. This, of course, makes it necessary to overcome the resistance of the working class. In short, speaking theoretically and abstractly, the restoration of capitalist equilibrium is possible. But it does not take place in a social and political vacuum—it can take place only through the classes. Every step, no matter how tiny, toward the restoration of equilibrium in economic life is a blow to the unstable social equilibrium upon which the Messrs. Capitalists still continue to maintain themselves. And this is the most important thing.

The aggravation of social contradictions

Economic development is thus not an automatic process. The issue is not restricted solely to the productive foundations of society. Upon these foundations there live and work human beings and the development occurs through these human beings. What, then, has taken place in the field of relations between human beings, or, more precisely, between classes?

We have seen that Germany and other European countries too have been thrown back twenty or thirty years in terms of their economic level. Have they perhaps been simultaneously thrown back in social terms, in the class sense? Not at all. The classes of Germany, the number of workers and their concentration, the concentration of capital and its degree of organization—all this had taken shape prior to the war, and in particular as a result of the last two decades of prosperity (1894–1913). And later on, all this became still more aggravated: during the war— with the aid of the state intervention; after the war— through the fever of speculation and the growing concentration of capital.

We thus have two processes of development. National wealth and national income keep falling, *but the development of classes continues therewith not to regress but to progress.* More and more people are becoming proletarianized, capital is being concentrated in fewer and fewer hands, banks keep merging, industrial enterprises become concentrated in trusts. As a result, the class struggle inevitably becomes sharper on the basis of a declining national income.

Herein is the whole gist of the matter. The more restricted becomes the material foundation under their feet, the more fiercely must classes and groups fight for their share of this national income. We must not lose sight of this circumstance for a single moment. While Europe has been thrown back thirty years with regard to its national wealth this does not at all mean that she has grown thirty years younger. No, in the class sense, she has become thirty years older.

The peasantry

During the first period of the war it was said and written that the peasantry throughout Europe was profiting by the war. And indeed the state was in critical need of bread and meat for the army. For all this, insane prices that kept soaring were paid, and the peasants stuffed their pockets with paper money. With this paper money, which kept depreciating, the peasants paid debts that they had previously contracted when currency was at par. Of course this was a very profitable operation for them.

Bourgeois economists reckoned that the prosperity of the peasant economy would secure the stability of capitalism after the war. But they miscalculated. The peasants paid off their mortgages, but agriculture in no way consists solely of paying off debts to bankers. It consists of cultivating the soil, fertilizing it, acquiring inventory and good seeds, making technological improvements, and so on. This was either not done at all, or it cost wild sums of money. Moreover, there was a scarcity of labor, agriculture declined, and the peasants, after the initial semifictitious boom, began to face ruin.

This process is to be observed in its various stages throughout Europe. But it has also manifested itself very acutely in America. There was extreme suffering among the American, Canadian, Australian, and South American farmers when it was revealed that ruined Europe was no longer able to buy their grain. The price of grain dropped. Among farmers there is ferment and dissatisfaction throughout the world.

The peasantry thus ceases to be one of the mainstays of law and order. Before the working class opens up the possibility of attracting to its side in the struggle at least a section of the peasantry (the lowest ranks), of neutralizing another section (the middle peasants), and of isolating and paralyzing the tops (the kulaks, the well-to-do farmers).

The new middle estate

The reformists pinned great hopes upon the so-called middle estate. Engineers, technicians, doctors, lawyers, bookkeepers, accountants, functionaries, civilian and government employees alike, and so on—all these constitute a semiconservative stratum that stands between capital and labor and that must, in the opinion of reformists, reconcile both sides, while directing and at the same time supporting democratic regimes.

This class has suffered even more than the working class during the war and after, that is, its living standards have deteriorated to an even greater degree than the living standards of the working class. The main reason for this is the decline in the purchasing power of money, the depreciation of paper currency. In all European countries this has given rise to sharp discontent among the lowest and even middle ranks of functionaries and the technological intelligentsia. In Italy, for example, the functionaries are engaged in a bitter strike at this very hour. Of course, functionaries in government or civil employ, bank clerks, and so on have not become a proletarian class, but they have shed their former conservative character. They do not prop up the state so much as shake and convulse its apparatus by their dissatisfaction and protests.

The discontent of the bourgeois intelligentsia is further aggravated by its intimate ties with the commercial-industrial petty and middle bourgeoisie. The latter feel themselves slighted, cheated of their rightful share. The monopoly bourgeoisie continues to wallow in wealth, notwithstanding the country's ruination. It arrogates to itself an ever-increasing portion of the declining national income. The nonmonopoly bourgeoisie and the new middle estate are sinking both absolutely and relatively.

As regards the proletariat, it is quite probable that despite the deterioration of its living standards, its common share in the declining national income is greater today than before the war. Monopoly capital seeks to slash the worker's share by driving it down to prewar levels. The worker, however, takes as his starting point not the statistical charts but his reduced living standards and strives to increase his share of the national income. *And so, the peasants are disgruntled by the decline of the economy; the intelligentsia is growing poorer and sinking; the petty and middle bourgeoisie are ruined and discontented. The class struggle is sharpening.*

International relations

International relations of course play an enormous role in the life of the capitalist world. The latter had this brought home to it all too clearly during the world war. And at the present time, when we pose the question of whether it is possible or impossible for capitalism to restore its world equilibrium, we must take note of the international conditions under which this work of reconstruction is being done. It is not hard to ascertain that international relations have become far more strained, far less compatible with the "peaceful" evolution of capitalism than was the case prior to the war.

Why did the war occur? Because the productive forces found themselves too constricted within the frameworks of the most powerful capitalist states. The inner urge of imperialist capital was to eradicate the state boundaries and to seize the entire globe, abolishing tariffs and other barriers that restrict the development of the productive forces. Herein are the economic foundations of imperialism and the root causes of the war. What were the results? Europe is now richer in boundaries and tariff walls than ever before. A whole galaxy of tiny states has been formed. The territories of the former Austro-Hungarian empire are now crisscrossed by a dozen tariff lines. The

Englishman Keynes has called Europe a madhouse,[16] and indeed from the standpoint of economic development this entire particularism of tiny insular states, their tariff systems, and so on, represents a monstrous anachronism, an insane implantation of medievalism into the twentieth century. While the Balkan peninsula is being barbarianized, Europe is becoming Balkanized.

The relations between Germany and France militate up to now against the possibility of any kind of European equilibrium. France is compelled to loot and rape Germany in order to maintain its own class equilibrium, which is not commensurate to the depleted foundation of the French economy. Germany will not and cannot remain the object of this pillage. At the present time, true enough, an agreement has been reached. Germany has pledged to pay annually two billion gold marks, plus 26 percent of its exports. This transaction represents a victory for England's policy, which aims to prevent the occupation of the Ruhr by France.[17] At the present time the bulk of European iron ore is in the hands of France; the bulk of coal—in Germany's hands. The cardinal condi-

---

16. John Maynard Keynes, a prominent British economist, served as an adviser to Prime Minister David Lloyd George at the Versailles Peace Conference in 1919, following World War I. Convinced that the tens of billions in reparations on Germany and other debt burdens imposed by the victors would result in the "devastation of Europe," Keynes resigned from that post. Later that year he wrote the widely publicized booklet, *The Economic Consequences of Peace*, referred to here by Trotsky.

17. As sanctioned by the Treaty of Versailles, the French imperialist government threatened to occupy the Ruhr Valley, Germany's industrial heartland, if Berlin fell behind on its reparations payments. Paris did so in January 1923, in collaboration with the government of Belgium.

tion for the regeneration of the European economy is the productive combination of French ore with German coal, but such a combination, unconditionally essential for economic development, happens to be mortally dangerous to English capitalism. All the efforts of London are for this reason directed to prevent either a warlike or peaceable combination of French ore with German coal. But this leads to a still greater aggravation of the antagonism between England and France.

FRANCE HAS TEMPORARILY accepted the compromise, all the more so since its disorganized productive apparatus is incapable of digesting even the coal Germany is now forcibly compelled to supply it. But this does not at all mean that the question of the Ruhr has been definitively settled. The very first infraction by Germany of its reparation obligations will inevitably raise once again the question of the Ruhr's fate.

The growth of France's influence in Europe, and partly in the world as well, during the past year is due not to the strengthening of France but to the patent progressive weakening of England.

Great Britain has conquered Germany. This was the chief issue settled by the last war. And in essence the war was not a world war but a European war, even though the struggle between the two mightiest European states—England and Germany—was resolved with the participation of the forces and resources of the entire world. England has conquered Germany. But today, England is much weaker in the world market, and generally in the world situation, than she was before the war. The United States has grown at England's expense much more than England has at the expense of Germany.

America is battering England down, first of all by the more rationalized and more progressive character of its industry. The productivity of an American worker is 150 percent above the productivity of an English worker. In other words, thanks to a more perfectly equipped industry, two American workers produce as much as five English workers. This fact alone, established by English statistical research, testifies that England is doomed in a struggle with America; and this alone suffices to push England toward a war with America, so long as the English fleet preserves its dominance on the oceans.

American coal is crowding out English coal throughout the world and even in Europe. Yet, England's world trade has been based primarily on its export of coal. In addition, oil is now of decisive significance for industry and defense; oil not only runs automobiles, tractors, submarines, airplanes, but is greatly superior to coal even for the big ocean liners. Up to 70 percent of the world's oil is produced within the boundaries of the United States. Consequently, in the event of war all this oil would be in the hands of Washington. In addition America holds in its hands Mexican oil, which supplies up to 12 percent of the world output. True, Americans are accusing England of having cornered, outside the United States borders, up to 90 percent of the world oil sources and of shutting off the Americans from access to them, while American oil fields face exhaustion within the next few years. But all these geological and statistical computations are quite dubious and arbitrary. They are compiled to order so as to justify American pretensions to the oil of Mexico, Mesopotamia, and so on. But were the danger of exhaustion of American oil fields actually to prove real, it would constitute one more reason for speeding up the war between the United States and England.

Europe's indebtedness to America is a touchy question. The debts on the whole amount to $18 billion. The United States always has the opportunity of creating the greatest difficulties in the English money market by presenting its demands for payment. As is well known, England has even proposed that America cancel English debts, promising in turn to cancel Europe's debt to England. Since England owes America much more than the continental countries of the Entente owe it, she stands to profit from such a transaction. America has refused. The capitalist Yankees showed no inclination to finance with their own funds Great Britain's preparations for war with the United States.

The alliance between England and Japan, which is fighting America for dominance on the Asiatic continent, has likewise aggravated in the extreme the relations between the United States and England.

B∪т мost acute in character, in view of all the indicated circumstances, is the question of the navy. Wilson's government, upon running up against England's opposition in world affairs, launched a gigantic program of naval construction. [President Warren G.] Harding's government has taken this program over from its predecessor, and this program is being rushed through at top speed. By 1924 the U.S. Navy will not only be far more powerful than that of England, but also superior to the English and Japanese fleets put together, if not in tonnage, then in firepower.

What does this mean from the English point of view? It means that by 1924 England must either accept the challenge and try to destroy the military, naval, and economic might of the United States by taking advantage of its present superiority, or she must passively become converted into a second- or third-rate power, surrendering once and for all domination of the oceans and seas to the United States. Thus the last slaughter of the peoples, which "settled" in its own way the European question, has for this very reason raised in all its scope the world question, namely: will England or the United States rule the world? The preparations for the new world war are proceeding full speed ahead. The expenditures for the army and the navy have grown extraordinarily as compared with prewar times. The English military budget has increased threefold, the American—three and a half times.

The contradictions between England and America are being transformed into a process of automatic proliferation, an automatic approach closer and closer to tomorrow's bloody conflict. Here we actually are dealing with automatism.

On January 1, 1914, that is, at the moment when the "armed peace" was under its greatest strain, there were approximately seven million soldiers with bayonets throughout the world. At the beginning of the current year there were about eighteen million soldiers with bayonets. The bulk of these armies weighs down, of course, upon exhausted Europe.

Consequently, militarism has grown. All this is one of the most important obstacles in the way of economic progress. One of the main causes of the war was the intolerable burden of armed peace upon the European economy. A horrible end was preferable to horror without end. But it turned out that this is no end at all, that horror *after* the end is even more horrible than it was before the horrible end, that is, before the last war.

The grave crisis, arising from the constriction of the

world market, acts to aggravate extremely the struggle between the capitalist states, depriving world relations of any kind of stability. Not only Europe but the whole world is being turned into a madhouse! Under these conditions there is hardly any necessity to speak of the restoration of capitalist equilibrium.

The working class after the war

From the standpoint of the revolution, in general and on the whole, all this creates for the working class a very favorable and at the same time an extremely complex situation. After all, what lies ahead of us is not a chaotic, spontaneous assault, the first stage of which we observed in Europe in 1918–19. It seemed to us (and there was some historical justification for it) that in the period when the bourgeoisie was disorganized this assault could mount in ever-rising waves, that in this process the consciousness of the leading layers of the working class would become clarified, and that in this way the proletariat would attain state power in the course of one or two years. That was a historical possibility. But it did not materialize.

History has—with the assistance of the bourgeoisie's bad or good will, its cunning, its experience, its organization, and its instinct for power—granted the bourgeoisie a fairly prolonged breathing space. No miracles have taken place. What has been destroyed, or burned, or ruined, has not come to life again; but the bourgeoisie proved well able to find its bearings in these straitened conditions; it restored its state apparatus and managed to utilize the weakness of the working class. From the standpoint of revolutionary perspectives, the situation has become more complicated, but still remains favorable. It is perhaps with greater assurance that we can say today that on the whole the situation is fully revolutionary. But the revolution is not so docile, nor so domesticated as to be led on a leash, as we once imagined. The revolution has its own fluctuations, its own crises, and its own favorable conjunctures.

Immediately after the war, the bourgeoisie was in a state of highest confusion and alarm—the workers, especially those returning from the army, were in a peremptory mood. But the working class as a whole was disoriented, uncertain of just what forms life would take after the war, unsure of what and how to demand, dubious of what road to take. . . . The movement, as we saw at the beginning of this report, assumed an extremely stormy character, but the working class lacked a firm leadership. On the other hand, the bourgeoisie was ready to make very great concessions. It kept up the financial and economic war regime (loans, emission of paper currency, grain monopoly, relief for the unemployed working masses, etc.). In other words, the ruling bourgeoisie continued to disorganize the economic foundation and to disrupt more and more the productive and financial equilibrium in order to bolster the equilibrium between the classes during the most critical period. Up to now it has more or less succeeded in accomplishing this.

At the present time the bourgeoisie is proceeding to solve the question of restoring the economic equilibrium. Involved here are not temporary concessions or sops to the working class but measures of a fundamental character. The disorganized productive apparatus must be restored. Currency must be stabilized, since the world market is unthinkable without a universal world equivalent, and, therefore, equally unthinkable without a universal equivalent is a "balanced" national industry, one tied up with the world market.

To restore the productive apparatus is to curtail work

on consumer goods and to step up work on the means of production. It is necessary to augment accumulation, that is, to intensify labor and slash wages.

To stabilize the currency it is necessary, apart from refusing to pay intolerable debts, to improve the trade balance, that is, import less and export more. And to this end it is necessary to consume less and produce more, that is, once again slash wages and intensify labor.

EVERY STEP TOWARD the restoration of the capitalist economy is bound up with boosting the rate of exploitation and will therefore unfailingly provoke resistance on the part of the working class. In other words, every effort by the bourgeoisie to restore the equilibrium in production or in distribution or in state finances must inescapably disrupt the unstable equilibrium between the classes. Whereas during the two postwar years, the bourgeoisie was guided in its economic policy primarily by the desire to mollify the proletariat, even at the cost of further economic ruination, at the present time, in the epoch of unprecedented crisis, the bourgeoisie has begun mending the economic situation by steadily increasing the pressure on the working class.

England provides us with a most graphic illustration of how this pressure engenders resistance. And the resistance of the working class acts to disrupt economic stability and to transform all speeches about the restoration of equilibrium into so many empty sounds.

The struggle of the proletariat for power has been unquestionably protracted. We did not get an overwhelming onslaught, we did not see a picture of wave mounting upon wave, rolling onward incessantly until the capitalist system was swept away in the final surge.

In this struggle we observed both ups and downs, both offense and defense. Class maneuvering was far from always skillful on our part. The reason for the protracted and uneven character of the struggle is twofold: In the first place, the weakness of the Communist parties, which arose only after the war, which lacked the necessary experience and the necessary apparatus, which were without sufficient influence and—what is the most important—didn't know how to pay sufficient attention to the working masses. In this sphere we have in any case taken a big step forward during the recent years. The Communist parties have grown stronger and have developed. The second reason lies in the heterogeneous composition of the working class itself, as it emerged from the war.

LEAST SHAKEN BY THE WAR are the labor bureaucracy, the trade union and party bureaucracy, and the parliamentarians. Capitalist states in all countries have shown utmost attention to and solicitude for this superstructure, understanding excellently that without it the working class could not possibly have been kept in submission through the years of bloodletting. The labor bureaucracy received all sorts of privileges and emerged from the war with the same habits of bovine conservatism with which it had entered the war, but somewhat more discredited and more intimately bound up with the respective capitalist states. Skilled workers of the oldest generation, inured to their trade union and party organizations, especially in Germany, have by and large remained to this very day the main support of the labor bureaucracy, but their inertia is by no means absolute.

Those workers who have passed through the school of war—and they are the pith of the working class—have introduced a new psychology among the proletariat, new habits and new attitudes to the questions of struggle, to the questions of life and death. They are ready to solve questions by means of force, but they have firmly assimilated from the war that a successful application of force presupposes correct tactics and strategy. These elements will march into battle, but they want firm leadership and serious preparation. Many backward categories of workers, including women workers whose numbers have grown prodigiously during the war, have now become, as a consequence of an abrupt turn in their consciousness, the most militant, though not always the most class-conscious section of the working class. Finally, at the extreme left wing we see the working-class youth, who have grown up during the war amid the roar of battles and revolutionary paroxysms and who are destined to fill a great place in the coming struggle.

All these extraordinarily augmented proletarian masses —the old workers and the worker-recruits, the workers who remained in the rear and the workers who spent several years under fire—this entire multimillion-headed mass is passing through the school of revolution not in the same way and not at the same time. This was brought home to us again during the March events in Germany,[18]

18. In March 1921 the German Communist Party, in the midst of a defensive strike by thousands of coal miners in central Germany, issued a call for a nationwide insurrection to seize power. The party leadership was acting on the basis of what they called a "theory of the offensive" also advocated by leftists in parties affiliated with the Comintern in Italy and elsewhere in Europe. The "March action" was rapidly isolated and defeated by the bourgeois regime in Germany, with hundreds of working-class militants killed and thousands jailed. The Third Comintern Congress drew a balance sheet of the action and rejected the "theory of

where the workers of Central Germany, the most backward elements before the war, were eager to rush into battle in March without pausing to consider the chances for success, whereas the Berlin workers and those of Saxony had gained some experience in the course of revolutionary battles and become more cautious. It is undeniable that the general course of the postwar struggle, and especially the current offensive of capitalism, is fusing together all the layers of the working class with the sole exception of its privileged aristocracy. The Communist parties are getting more and more opportunities for establishing a genuine working-class united front.

Immediate perspectives and tasks

The revolution has three sources that are interconnected. The revolution's first source is the decline of Europe. Class equilibrium in Europe was maintained first of all by England's dominant position in the world market. Today Europe's dominant position has been completely lost, and irretrievably so. Hence the inevitability of powerful revolutionary paroxysms that can terminate either in the victory of the proletariat or in Europe's complete downfall.

The second source of the revolutionary struggle lies in the severe spasms of the entire economic organism of the

---

the offensive." In his speech to the congress in defense of the tactics of the Communist International, Lenin said it had been wrong "to begin talking in Germany *about the theory* of the revolutionary offensive when an actual offensive had not been prepared. Nevertheless, the March action was a great step forward in spite of the mistakes of its leaders. . . . [I]t is a real step forward if hundreds of thousands fight against the vile provocation of the social-traitors and against the bourgeoisie." (Lenin, *Collected Works*, vol. 32, p. 473.)

United States: an unprecedented boom, called forth by the European war, and next—a cruel crisis engendered by the drawn-out aftereffects of this war. Under these conditions, the revolutionary movement of the American proletariat can acquire the same tempo, unequaled in history, as the economic development of the United States in recent years.

The third source of revolutionary struggle is the industrialization of the colonies, above all India. The basis for the liberation struggle of the colonies is constituted by the peasant masses. But the peasants in their struggle need leadership. Such a leadership used to be provided by the native bourgeoisie. The latter's struggle against foreign imperialist domination cannot, however, be either consistent or energetic, inasmuch as the native bourgeoisie itself is intimately bound up with foreign capital and represents to a large measure an agency of foreign capital. Only the rise of a native proletariat strong enough numerically and capable of struggle can provide a real axis for the revolution. In comparison to the country's entire population, of course, the size of the Indian proletariat is numerically small. But those who have grasped the meaning of the revolution's development in Russia will never fail to take into account that the proletariat's revolutionary role in the Eastern countries will far exceed its actual numerical strength. This applies not only to purely colonial countries, like India, or semicolonial countries like China, but also to Japan where capitalist oppression blends with the bureaucratic absolutism of a feudal caste.

Thus both the world situation and the future perspectives are profoundly revolutionary in character.

When the bourgeoisie resorted after the war to throwing sops to the working class, the conciliators obsequiously converted these sops into reforms (the eight-hour day, unemployment insurance, and so on); and discovered—amid the ruins—the era of reformism. Today the bourgeoisie has passed over to a counteroffensive all along the line, and even the London *Times*—a supercapitalist daily—refers with alarm to capitalist Bolsheviks. The current epoch is the epoch of counterreformism.

The English pacifist Norman Angell has called the war a miscalculation.[19] The experience of the last war has shown that the calculation, from the bookkeeping standpoint, was indeed a false one. After the war it might have seemed that the triumph of pacifism was about to arrive and that the League of Nations was its manifestation.[20]

Today we see that the calculation of pacifism was a miscalculation. Never before has capitalist mankind engaged in such frenzied preparation for a new war as at the present time. Democracy is being stripped of its illusions even in the eyes of the most conservative layers of the working class. Not so long ago democracy used to be counterposed only to the dictatorship of the proletariat with its terror, its Cheka,[21] and so forth and so on. Nowa-

---

19. Sir Norman Angell was a British economist and journalist.

20. The establishment of the League of Nations, part of the victors' settlement at Versailles, was presented by Washington, London, and Paris as an instrument of world peace. Like its contemporary stepchild, the United Nations, it was in fact an auxiliary instrument used by the imperialist powers to maintain their world domination—"a den of thieves," as Lenin dubbed the League.

21. The All-Russia Extraordinary Commission, known by its Russian acronym Cheka, was established shortly after the triumph of the Bolshevik-led workers and peasants government, in December 1917, as a revolutionary tribunal and security force for the purpose of combating counterrevolution and sabotage. It was headed by Felix Dzerzhinsky.

days democracy is being ever more counterposed to any and all forms of the class struggle. Lloyd George has advised the coal miners to solicit Parliament with their grievances and has branded their strike an act of violence upon the will of the nation.

Under the Hohenzollern regime the German workers found a certain stability and well-defined limits. The workers knew on the whole what could be done and what was forbidden. In Ebert's republic a worker-striker always incurs the risk of having his throat cut in the streets or in a police station, without further ado. Ebertian "democracy" offers the German workers as little as do high wages paid in completely worthless currency.

The task of the Communist parties lies in comprehending the existing situation as a whole, and intervening actively in the struggle of the proletariat in order to conquer the majority of the working class on the basis of this struggle. *Should the situation in one or another country become extremely exacerbated, we must pose the basic question point-blank, and we must join battle in whatever condition the events catch us.*

If the march of events proceeds more evenly and smoothly, however, then we must utilize all the possibilities in order *to gain the majority of the working class prior to the decisive events.*

W E DO NOT AS YET have the majority of the working class throughout the world; but a much larger section of the proletariat is with us today than a year or two ago. After we have actually analyzed the existing situation, which is one of the important tasks of our congress; after we have reviewed the situation in each given country, we must say to ourselves: The struggle will perhaps be long and we shall not advance at so feverish a pace as we should like. The struggle will be very harsh and will exact many sacrifices. We have become stronger through accumulated experience. We shall know how to maneuver in this struggle. We shall know how to plot for our tactics not only an ideal mathematical line, but also the curves of a shifting situation, amid which the revolutionary line must cut its way. We shall understand how to maneuver actively amid the decomposition of the capitalist class; we shall be able to mobilize the forces of the workers for the social revolution.

I believe that our successes as well as our failures have demonstrated that the difference between us and the Independent Social Democrats does not consist in our having said that we would make the revolution in the year 1919, while they kept maintaining that the revolution would come much later. No, that's not where the difference lies. The difference lies in this, that the Social Democracy and the Independent Social Democrats support the bourgeoisie against the revolution under any and all circumstances. Whereas we were and are ready to utilize every situation, no matter what changes it may undergo, for the revolutionary offensive and for the conquest of political power. [*Long, enthusiastic applause.*]

In today's defensive economic struggles unfolding on the basis of the crisis, the Communists must participate most actively in all the trade unions, in all the strikes and demonstrations, and in all kinds of movements, always maintaining their inner ties unbroken in their work, and always stepping to the forefront as the most resolute and best disciplined wing of the working class. Depending upon the course of the crisis and the shifts in the political situation, the defensive economic struggle may become extended, embracing ever-newer layers among the working class, among the population, and among the army of the unemployed; and on becoming transformed at a certain stage into a revolutionary offensive struggle, it may be crowned with victory. It is precisely to this end that our efforts must be directed.

B UT WHAT IF IN PLACE of the crisis an improvement should come in the world economic conjuncture? What then? Would this signify that the revolutionary struggle is checked for an indefinite period?

From my entire report, comrades, it follows that a new upswing, which can be neither prolonged nor profound, can by no means act as a check upon the revolutionary development. The industrial boom of 1849–51 dealt a blow to the revolution only because the revolution of 1848 had expanded the framework of capitalist development. As to the events of 1914–21, they have acted not to expand but to contract in the extreme the framework of the world market, and therefore the curve of capitalist development as a whole will much sooner slope downwards in the next period. In these conditions a temporary boom can only strengthen the class self-confidence of the workers and fuse their ranks not only in the factories but also in struggles. And it can provide the impulse not only for their economic counteroffensive but also for their revolutionary struggle for power.

The situation is becoming more and more favorable for us, but it is also growing extremely complex. Victory will not come to us automatically. The ground under the enemy's feet is undermined, but our enemy remains strong, our enemy keenly discerns our weak spots, veers and maneuvers, always guided by icy calculation. We—the entire Communist International—have a great deal to learn from the experience of our battles during these three years, and especially from the experience of our mistakes and our failures. Civil war demands political, tactical, and strategic maneuvering; it demands that the peculiarities of each given situation, the strong and the weak sides of the enemy, be taken into account; it demands a combination of enthusiasm with icy calculation; it demands not only the ability to assume the offensive but also the readiness to temporarily retreat in order to preserve one's forces, so as to deal all the surer a blow.

Let me repeat, the world situation and the future perspectives remain profoundly revolutionary. This creates the necessary premises for our victory. But full guarantees can be given only by our skillful tactics, by our strong organization. To raise the Communist International to a higher level, to make it more effective tactically—that is the basic task of the Third World Congress of the Communist International.

Delegates to Third Comintern Congress, 1921, at Moscow welcoming parade. Leon Trotsky, organizer of Red Army (in uniform), is at front, center.

"Capitalist equilibrium is an extremely complex phenomenon," Trotsky explained in his report to the congress. "Capitalism produces this equilibrium, disrupts it, restores it anew in order to disrupt it anew, concurrently extending the limits of its domination. In the economic sphere these constant disruptions and restorations take the shape of crises and booms; in interclass relations, the form of strikes, lockouts, revolutionary struggle; in interstate relations, war or—in a weaker form— tariff war, economic war, or blockade."

V.I. Lenin presents report on tactics of Russian Communist Party to Third Congress of Communist International, July 5, 1921.

"Our job is to learn from and apply Lenin and Trotsky's living, practical example of how Marxists approach the interrelationship between deep-going economic and financial trends in international capitalism, shifts in long-term patterns of imperialist politics and the worldwide class struggle, and changes in working-class resistance. Our job is to act accordingly, in response to today's trends."

A VERY UNSTABLE EQUILIBRIUM:

REPORT ON THE TACTICS

OF THE RUSSIAN COMMUNIST PARTY

by V.I. Lenin

July 5, 1921

C OMRADES, STRICTLY SPEAKING I was unable to prepare properly for this report. All I was able to prepare for you in the way of systematic material was
a translation of my pamphlet on the tax in kind and the
theses on the tactics of the Russian Communist Party.[22] To
this I merely want to add a few explanations and remarks.

I think that to make a case for our party's tactics we must
first of all examine the *international situation*. We have already had a detailed discussion of the economic position
of capitalism internationally, and the congress has adopted the corresponding resolutions on this subject.[23] I deal

22. Lenin's pamphlet "The Tax in Kind: The Significance of the
New Policy and Its Conditions," published in April 1921, and his
"Theses for a Report on the Tactics of the Russian Communist
Party," prepared in June 1921 for the Third Congress of the Com-
munist International, both appear in Lenin's *Collected Works*, vol.
32, pp. 329–65 and pp. 453–61 respectively.

23. Lenin is referring to the "Report on the World Economic Crisis and the New Tasks of the Communist International," presented
to the congress by Leon Trotsky, major excerpts from which are
printed here.

with this subject in my theses very briefly, and only from the political standpoint. I leave aside the economic basis, but I think that in discussing the international position of our republic we must, politically, take into account the fact that a certain equilibrium has now undoubtedly set in between the forces that have been waging an open struggle, arms in hand, against each other for the supremacy of one or another leading class. It is an equilibrium between bourgeois society, the international bourgeoisie as a whole, and Soviet Russia. It is, of course, an equilibrium only in a limited sense. It is only in respect to this military struggle, I say, that a certain equilibrium has been brought about in the international situation.

I T MUST BE EMPHASIZED, of course, that this is only a relative equilibrium, and a very unstable one. Much inflammable material has accumulated in capitalist countries, as well as in those countries that up to now have been regarded merely as the objects and not as the subjects of history, i.e., the colonies and semicolonies. It is quite possible, therefore, that insurrections, great battles, and revolutions may break out in these countries sooner or later, and quite unexpectedly too. During the past few years we have witnessed the direct struggle waged by the international bourgeoisie against the first proletarian republic. This struggle has been at the center of the world political situation, and it is there that a change has taken place. Inasmuch as the attempt of the international bourgeoisie to strangle our republic has failed, an equilibrium has set in, and a very unstable one it is, of course.

We know perfectly well, of course, that the international bourgeoisie is at present much stronger than our republic, and that it is only the peculiar combination of circumstances that is preventing it from continuing the war against us. For several weeks now, we have witnessed fresh attempts in the Far East to renew the invasion, and there is not the slightest doubt that similar attempts will continue.[24] Our party has no doubts whatever on that score. The important thing for us is to establish that an unstable equilibrium does exist, and that we must take advantage of this respite, taking into consideration the characteristic features of the present situation, adapting our tactics to specific features of this situation, and never forgetting for a minute that the necessity for armed struggle may arise again quite suddenly. Our task is still to organize and build up the Red Army. In connection with the question of food supplies, too, we must continue to think first of all of our Red Army. We can adopt no other line in the present international situation, when we must still be prepared for fresh attacks and fresh attempts at invasion on the part of the international bourgeoisie. In regard to our practical policy, however, the fact that a certain equilibrium has been reached in the international situation has some significance, but only in the sense that we must admit that, although the revolutionary movement has made progress, the development of the international revolution this year has not proceeded along as straight a line as we had expected.

When we started the international revolution, we did

----

24. In April 1921, after the Red Army's victory over the strongest counterrevolutionary armies and their imperialist backers, Tokyo overturned the local government in the Pacific Coast city of Vladivostok and threatened to renew the war in Russia's Far East. Faced with the weakness of its local puppets and lack of support from the U.S. or European imperialist governments, Tokyo withdrew its invasion force in October 1922.

so not because we were convinced that we could foresee its development, but because we were compelled to do so by a number of circumstances. We thought: either the international revolution comes to our assistance, and in that case our victory will be fully assured, or we shall do our modest revolutionary work in the conviction that even in the event of defeat we shall have served the cause of the revolution and that our experience will benefit other revolutions. It was clear to us that without the support of the international world revolution the victory of the proletarian revolution was impossible. Before the revolution, and even after it, we thought: either revolution breaks out in the other countries, in the more developed capitalist countries, immediately, or at least very quickly, or we must perish. In spite of this conviction, we did all we possibly could to preserve the Soviet system under all circumstances, come what may, because we knew that we were not only working for ourselves, but also for the international revolution. We knew this, we repeatedly expressed this conviction before the October Revolution, immediately after it, and at the time we signed the Brest-Litovsk Peace Treaty.[25] And, generally speaking, this was correct.

Actually, however, events did not proceed along as straight a line as we had expected. In the other big, more developed

---

25. The Bolshevik-led workers and peasants republic signed the Brest-Litovsk Treaty with the government of Germany in March 1918, ending the state of war that had existed between the two countries since August 1914. The government of Soviet Russia accepted substantial territorial conquests by imperialist Germany in order to halt the war and concentrate on organizing the workers and peasants to carry out the tasks of defense, reconstruction, and the first steps in the building of socialism.

capitalist countries the revolution has not broken out to this day. True, we can say with satisfaction that the revolution is developing all over the world, and it is only thanks to this that the international bourgeoisie is unable to strangle us, in spite of the fact that, militarily and economically, it is a hundred times stronger than we are. [*Applause.*]

In Paragraph 2 of the theses I examine the manner in which this situation arose, and the conclusions that must be drawn from it.[26] Let me add that my final conclusion

---

26. In paragraph 2 of the theses, Lenin wrote that the international alignment of class forces at the time was as follows: "The international bourgeoisie, deprived of the opportunity of waging open war against Soviet Russia, is waiting and watching for the moment when circumstances will permit it to resume the war.

"The proletariat in all the advanced capitalist countries has already formed its vanguard, the Communist Parties, which are growing, making steady progress toward winning the majority of the proletariat in each country, and destroying the influence of the old trade union bureaucrats and of the upper stratum of the working class of America and Europe, which has been corrupted by imperialist privileges.

"The petty-bourgeois democrats in the capitalist countries . . . serve today as the mainstay of capitalism, since they retain an influence over the majority, or a considerable section, of the industrial and commercial workers and office employees who are afraid that if revolution breaks out they will lose the relative petty-bourgeois prosperity created by the privileges of imperialism. But the growing economic crisis is worsening the condition of broad sections of the people everywhere, and this, with the looming inevitability of new imperialist wars if capitalism is preserved, is steadily weakening this mainstay.

"The masses of the working people in the colonial and semi-colonial countries, who constitute the overwhelming majority of the population of the globe [are becoming] an active factor in world politics and in the revolutionary destruction of imperialism. . . ."

is the following: the development of the international revolution, which we predicted, is proceeding, but not along as straight a line as we had expected. It becomes clear at the first glance that after the conclusion of peace, bad as it was, it proved impossible to call forth revolution in other capitalist countries, although we know that the signs of revolution were very considerable and numerous, in fact, much more considerable and numerous than we thought at the time. Pamphlets are now beginning to appear that tell us that during the past few years and months these revolutionary symptoms in Europe have been much more serious than we had suspected.

What, in that case, must we do now? We must now thoroughly prepare for revolution and make a deep study of its concrete development in the advanced capitalist countries. This is the first lesson we must draw from the international situation. As for our Russian republic, we must take advantage of this brief respite in order to adapt our tactics to this zigzag line of history. This equilibrium is very important politically, because we clearly see that in many West European countries, where the broad mass of the working class, and very likely the overwhelming majority of the population, are organized, the main bulwark of the bourgeoisie consists of the hostile working-class organizations affiliated to the Second and the Two-and-a-Half Internationals.[27] I speak of this in Paragraph 2 of

---

27. In August 1914, when the leaderships of the majority of the national parties comprising the Second, or Socialist, International patriotically rallied behind the war effort of "their own" bourgeoisies at the opening of World War I, Lenin and the Bolshevik Party of Russia broke from that world organization. The Bolsheviks remained on a proletarian internationalist course that three years later culminated in the conquest of power by the workers and peasants of Russia and less than two years after that, in 1919, to

the theses, and I think that in this connection I need to deal with only two points, which were clarified during the discussion on the question of tactics.

First, winning over the majority of the proletariat. The more organized the proletariat is in a developed capitalist country, the greater thoroughness does history demand of us in preparing for revolution, and the more thoroughly must we win over the majority of the working class. Second, the main bulwark of capitalism in the industrially developed capitalist countries is the part of the working class that is organized in the Second and the Two-and-a-Half Internationals. If it weren't for the support of this section of the workers, these counterrevolutionary elements within the working class, the international bourgeoisie would be altogether unable to retain its position. [*Applause.*]

H ERE I WOULD also like to emphasize the significance of *the movement in the colonies.* In this respect we see in all the old parties, in all the bourgeois and petty-bourgeois labor parties affiliated to the Second and the Two-and-a-Half Internationals, remnants of the old sentimental views: they insist on their profound sympathy for oppressed colonial and semicolonial peoples. The movement in the colonial countries is still regarded as an insignificant national and totally peaceful movement. But this is not so. It has undergone great change since the

the formation of the Communist International. In 1921 various centrist currents in the Second International briefly split to form what became known as the Two-and-a-Half International, but the class-collaborationist officials of the two organizations patched up their conflicts and reunited in 1923.

beginning of the twentieth century: millions and hundreds of millions, in fact the overwhelming majority of the population of the globe, are now coming forward as independent, active, and revolutionary factors. It is perfectly clear that in the impending decisive battles in the world revolution, the movement of the majority of the population of the globe, initially directed towards national liberation, will turn against capitalism and imperialism and will, perhaps, play a much more revolutionary part than we expect. It is important to emphasize the fact that, for the first time in our International, we have taken up the question of preparing for this struggle. Of course, there are many more difficulties in this enormous sphere than in any other, but at all events the movement is advancing. And in spite of the fact that the masses of toilers—the peasants in the colonial countries—are still backward, they will play a very important revolutionary part in the coming phases of the world revolution. [*Animated approval.*]

As regards the internal political position of our republic I must start with a close examination of class relationships. During the past few months a change has taken place in this sphere, and we have witnessed the formation of new organizations of the exploiting class directed against us. The aim of socialism is to abolish classes. In the front ranks of the exploiting class we find the big landowners and the industrial capitalists. In regard to them, the work of destruction is fairly easy; it can be completed within a few months, and sometimes even a few weeks or days. We in Russia have expropriated our exploiters, the big landowners as well as the capitalists. They had no organizations of their own during the war and operated merely as appendages of the military forces of the international bourgeoisie. Now, after we have repulsed the attacks of the international counterrevolution, organizations of the Russian bourgeoisie and of all the Russian counterrevolutionary parties have been formed abroad. The number of Russian émigrés scattered in all foreign countries may be estimated at one-and-a-half to two million. In nearly every country they publish daily newspapers, and all the parties, landowner and petty-bourgeois, not excluding the Socialist Revolutionaries and the Mensheviks, have numerous ties with foreign bourgeois elements, that is to say, they obtain enough money to run their own press. We find the collaboration abroad of absolutely all the political parties that formerly existed in Russia, and we see how the "free" Russian press abroad, from the Socialist Revolutionary and Menshevik press to the most reactionary monarchist press, is championing the great landed interests.

This, to a certain extent, facilitates our task, because we can more easily observe the forces of the enemy, his state of organization, and the political trends in his camp. On the other hand, of course, it hinders our work, because these Russian counterrevolutionary émigrés use every means at their disposal to prepare for a fight against us. This fight again shows that, taken as a whole, the class instinct and class-consciousness of the ruling classes are still superior to those of the oppressed classes, notwithstanding the fact that the Russian revolution has done more than any previous revolution in this respect. In Russia, there is hardly a village in which the people, the oppressed, have not been roused. Nevertheless, if we take a cool look at the state of organization and political clarity of views of the Russian counterrevolutionary émigrés, we shall find that the class-consciousness of the bourgeoisie is still superior to that of the exploited and the oppressed. These people make every possible attempt and skillfully take advantage of every opportunity to attack Soviet Russia in one way or another, and to dismember it. It would be very instructive—and I think the foreign comrades will do that—systematically to watch the most important aspirations, the most important tactical moves, and the most important trends of this Russian counterrevolution. It operates chiefly abroad, and it will not be very difficult for the foreign comrades to watch it. In some respects, we ought to learn from this enemy. These counterrevolutionary émigrés are very well informed, they are excellently organized and are good strategists. And I think that a systematic comparison and study of the manner in which they are organized and take advantage of every opportunity may have a powerful propaganda effect upon the working class. This is not general theory, it is practical politics; here we can see what the enemy has learned.

During the past few years, the Russian bourgeoisie has suffered a terrible defeat. There is an old saying that a beaten army learns a great deal. The beaten reactionary army has learned a great deal, and has learned it thoroughly. It is learning with great avidity, and has really made much headway. When we took power at one swoop, the Russian bourgeoisie was unorganized and politically undeveloped. Now, I think, its development is on a par with modern, West European development. We must take this into account, we must improve our own organization and methods, and we shall do our utmost to achieve this. It was relatively easy for us, and I think that it will be equally easy for other revolutions, to cope with these two exploiting classes.

But, in addition to this class of exploiters, there is in nearly all capitalist countries, with the exception, perhaps, of Britain, a class of small producers and small farmers. The main problem of the revolution now is how to fight these two classes. In order to be rid of them, we must adopt methods other than those employed against the big landowners and capitalists. We could simply expropriate and banish both of these classes, and that is what we did. But we cannot do the same thing with the remaining capitalist classes, the small producers and the petty bourgeoisie, which are found in all countries. In most capitalist countries, these classes constitute a very considerable minority, approximately from 30 to 45 percent of the population. Add to them the petty-bourgeois elements of the working class, and you get even more than 50 percent. These cannot be expropriated or banished; other methods of struggle must be adopted in their case. From the international standpoint, if we regard the international revolution as one process, the significance of the period into which we are now entering in Russia is, in essence, that we must now find a practical solution for the problem of the relations the proletariat should establish with the last capitalist class in Russia.

ALL MARXISTS HAVE a correct and ready solution for this problem in theory. But theory and practice are two different things, and the practical solution of this problem can by no means be reduced to the theoretical solution. We know definitely that we have made serious mistakes. From the international standpoint, it is a sign of great progress that we are now trying to determine the attitude the proletariat in power should adopt towards the last capitalist class—the rock-bottom of capitalism— small private property, the small producer. This problem now confronts us in a practical way. I think we shall solve it. At all events, the experiment we are making will be useful for future proletarian revolutions, and they will be able to make better technical preparations for solving it.

In my theses I tried to analyze *the problem of the relations between the proletariat and the peasantry.* For the first time in history there is a state with only two classes, the proletariat and the peasantry. The latter constitutes the overwhelming majority of the population. It is, of course, very backward. How do the relations between the peasantry and the proletariat, which holds political power, find practical expression in the development of the revolution? The first form is alliance, close alliance. This is a very difficult task, but at any rate it is economically and politically feasible.

Η ow DID WE approach this problem practically? We concluded an alliance with the peasantry. We interpret this alliance in the following way: the proletariat emancipates the peasantry from the exploitation of the bourgeoisie, from its leadership and influence, and wins it over to its own side in order jointly to defeat the exploiters.

The Menshevik argument runs like this: the peasantry constitutes a majority; we are pure democrats, therefore, the majority should decide. But as the peasantry cannot operate on its own, this, in practice, means nothing more nor less than the restoration of capitalism. The slogan is the same: alliance with the peasantry. When we say that, we mean strengthening and consolidating the proletariat. We have tried to give effect to this alliance between the proletariat and the peasantry, and the first stage was a military alliance. The three years of the civil war created enormous difficulties, but in certain respects the war facilitated our task. This may sound odd, but it is true. The war was not something new for the peasants; a war against the exploiters, against the big landowners, was something they quite understood. The overwhelming majority of the peasants were on our side. In spite of the enormous distances, and the fact that the overwhelming majority of our peasants are unable to read or write, they assimilate our propaganda very easily. This proves that the broad masses—and this applies also to the most advanced countries—learn more readily from their own practical experience than from books. In Russia, moreover, learning from practical experience was facilitated for the peasantry by the fact that the country is so exceptionally large that in the same period different parts of it were passing through different stages of development.

In Siberia and in the Ukraine the counterrevolution was able to gain a temporary victory because there the bourgeoisie had the peasantry on its side, because the peasants were against us. The peasants frequently said, "We are Bolsheviks, but not Communists. We are for the Bolsheviks because they drove out the landowners: but we are not for the Communists because they are opposed to individual farming." And for a time, the counterrevolution managed to win out in Siberia and in the Ukraine because the bourgeoisie were successful in the struggle for influence over the peasantry.

But it took only a very short time to open the peasants' eyes. They quickly acquired practical experience and soon said, "Yes, the Bolsheviks are rather unpleasant people, we don't like them, but still they are better than the white guards and the Constituent Assembly." "Constituent Assembly" is a term of abuse not only among the educated Communists, but also among the peasants. They know from practical experience that the Constituent Assembly and the white guards stand for the same thing, that the former is inevitably followed by the latter.[28] The Mensheviks also resort to a military alliance with the peasantry, but they fail to understand that a military alliance alone is inadequate. There can be no military alliance without an economic alliance. It takes more than air to keep a man alive; our alliance with the peasantry could not possibly have lasted any length of time without the economic foundation, which was the basis of our victory in the war against our bourgeoisie. After all our bourgeoisie had been united with the whole of the international bourgeoisie.

The basis of our economic alliance with the peasantry was, of course, very simple, and even crude. The peasant obtained from us all the land and support against the big landowners. In return for this, we were to obtain food.

---

28. Following the revolutionary conquest of power by delegated mass councils—or "soviets," in the Russian language—of workers, peasants, and soldiers in October 1917, the landlords and capitalists in Russia initially sought to restore their rule by organizing elections to a Constitutent Assembly in mid-November. When the tsarist regime had been overturned in February of that year, the provisional government representing the class interests of these same exploiting classes had repeatedly put off holding such elections. The assembly met in January 1918 and immediately refused to recognize the power of the workers, peasants, and soldiers soviets. The assembly also rejected the initial steps of the revolutionary government expropriating the landlords, establishing workers' control in the factories, nationalizing the banks, decreeing self-determination for oppressed nations and nationalities, and arming the toilers. In response to these counterrevolutionary actions, the Soviet republic dissolved the Constituent Assembly on January 19. (See Lenin's "Draft Decree on the Dissolution of the Constituent Assembly" in *Collected Works*, vol. 26, pp. 434–36.)

This alliance was something entirely new and did not rest on the ordinary relations between commodity producers and consumers. Our peasants had a much better understanding of this than the heroes of the Second and the Two-and-a-Half Internationals. They said to themselves, "These Bolsheviks are stern leaders, but after all they are our own people." Be that as it may, we created in this way the foundations of a new economic alliance. The peasants gave their produce to the Red Army and received from the latter assistance in protecting their possessions. This is always forgotten by the heroes of the Second International, who, like Otto Bauer, totally fail to understand the actual situation. We confess that the initial form of this alliance was very primitive and that we made very many mistakes. But we were obliged to act as quickly as possible, we had to organize supplies for the army at all costs. During the civil war we were cut off from all the grain districts of Russia. We were in a terrible position, and it looks like a miracle that the Russian people and the working class were able to endure such suffering, want, and privation, sustained by nothing more than a deep urge for victory. [*Animated approval and applause.*]

WHEN THE CIVIL WAR came to an end, however, we faced a different problem. If the country had not been so laid waste after seven years of incessant war, it would perhaps have been possible to find an easier transition to the new form of alliance between the proletariat and the peasantry. But bad as conditions in the country were, they were still further aggravated by the crop failure, the fodder shortage, etc. In consequence, the sufferings of the peasants became unbearable. We had to show the broad masses of the peasants immediately that we were

prepared to change our policy, without in any way devi-
ating from our revolutionary path, so that they could say,
"The Bolsheviks want to improve our intolerable condition immediately, and at all costs."

And so, *our economic policy was changed*; the tax in kind
superseded the requisitions. This was not invented at one
stroke. You will find a number of proposals in the Bolshevik press over a period of months, but no plan that
really promised success. But this is not important. The
important thing is that we changed our economic policy,
yielding to exclusively practical considerations, and impelled by necessity. A bad harvest, fodder shortage and
lack of fuel—all, of course, have a decisive influence on
the economy as a whole, including the peasant economy.
If the peasantry goes on strike, we get no firewood; and
if we get no firewood, the factories will have to idle. Thus,
in the spring of 1921, the economic crisis resulting from
the terrible crop failure and the fodder shortage assumed
gigantic proportions. All that was the aftermath of the
three years of civil war. We had to show the peasantry that
we could and would quickly change our policy in order
immediately to alleviate their distress.

We have always said—and it was also said at the Second
Congress—that revolution demands sacrifices. Some
comrades in their propaganda argue in the following way:
we are prepared to stage a revolution, but it must not be
too severe. Unless I am mistaken, this thesis was put forward by Comrade Smeral in his speech at the congress
of the Communist Party of Czechoslovakia. I read about
it in the report published in the Reichenberg *Vorwärts*.
There is evidently a slightly Leftist wing there; hence this
source cannot be regarded as being quite impartial. At all
events, I must say that if Smeral did say that, he was wrong.
Some comrades who spoke after Smeral at this congress

said, "Yes, we shall go along with Smeral because in this
way we shall avoid civil war." [*Laughter.*] If these reports
are true, I must say that such agitation is neither Communist nor revolutionary. Naturally, every revolution entails enormous sacrifice on the part of the class making
it. Revolution differs from ordinary struggle in that ten
and even a hundred times more people take part in it.
Hence every revolution entails sacrifices not only for individuals, but for a whole class. The dictatorship of the
proletariat in Russia has entailed for the ruling class—
the proletariat—sacrifices, want, and privation unprecedented in history, and the case will, in all probability,
be the same in every other country.

THE QUESTION ARISES: How are we to distribute this
burden of privation? We are the state power. We are able
to distribute the burden of privation to a certain extent,
and to impose it upon several classes, thereby relatively
alleviating the condition of certain strata of the population. But what is to be our principle? Is it to be that of
fairness, or of a majority? No. We must act in a practical
manner. We must distribute the burdens in such a way as
to preserve the power of the proletariat. This is our only
principle. In the beginning of the revolution the working class was compelled to suffer incredible want. Let me
state that from year to year our food policy has been
achieving increasing success. And the situation as a whole
has undoubtedly improved. But the peasantry in Russia
has certainly gained more from the revolution than the
working class. There is no doubt about that at all. From
the standpoint of theory, this shows, of course, that our
revolution was to some degree a bourgeois revolution.
When Kautsky used this as an argument against us, we

laughed. Naturally, a revolution that does not expropriate the big landed estates, expel the big landowners, or divide the land is only a bourgeois revolution and not a socialist one. But we were the only party able to carry the bourgeois revolution to its conclusion and to facilitate the struggle for the socialist revolution. The Soviet power and the Soviet system are institutions of the socialist state. We have already established these institutions, but we have not yet solved the problem of economic relations between the peasantry and the proletariat. Much remains to be done, and the outcome of this struggle depends upon whether we solve this problem or not. Thus, the distribution of the burden of privation is one of the most difficult practical problems. On the whole, the condition of the peasants has improved, but dire suffering has fallen to the lot of the working class, precisely because it is exercising its dictatorship.

I HAVE ALREADY SAID that in the spring of 1921 the most appalling want caused by the fodder shortage and the crop failure prevailed among the peasantry, which constitutes the majority of our population. We cannot possibly exist unless we have good relations with the peasant masses. Hence, our task was to render them immediate assistance. The condition of the working class is extremely hard, it is suffering horribly. Those who have more political understanding, however, realize that in the interest of the dictatorship of the working class we must make tremendous efforts to help the peasants at any price. The vanguard of the working class has realized this, but in that vanguard there are still people who cannot understand it, and who are too weary to understand it. They regarded it as a mistake and began to use the word "opportunism."

They said, "The Bolsheviks are helping the peasants. The peasants, who are exploiting us, are getting everything they please, while the workers are starving." But is that opportunism? We are helping the peasants because without an alliance with them the political power of the proletariat is impossible, its preservation is inconceivable. It was this consideration of expediency and not that of fair distribution that was decisive for us. We are assisting the peasants because it is absolutely necessary to do so in order that we may retain political power. The supreme principle of the dictatorship is the maintenance of the alliance between the proletariat and the peasantry in order that the proletariat may retain its leading role and its political power.

The only means we found for this was the adoption of the tax in kind, which was the inevitable consequence of the struggle. This year, we shall introduce this tax for the first time. [29] This principle has not yet been tried in practice. From the military alliance we must pass to an economic alliance, and, theoretically, the only basis for the latter is the introduction of the tax in kind. It provides the only theoretical possibility for laying a really solid economic foundation for socialist society. The socialized factory gives the peasant its manufactures and in return the peasant gives his grain. This is the only possible form of

---

29. In order to feed and clothe the soldiers and urban workers during the civil war, the revolutionary government had implemented a policy of compulsory requisitions of farm products beyond what peasant families needed for their own use. Under the government's New Economic Policy, peasants paid an established tax in the form of agricultural produce—a tax in kind, rather than a money tax—and could sell the remainder of their output on the market or to the government in return for industrial goods.

existence of socialist society, the only form of socialist development in a country in which the small peasants constitute the majority, or at all events a very considerable minority. The peasants will give one part of their produce in the form of tax and another either in exchange for the manufactures of socialist factories, or through the exchange of commodities.

This brings us to the most difficult problem. It goes without saying that the tax in kind means freedom to trade. After having paid the tax in kind, the peasant will have the right freely to exchange the remainder of his grain. This freedom of exchange implies freedom for capitalism. We say this openly and emphasize it. We do not conceal it in the least. Things would go very hard with us if we attempted to conceal it. Freedom to trade means freedom for capitalism, but it also means a new form of capitalism. It means that, to a certain extent, we are recreating capitalism. We are doing this quite openly. It is state capitalism. But state capitalism in a society where power belongs to capital, and state capitalism in a proletarian state, are two different concepts. In a capitalist state, state capitalism means that it is recognized by the state and controlled by it for the benefit of the bourgeoisie, and to the detriment of the proletariat. In the proletarian state, the same thing is done for the benefit of the working class, for the purpose of standing up to and fighting against the as yet strong bourgeoisie. It goes without saying that we must grant concessions to the foreign bourgeoisie, to foreign capital. Without the slightest denationalization, we shall lease mines, forests, and oilfields to foreign capitalists, and receive in exchange manufactured goods, machinery, etc., and thus restore our own industry.

Of course, we did not all agree right away on the question of state capitalism. But we are very pleased to note in this connection that our peasantry has been developing, that it has fully realized the historical significance of the struggle we are waging at the present time. Ordinary peasants from the most remote districts have come to us and said: "What! We have expelled our capitalists, the capitalists who speak Russian, and now foreign capitalists are coming!" Does not this show that our peasants have developed? There is no need to explain to a worker who is versed in economics why this is necessary. We have been so ruined by seven years of war that it will take many years to restore our industry. We must pay for our backwardness and weakness, and for the lessons we are now learning and must learn. Those who want to learn must pay for the tuition. We must explain this to one and all, and if we prove it in practice, the vast masses of the peasants and workers will agree with us, because in this way their condition will be immediately improved, and because it will ensure the possibility of restoring our industry.

W<small>HAT COMPELS US</small> to do this? We are not alone in the world. We exist within a system of capitalist states. . . . On one side, there are the colonial countries, but they cannot help us yet. On the other side, there are the capitalist countries, but they are our enemies. The result is a certain equilibrium, a very poor one, it is true. Nevertheless, we must reckon with this fact. We must not shut our eyes to it if we want to exist. Either we score an immediate victory over the whole bourgeoisie, or we pay the tribute.

We admit quite openly, and do not conceal the fact, that concessions in the system of state capitalism mean paying a tribute to capitalism. But we gain time, and gaining time means gaining everything, particularly in the period of equilibrium, when our comrades abroad are preparing thoroughly for their revolution. The more thorough their preparations, the more certain will the victory be. Meanwhile, however, we shall have to pay tribute.

A FEW WORDS ABOUT our food policy. Undoubtedly, it was a bad and primitive policy. But we can also point to some achievements. In this connection I must once again emphasize that the only possible economic foundation of socialism is large-scale machine industry. Whoever forgets this is no communist. We must analyze this problem concretely. We cannot present problems in the way the theoreticians of the old school of socialism do. We must present them in a practical manner. What is modern large-scale industry? It is *the electrification of the whole of Russia.* Sweden, Germany, and America have almost achieved this, although they are still bourgeois. A Swedish comrade told me that in Sweden a large part of industry and 30 percent of agriculture are electrified. In Germany and America, where capitalism is even more developed, we see the same thing on a larger scale. Large-scale machine industry is nothing more nor less than the electrification of the whole country. We have already appointed a special commission consisting of the country's best economists and engineers. It is true that nearly all of them are hostile to the Soviet power. All these specialists will come over to communism, but not our way, not by way of twenty years of underground work, during which we unceasingly studied and repeated over and over again the ABC of communism.

Nearly all the Soviet government bodies agreed that we had to draw on the specialists. The expert engineers will come to us when we give them practical proof that this will increase the country's productive forces. It is not enough to prove it to them in theory; we must prove it to them in practice, and we shall win these people over to our side if we present the problem differently, not from the standpoint of the theoretical propaganda of communism. We say: large-scale industry is the only means of saving the peasantry from want and starvation. Everyone agrees with this. But how can it be done? The restoration of industry on the old basis will entail too much labor and time. We must give industry a more modern form, that is, we must adopt electrification. This will take much less time. We have already drawn up the plans for electrification. More than two hundred specialists—almost to a man opposed to the Soviet power—worked on it with keen interest, although they are not communists. From the standpoint of technical science, however, they had to admit that this was the only correct way. Of course, we have a long way to go before the plan is achieved. The cautious specialists say that the first series of works will take at least ten years. Professor Ballod has estimated that it would take three to four years to electrify Germany. But for us even ten years is not enough. In my theses I quote actual figures to show you how little we have been able to do in this sphere up to now. The figures I quote are so modest that it immediately becomes clear that they are more of propaganda than scientific value. But we must begin with propaganda. The Russian peasants who fought in the world war and lived in Germany for several years learned how modern farming should be carried on in order to conquer famine. We must carry on extensive propaganda in this direction. Taken by themselves, these plans are not yet of great practical value, but their propaganda value is very great.

The peasants realize that something new must be created. They realize that this cannot be done by everybody working separately, but by the state working as a whole. The peasants who were prisoners of war in Germany found out what the real basis is for cultural life. Twelve thousand kilowatts is a very modest beginning.   Probably a foreigner who is familiar with electrification in America, Germany, or Sweden would laugh at this. But he laughs best who laughs last. It is, indeed, a modest beginning. But the peasants are beginning to understand that new work must be carried out on a grand scale, and that this work has already begun. Enormous difficulties will have to be overcome. We shall try to establish relations with the capitalist countries. We must not regret having to give the capitalists several hundred million kilograms of oil on condition that they help us to electrify our country.

AND NOW, IN CONCLUSION, a few words about "*pure democracy.*" I will read you a passage from Engels's letter to Bebel of December 11, 1884. He wrote:

> "As regards pure democracy, . . . [t]hat it plays a far more subordinate role in Germany than in countries long since industrialised goes without saying. But that will not prevent it *qua* extreme *bourgeois* party—which, after all, it had made itself out to be at Frankfurt—from acquiring at the moment of revolution, a temporary significance as the last sheet-anchor of the bourgeois and, indeed, feudal economy. . . . It was thus that from March to September 1848, the entire feudal-bureaucratic mass swelled the ranks of the Liberals in order to keep down the revolutionary masses. . . . At all

events, on the crucial day and the day after that, our only adversary will be *collective reaction centred round pure democracy* and this, I think, ought never to be lost from view."[30]

Our approach must differ from that of the theoreticians. The whole reactionary mass, not only bourgeois, but also feudal, groups itself around "pure democracy." The German comrades know better than anyone else what "pure democracy" means, for Kautsky and the other leaders of the Second and the Two-and-a-Half Internationals are defending this "pure democracy" from the wicked Bolsheviks. If we judge the Russian Socialist Revolutionaries[31] and Mensheviks, not by what they say, but by what they do, we shall find that they are nothing but representatives of petty-bourgeois "pure democracy." In

---

30. Engels is referring to the representatives of the most radical layers of the bourgeoisie who served in the Prussian National Assembly during the 1848–49 revolution in Germany and served as the front behind which the propertied classes in countryside and city held off the demands of the peasantry, the artisans and small masters, and the emerging industrial working class. Engels's letter to Bebel can be found in Marx and Engels, *Collected Works*, vol. 47, pp. 231–35.

31. The Socialist Revolutionary Party (SR), formed in 1901–2, was a peasant-based party that had majority support of peasant delegates in the soviets after the February 1917 revolution in Russia that toppled the tsarist regime. The party split later that year, when its left wing supported the October Revolution and initially joined with the Bolsheviks in the new workers and peasants government. Like the Mensheviks, Right SRs joined the capitalists and landlords in taking up arms against the Soviet republic. In July 1918 the Left SRs, too, took up arms against the government, ostensibly in opposition to the Bolsheviks' signing of the Brest-Litovsk Treaty.

the course of our revolution they have given us a classic example of what "pure democracy" means, and again during the recent crisis, in the days of the Kronstadt mutiny.[32] There was serious unrest among the peasantry, and discontent was also rife among the workers. They were weary and exhausted. After all, there is a limit to human endurance. They had starved for three years, but you cannot go on starving for four or five years. Naturally, hunger has a tremendous influence on political activity. How did the Socialist Revolutionaries and the Mensheviks behave? They wavered all the time, thereby strengthening the bourgeoisie.

The organization of all the Russian parties abroad has revealed the present state of affairs. The shrewdest of the leaders of the Russian big bourgeoisie said to themselves: "We cannot achieve victory in Russia immediately. Hence our slogan must be: 'Soviets without the Bolsheviks.'" Milyukov, the leader of the Constitutional Democrats,[33] defended the Soviet power from the attacks of the Socialist Revolutionaries. This sounds very strange; but such are the practical dialectics that we, in our revolution, have been studying in a peculiar way, from the practical expe-

---

32. In 1921, just as the civil war was coming to a close, anarchists organized a rebellion against the Soviet government by sailors at the Kronstadt naval base, northwest of Petrograd. The counterrevolutionary uprising, which was quelled by the Red Army, was hailed by the Mensheviks, imperialist propagandists, and spokespersons for Russia's overturned landlords and capitalists.

33. The Constitutional Democrats were the main party of the bourgeoisie in Russia prior to the October Revolution. They continued to function in exile for sometime afterwards as an organizing center of the counterrevolutionary armies working to overthrow the workers and peasants government. Pavel Milyukov was the party's central leader.

rience of our struggle and of the struggle of our enemies. The Constitutional Democrats defend "Soviets without the Bolsheviks" because they understand the position very well and hope that a section of the people will rise to the bait. That is what the clever Constitutional Democrats say. Not all the Constitutional Democrats are clever, of course, but some of them are, and these have learned something from the French Revolution. The present slogan is to fight the Bolsheviks, whatever the price, come what may. The whole of the bourgeoisie is now helping the Mensheviks and Socialist Revolutionaries, who are now the vanguard of all reaction. In the spring we had a taste of the fruits of this counterrevolutionary cooperation.

THAT IS WHY WE MUST continue our relentless struggle against these elements. Dictatorship is a state of intense war. That is just the state we are in. There is no military invasion at present; but we are isolated. On the other hand, however, we are not entirely isolated, since the whole international bourgeoisie is incapable of waging open war against us just now, because the whole working class, even though the majority is not yet communist, is sufficiently class-conscious to prevent intervention. The bourgeoisie is compelled to reckon with the temper of the masses even though they have not yet entirely developed to the point of embracing communism. That is why the bourgeoisie cannot now start an offensive against us, although one is never ruled out.

Until the final issue is decided, this awful state of war will continue. And we say: "When at war, act as if at war; we do not promise any freedom, or any democracy." We tell peasants quite openly that they must choose between the rule of the bourgeoisie, and the rule of the Bolshe-

viks—in which case we shall make every possible conces-
sion within the limits of retaining power, and later we shall
lead them to socialism. Everything else is deception and
pure demagogy. Ruthless war must be declared against
this deception and demagogy. Our point of view is: for
the time being—big concessions and the greatest caution,
precisely because a certain equilibrium has set in, precisely because we are weaker than our combined enemies,
and because our economic basis is too weak and we need
a stronger one.

That, comrades, is what I wanted to tell you about our
tactics, the tactics of the Russian Communist Party. [*Prolonged applause.*]

Russian Revolution's world example

Lenin's Final Fight

Speeches and Writings, 1922–23
V.I. LENIN

In the early 1920s Lenin waged a battle in the Communist Party leadership to maintain the course that had enabled workers and peasants to carry out the first socialist revolution, and begin building a world communist movement. The issues posed in this fight—from the leadership's class composition, to the worker-peasant alliance and battle against national oppression—remain central to world politics today. $19.95

The First Five Years of the Communist International

LEON TROTSKY

During its first five years, the Communist International, guided by V.I. Lenin, Leon Trotsky, and other central Bolshevik leaders, sought to build a world movement of Communist Parties capable of leading the toilers to overthrow capitalist exploitation and colonial oppression. This two-volume collection contains Trotsky's speeches and writings from the first four Comintern congresses. 2 vols., $28 each

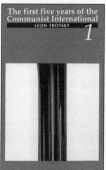

The History of the Russian Revolution

LEON TROTSKY

A classic account of the social and political dynamics of the first socialist revolution as told by one of its central leaders. "The history of a revolution is first of all a history of the forcible entrance of the masses into the realm of rulership over their own destiny," says Trotsky. Unabridged, 3 vols. in one. $35.95

The Revolution Betrayed

What Is the Soviet Union and Where Is It Going?
LEON TROTSKY

In 1917 the workers and peasants of Russia carried out one of the greatest revolutions in history. Yet within ten years a political counterrevolution by a privileged social layer whose chief spokesperson was Joseph Stalin was being consolidated. This study of the Soviet workers state and the degeneration of the revolution illuminates the roots of the social and political crisis shaking the former USSR today. $15

"Without revolutionary theory

NEW INTERNATIONAL NO. 11

U.S. Imperialism Has Lost the Cold War

Jack Barnes

Contrary to imperialist expectations at the opening of the 1990s in the wake of the collapse of regimes across Eastern Europe and the USSR claiming to be communist, the workers and farmers there have not been crushed. Nor have capitalist social relations been stabilized. The toilers remain an intractable obstacle to imperialism's advance, one the exploiters will have to confront in class battles and war. $15

NEW INTERNATIONAL NO. 7

Opening Guns of World War III: Washington's Assault on Iraq

Jack Barnes

The murderous assault on Iraq in 1990–91 heralded increasingly sharp conflicts among imperialist powers, growing instability of international capitalism, and more wars. $12

there can be no revolutionary practice"
—Lenin

NEW INTERNATIONAL NO. 9
The Rise and Fall of the Nicaraguan Revolution

Based on ten years of socialist journalism from inside Nicaragua, this special issue recounts the achievements and worldwide impact of the 1979 Nicaraguan revolution. It traces the political retreat of the Sandinista National Liberation Front leadership that led to the downfall of the workers and farmers government in the closing years of the 1980s. Documents of the Socialist Workers Party. $16

NEW INTERNATIONAL NO. 8
Che Guevara, Cuba, and the Road to Socialism

Articles by Ernesto Che Guevara, Carlos Rafael Rodríguez, Carlos Tablada, Mary-Alice Waters, Steve Clark, Jack Barnes
Exchanges from the early 1960s and today on the political perspectives defended by Guevara as he helped lead working people to advance the transformation of economic and social relations in Cuba. $10

NEW INTERNATIONAL NO. 6
Washington's 50-year Domestic Contra Operation

As the U.S. rulers prepared to smash working-class resistance and join the interimperialist slaughter of World War II, the federal political police apparatus as it exists today was born, together with vastly expanded executive powers of the imperial presidency. This article describes the consequences for the labor, Black, antiwar, and other social movements and how communists have fought to defend workers rights against government and employer attacks. $16

Do you have a friend, coworker, or relative whose first language is Spanish, French, Swedish, or Icelandic?
If so, many issues of New International are available as
Nueva Internacional, Nouvelle Internationale,
Ny International, and Nýtt Alþjóðlegt.

See full listing at www.pathfinderpress.com

NEW INTERNATIONAL IS ALSO PUBLISHED IN SPANISH AS
NUEVA INTERNACIONAL
AND IN FRENCH AS
NOUVELLE INTERNATIONALE

... AND SELECTED ISSUES ARE AVAILABLE IN THE SWEDISH

NY INTERNATIONAL
AND ICELANDIC
NÝTT ALÞJÓÐLEGT

WWW.PATHFINDERPRESS.COM
OR VISIT ONE OF THE LOCATIONS
LISTED AT THE BACK OF THE MAGAZINE

INDEX

military
Norway, 219
Nuclear power, 53–54
Nuclear weapons, 49, 51–52, 53–54, 114; U.S.-led campaign around, 54–55, 114

O

O'Neill, Paul, 140–41
October 1962: The 'Missile' Crisis as Seen from Cuba (Diez), 167
Oil, 115, 133, 250
Orange County, 179–80

P

Pacifism, 260
Pakistan, 48, 51
Palestine Liberation Organization (PLO), 66
Palestinians, 45, 53, 66, 67–68, 168
Palmer Raids, 43–44, 216
Pathfinder Press, 11, 14–15, 85, 152–57, 200; political centrality of, 82, 151–55; vanguard workers and, 156–57, 204
Pathfinder Reprint Project, 11–12, 157–60
Patriotism, 23, 42, 59, 106, 109–11, 175, 176
"Peace dividend," 44, 62–63
Pearl Harbor, 113
Peasants, 244–45, 259, 274, 276–77; in Soviet Russia, 277–82, 283, 286, 289, 292, 293–94. *See also* Farmers
Pensions, 193–94; attacks on workers', 19, 61, 186, 196; funds, 126, 131, 133, 145–46, 189. *See also* Social Security
Perspectiva Mundial, 107, 150, 200, 204
Philippines, 107, 121; U.S. military and, 24, 63, 115–16
Playa Girón/Bay of Pigs: Washing-

ton's First Military Defeat in the Americas (Castro and Fernández), 11, 153–54
Point Blank Body Armor, 76, 109
Pol Pot, 162
Poland, 47, 48, 217–18
Pombo: A Man of Che's "guerrilla" (Villegas), 11
Pornographication. *See* United States, factionalism in politics of
Productivity, 140, 250; capitalist efforts to raise, 57, 185, 242
Profit rates, 77, 126, 134–35
Proliferation Security Initiative (PSI), 46
Propaganda work, 82, 149–50, 167, 200, 289; Marx and Engels on, 202
Protocols of the Elders of Zion, 199–200
Puerto Rico, 30, 121
Putin, Vladimir, 50–51

Q

Qaddafi, Muammar el-, 52

R

Reagan, Ronald, 49, 114
Recessions, 101, 126, 183–84
Red Army (Soviet Russia), 8, 269
Red Brigades (Italy), 70
Religion, 57, 68, 88
Republican Party, 61, 63, 75, 88, 192; and military transformation, 21–22, 23, 39–40
Resentment, politics of, 147
Revolution: and economics, 6, 236–41, 262–63; of 1848, 228, 236–37, 263, 290; post–WWI predictions about, 222–23, 272; prospects for, 214–20, 241, 253–54, 255–56, 258–59, 264, 271–72. *See also* Russia, 1917 revolution

Also from **PATHFINDER**

Fighting Racism in World War II

**C.L.R. JAMES, GEORGE BREITMAN,
EDGAR KEEMER, AND OTHERS**

A week-by-week account of the struggle against lynch-mob terror and racist discrimination in U.S. war industries, the armed forces, and society as a whole from 1939 to 1945, taken from the pages of the *Militant* newsweekly. These struggles helped lay the basis for the rise of the mass civil rights movement in the subsequent two decades. $21.95

Puerto Rico: Independence Is a Necessity

RAFAEL CANCEL MIRANDA

In two interviews, one of five Puerto Rican Nationalists imprisoned by Washington for more than 25 years until 1979 speaks out on the brutal reality of U.S. colonial domination, the campaign to free Puerto Rican political prisoners, the example of Cuba's socialist revolution. $3

On the Jewish Question

LEON TROTSKY

"Never was it so clear as it is today that the salvation of the Jewish people is bound up inseparably with the overthrow of the capitalist system"—Leon Trotsky, 1940. $4.50

America's Revolutionary Heritage

EDITED BY GEORGE NOVACK

A historical materialist analysis of the genocide against Native Americans, the American Revolution, the Civil War, the rise of industrial capitalism, and the first wave of the fight for women's rights. $22.95

W W W . P A T H F I N D E R P R E S S . C O M

Further Reading from **PATHFINDER**

Out Now!

*A Participant's Account of the Movement
in the United States against the Vietnam War*

FRED HALSTEAD

The fight for a political course to organize working people, GIs, and youth and help lead growing world opposition to the Vietnam War. Gaining momentum from the mass struggle for Black civil rights at home, together with the unyielding revolutionary resistance by Vietnamese national liberation fighters, the antiwar movement helped force Washington to bring the troops home, altering the dynamic of the class struggle in the U.S. $30.95

FBI on Trial

*The Victory in the Socialist Workers Party
Suit against Government Spying*

EDITED BY MARGARET JAYKO

The 1987 victory in the 14-year SWP legal battle against the FBI, CIA, and other government spy agencies "increases the space for politics, expands the de facto use of the Bill of Rights, increases the confidence of working people that you can be political and hold the deepest convictions against the government and it's your right to do so and act upon them."—From the introduction. $18.95

Israel and the Arab Revolution

Fundamental Principles of Revolutionary Marxism

GUS HOROWITZ

The fight for a democratic, secular Palestine and its place in advancing the struggle of workers and peasants against imperialist oppression and capitalist exploitation throughout the Middle East and the entire world. Socialist Workers Party resolutions and reports from 1971–72. $10

EDUCATION FOR SOCIALISTS

Israel and the Arab Revolution
Fundamental Principles of Revolutionary Marxism
by Gus Horowitz

WE FIGHT ISRAEL BECAUSE IT OCCUPIES OUR LAND
FATEH

W W W . P A T H F I N D E R P R E S S . C O M

THE CUBAN REVOLUTION AND WORLD POLITICS

Cuba and the
Coming American Revolution

JACK BARNES

"There will be a victorious revolution in the United States before there will be a victorious counterrevolution in Cuba." That statement, made by Fidel Castro in 1961, remains as accurate today as when it was spoken. This is a book about the class struggle in the United States, where the revolutionary capacities of workers and farmers are today as utterly discounted by the ruling powers as were those of the Cuban toilers. And just as wrongly. It is about the example set by the people of Cuba that revolution is not only necessary—it can be made. $13

Che Guevara Talks to Young People

In eight talks from 1959 to 1964, the Argentine-born revolutionary challenges youth of Cuba and the world to study, to work, to become disciplined. To join the front lines of struggles, small and large. To politicize their organizations and themselves. To become a different kind of human being as they strive together with working people of all lands to transform the world. And, along this course, to revel in the spontaneity and joy of being young. $15

Making History

Interviews with Four Generals of Cuba's Revolutionary Armed Forces

Through the stories of four outstanding Cuban generals—Néstor López Cuba, Enrique Carreras, José Ramón Fernández, and Harry Villegas—each with close to half a century of revolutionary activity, we see the class dynamics that have shaped our entire epoch. We understand how the people of Cuba, as they struggle to build a new society, have for four and a half decades held Washington at bay. $15.95

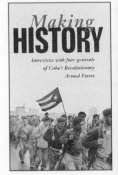

From the Escambray to the Congo

In the Whirlwind of the Cuban Revolution

VÍCTOR DREKE

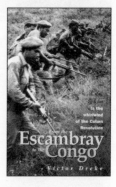

In this participant's account, Víctor Dreke describes how easy it became after the Cuban Revolution to take down a rope segregating blacks from whites at a dance in the town square, yet how enormous was the battle to transform social relations underlying all the "ropes" inherited from capitalism and Yankee domination. He recounts the creative joy with which working people have defended their revolutionary course from the Cuban Escambray mountains to Africa and beyond. $17

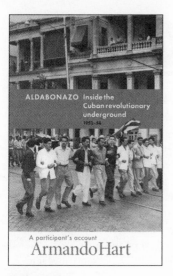

Aldabonazo

Inside the Cuban Revolutionary Underground, 1952–58

ARMANDO HART

In this firsthand account by a historic leader of the Cuban Revolution, we meet men and women who led the urban underground in the fight against the brutal U.S.-backed tyranny in the 1950s. Together with their comrades-in-arms in the Rebel Army, they not only overthrew the dictatorship. Their revolutionary actions and example worldwide changed the history of the 20th century—and the century to come. $25

The Second Declaration of Havana

In 1962 the workers and farmers who carried out a socialist revolution in Cuba refused to back down in face of the rapidly escalating military, economic, and political attack by the U.S. government. Instead, they pointed to the example of the Cuban revolution as the way forward for the oppressed and exploited throughout Latin America. Their ringing indictment of imperialist rule, read by Fidel Castro at a rally of a million people in Havana, remains a manifesto of revolutionary struggle for working people everywhere. $5

WWW.PATHFINDERPRESS.COM

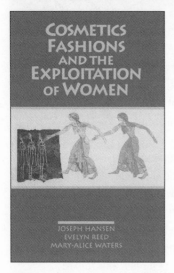

Cosmetics, Fashions, and the Exploitation of Women

Joseph Hansen, Evelyn Reed, Mary-Alice Waters

How big business plays on women's second-class status and social insecurities to market cosmetics and rake in profits. The introduction by Mary-Alice Waters explains how the entry of millions of women into the workforce during and after World War II irreversibly changed U.S. society and laid the basis for a renewed rise of struggles for women's emancipation. $15

Feminism and the Marxist Movement

Mary-Alice Waters

Since the founding of the modern revolutionary workers movement nearly 150 years ago, Marxists have championed the struggle for women's rights and explained the economic roots in class society of women's oppression. "The struggle for women's liberation," Waters writes, "was lifted out of the realm of the personal, the 'impossible dream,' and unbreakably linked to the progressive forces of our epoch"—the working-class struggle for power. $3.50

Marianas in Combat

Teté Puebla and the Mariana Grajales Women's Platoon in Cuba's Revolutionary War 1956–58
Teté Puebla

Brigadier General Teté Puebla, the highest-ranking woman in Cuba's Revolutionary Armed Forces, joined the struggle to overthrow the U.S.-backed dictatorship of Fulgencio Batista in 1956, when she was fifteen years old. This is her story—from clandestine action in the cities, to serving as an officer in the victorious Rebel Army's first all-women's unit—the Mariana Grajales Women's Platoon. For nearly fifty years, the fight to transform the social and economic status of women in Cuba has been inseparable from Cuba's socialist revolution. $14

Problems of Women's Liberation

Evelyn Reed

Six articles explore the social and economic roots of women's oppression from prehistoric society to modern capitalism and point the road forward to emancipation. $13

Women and the Family

Leon Trotsky

How the October 1917 Russian Revolution, the first victorious socialist revolution, transformed the fight for women's emancipation. Trotsky explains the Bolshevik government's steps to wipe out illiteracy, establish equality in economic and political life, set up child-care centers and public kitchens, guarantee the right to abortion and divorce, and more. $12

Communist Continuity and the Fight for Women's Liberation

Documents of the Socialist Workers Party
1971–86
**Edited with an introduction
by Mary-Alice Waters**

How did the oppression of women begin? What class benefits? What social forces have the power to end the second-class status of women? Why is defense of a woman's right to choose abortion a pressing issue for the labor movement? This three-part series helps politically equip the generation of women and men joining battles in defense of women's rights today. 3 volumes. $30

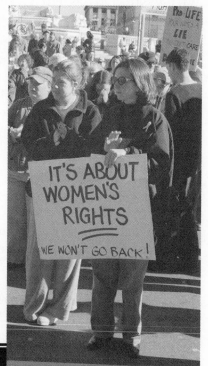

www.pathfinderpress.com

REVOLUTIONARY LEADERS IN THEIR OWN WORDS

MALCOLM X TALKS TO YOUNG PEOPLE

Four talks and an interview given to young people in Ghana, the United Kingdom, and the United States in the last months of Malcolm's life. This new edition contains the entire December 1964 presentation by Malcolm X at the Oxford Union in the United Kingdom, in print for the first time anywhere. The collection concludes with two memorial tributes by a young socialist leader to this great revolutionary. $15

TO SPEAK THE TRUTH

WHY WASHINGTON'S 'COLD WAR' AGAINST CUBA DOESN'T END
Fidel Castro, Ernesto Che Guevara

In historic speeches before the United Nations and UN bodies, Guevara and Castro address the workers of the world, explaining why the U.S. government so hates the example set by the socialist revolution in Cuba and why Washington's effort to destroy it will fail. $17

MAURICE BISHOP SPEAKS

THE GRENADA REVOLUTION AND ITS OVERTHROW, 1979–83
The triumph of the 1979 revolution in the Caribbean island of Grenada had "importance for all struggles around the world," said Maurice Bishop, its central leader. Invaluable lessons from that workers and farmers government, overturned in a Stalinist-led coup in 1983, can be found in this collection of Bishop's speeches and interviews. $24.95

THOMAS SANKARA SPEAKS

THE BURKINA FASO REVOLUTION, 1983–87

Imperialist domination has left a legacy of hunger, illiteracy, and economic backwardness in the West African country of Burkina Faso, as it has across the continent. In 1983 the peasants and workers of that country established a popular revolutionary government and began to combat the causes of such devastation. Thomas Sankara, the principal leader of that struggle, explains the example set for all of Africa. $20

ROSA LUXEMBURG SPEAKS

Edited by Mary-Alice Waters

From her political awakening as a high school student in tsarist-occupied Poland until her murder in 1919 during the German revolution, Rosa Luxemburg acted and wrote as a proletarian revolutionist. This collection of her writings and speeches takes us inside the political battles between revolution and class collaboration that still shape the modern workers movement. $27

EUGENE V. DEBS SPEAKS

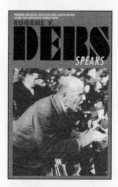

Speeches by the pioneer U.S. socialist agitator and labor leader, jailed for opposing Washington's imperialist aims in World War I. Debs speaks out on capitalism and socialism, anti-immigrant chauvinism, how anti-Black racism weakens the labor movement, Rockefeller's massacre of striking miners at Ludlow, Colorado, and more. $19.95

SOCIALISM ON TRIAL

James P. Cannon

The basic ideas of socialism, explained in testimony during the 1941 trial of leaders of the Minneapolis Teamsters union and the Socialist Workers Party framed up and imprisoned under the notorious Smith "Gag" Act during World War II. $16

To order any issue of **New International**
or any book or pamphlet advertised in this issue…

Visit us on the Web at:

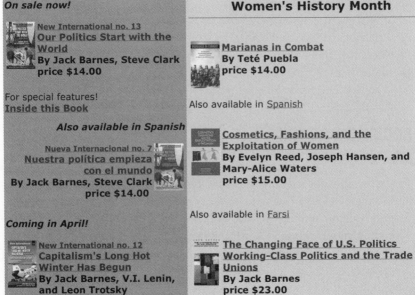

Pathfinderpress ● com

| Home | Author | Subject | Title | Language | Search | Shopping Cart |

- Log in
- New and Noteworthy
- News from Pathfinder
- Pathfinder Readers Club Discounts
- Promotional Materials
- How to

Revolutionary politics of the working class	The Cuban Revolution in the world	Trade unions: past, present, and future	Farmers and the workers movement
New International magazine	Writings of Marx and Engels	Lenin and the Communist International	Writings of Leon Trotsky
The materialist world view	Malcolm X, in his own words	Black liberation	Women's emancipation struggle
Fascism and how to fight it	U.S. politics and history	The Jewish Question and anti-Semitism	Latin America and Caribbean
Sub-Saharan Africa	Russia, Eastern Europe, and Balkans	China and Asia and the Pacific	Palestine, Israel, and the Middle East
Art and culture	Education for Socialists bulletins	www.pathfinderpress.com	

On sale now!

New International no. 13
Our Politics Start with the World
By Jack Barnes, Steve Clark
price $14.00

For special features!
Inside this Book

Also available in Spanish

Nueva Internacional no. 7
Nuestra política empieza con el mundo
By Jack Barnes, Steve Clark
price $14.00

Coming in April!

New International no. 12
Capitalism's Long Hot Winter Has Begun
By Jack Barnes, V.I. Lenin, and Leon Trotsky

Women's History Month

Marianas in Combat
By Teté Puebla
price $14.00

Also available in Spanish

Cosmetics, Fashions, and the Exploitation of Women
By Evelyn Reed, Joseph Hansen, and Mary-Alice Waters
price $15.00

Also available in Farsi

The Changing Face of U.S. Politics
Working-Class Politics and the Trade Unions
By Jack Barnes
price $23.00

NEW INTERNATIONAL #12 & #13

READ THEM TOGETHER . . .

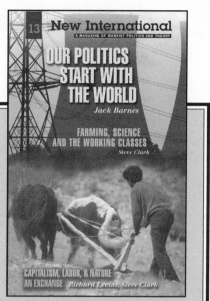

Electrification is an elementary precondition if modern industry and cultural life are to develop, and class-conscious workers fight for it to be extended to all the world's six billion people. This fight is a prime example of how proletarian politics, our politics, start with the world.

—*Jack Barnes*

The huge economic and cultural inequalities between imperialist and semicolonial countries, and among classes within almost every country, are produced, reproduced, and accentuated by the workings of capitalism. For vanguard workers to build parties able to lead a successful revolutionary struggle for power in our own countries, says Jack Barnes in the lead article, our activity must be guided by a strategy to close this gap.

"We are part of an international class that has no homeland. That's not a slogan or a moral imperative. It is a recognition of the class reality of economic, social, and political life in the imperialist epoch."

OUR POLITICS START WITH THE WORLD
by Jack Barnes

FARMING, SCIENCE, AND THE WORKING CLASSES
by Steve Clark

CAPITALISM, LABOR, AND NATURE: AN EXCHANGE
Richard Levins, Steve Clark

$14

SPECIAL OFFER!
BOTH ISSUES FOR
$25

AVAILABLE FROM WWW.PATHFINDERPRESS.COM

NEW INTERNATIONAL AROUND THE WORLD

New International is also published in Spanish as *Nueva Internacional* and French as *Nouvelle Internationale*. Selected issues are available in Swedish as *Ny International* and in Icelandic as *Nýtt Alþóðlegt*. All are distributed worldwide by Pathfinder Press.

Available at
www.pathfinderpress.com
and at the following locations

AUSTRALIA

(and Southeast Asia and the Pacific)
Pathfinder, Level 1, 3/281-287 Beamish St., Campsie, NSW 2194
Postal address: P.O. Box 164, Campsie, NSW 2194

CANADA

Pathfinder, 2238 Dundas St. West, Suite 201,
Toronto, ON M6R 3A9

ICELAND

Pathfinder, Skolavordustig 6B, Reykjavík
Postal address: P. Box 0233, IS 121 Reykjavík

NEW ZEALAND

Pathfinder, Suite 3, 7 Mason Ave., Otahuhu, Auckland
Postal address: P.O. Box 3025, Auckland

SWEDEN

Pathfinder, Bjulevägen 33, kv, S-122 41 Enskede

UNITED KINGDOM

(and Europe, Africa, Middle East, and South Asia):
Pathfinder, First Floor, 120 Bethnal Green Road
(entrance in Brick Lane), London E2 6DG

UNITED STATES

(and Caribbean, Latin America, and East Asia):
Pathfinder Books, 306 W. 37th St., 10th Floor,
New York, NY 10018-2852